BECOMING
DEVIANT

BECOMING DEVIANT

David Matza

With a new introduction by **Thomas G. Blomberg**

Transaction Publishers
New Brunswick (U.S.A.) and London (U.K.)

New material this edition copyright © 2010 by Transaction Publishers, New Brunswick, New Jersey. Originally published in 1969 by Prentice-Hall, Inc.

This book is printed on acid-free paper that meets the American National Standard for Permanence of Paper for Printed Library Materials.

Library of Congress Catalog Number: 2010012610
ISBN: 978-1-4128-1446-1
Printed in the United States of America

Library of Congress Cataloging-in-Publication Data

Matza, David.
    Becoming deviant / David Matza ; with an introduction by Thomas G. Blomberg. -- Rev. ed.
        p. cm.
    Originally published: Englewood Cliffs, N.J. : Prentice-Hall, [1969]
    Includes bibliographical references and index.
    ISBN 978-1-4128-1446-1
        1. Deviant behavior. I. Title.

HM811.M388 2010
302.5'42--dc22
                                                                2010012610

to Abraham

Contents

Introduction to the Transaction Edition

It is my pleasure to introduce the second edition of *Becoming Deviant* and its author David Matza to a new generation of scholars and students. In the years since its original publication in 1969, *Becoming Deviant* has become a "criminological classic" and its author David Matza recognized as a major criminological theorist. *Becoming Deviant* was at once original while simultaneously grounded and informed by previous criminological research and theory. It was original in its efforts to give the subject a prominent role in the process of becoming deviant. It was grounded and informed by previous research and theory through its successful integration of functional, learning, and labeling perspectives to conceptualize and interpret the process of becoming deviant.

Throughout the twentieth century, a series of theories emerged in the ongoing effort to explain crime. These theories included the Chicago School's "culture conflict" theme (i.e., Park and Burgess, 1924; Shaw, 1931) followed by the widely recognized contributions of Merton (1938) with "anomie" theory and Sutherland (1939) with "differential association" theory. Anomie and differential association theories were subsequently employed, individually or in combination, (i.e., Cohen,

1955; Cloward and Ohlin, 1960) to explain delinquent subcultures. Additionally, labeling theory (i.e., Lemert, 1951; Becker, 1963), with it's shift in theoretical focus from the deviant to society's reaction to deviance and the consequences of this "societal reaction" for subsequent behavior, competed for theoretical prominence in the early 1960s. It was from this theoretical context that David Matza's first book, *Delinquency and Drift* (1964), followed by *Becoming Deviant* (1969) emerged and to which they were responsive.

Delinquency and Drift differed from established subcultural theories through its assertion that delinquents were, in fact, more integrated into American mainstream culture than previous subcultural theorists acknowledged. *Becoming Deviant* provided yet another theoretical account in which the process of becoming deviant was conceptualized not as deterministic but rather as sequential and open, thereby allowing for both offending and non-reoffending through its focus upon the thinking, meaning, and action of the subject. In sum, in *Becoming Deviant*, Matza gave the subject a voice and active role in the process of becoming deviant that while necessarily complex, was altogether understandable.

To introduce new readers to David Matza and *Becoming Deviant*, what follows are a biographical sketch of Matza, a description of his becoming a criminologist, a review of his criminological contributions culminating in *Becoming Deviant*, and reflections from a number of criminologists regarding *Becoming Deviant*'s original and continuing contributions to criminological theory. Much of the material on Matza's biography and career was drawn from a series of interviews I conducted with him during 2008-2009. The reflections from criminologists on *Becoming Deviant* were drawn from responses to a survey I administered in 2009.

A Biographical Sketch of David Matza

David Matza was born on May 1, 1930 in New York City. He grew up in Harlem and the East Bronx with his parents, and an older brother and sister. His father had emigrated to the U.S. from Turkey in 1906 and his mother from Greece in 1921. David recounts that while his father experienced long periods of unemployment during his childhood, he remembers his family life, particularly during the Great Depression, as being normal for the times, until his brother Abraham was killed in the Battle of the Bulge in early January 1945, a few months before the end of World War Two. His brother's death had a major and lasting effect that contiues today.

While living in Harlem, David attended a religious community center and a public school up to the 6th grade where he described himself as "a good boy." He was a high-performing and gifted student. David's family moved from Harlem to the East Bronx in 1941. In the East Bronx, he divided his time between public Junior High and High School and a Jewish community center and spent the remainder of his time with friends, playing ball and hanging out in the streets and playgrounds.

Following graduation from high school, David attended CCNY Business School but quickly dropped out to work. He re-enrolled in college at CCNY as a social science major after working for several years.

The social science major at CCNY included requirements for courses in sociology, economics, philosophy, and history. David completed the honors program at CCNY, which included a great books reading course. The works of Plato, Machiavelli, Marx, Schumpeter, and others were required course readings. He recalls that the course had considerable influence on him because it exposed him to the works of a series of remarkable writers. The most important influences in shaping his interest in sociology were Marx and Veblen and, to a lesser degree, C. Wright Mills. Additionally, David explains that while he read numerous novels, he found Dostoyevsky to be one of his favorite novelists. Up until his last year of study in the honors program, he had planned to become a social worker. However, David did not truly aspire to be a social worker but rather, because of his experiences and work in a settlement house, it seemed like a logical career choice. To elaborate, David had been helped and influenced by many social workers who worked with him and his friends in Club Freeman at the East Bronx Y. Moreover, many of his closest friends had chosen social work careers. Nonetheless, by the time he graduated from CCNY, he had decided to become a writer. The fields of economics and sociology seemed closer to a writing career than social work, which seemed more like an applied career working with people for which he believed he was not ideally suited. During his last year of study at CCNY, David was advised by Professor Charles Page to seriously consider going into graduate school to study sociology. He followed that advice.

Becoming a Criminologist

David chose to attend Princeton University because it was the only program at the time with a joint department of economics and sociology. As David explains, he was very interested in the relationship between economics and sociology. However, he soon discovered that economics was not well-integrated with sociology at Princeton. David recounted that while he took Jacob Viner's course on the history of economic theory, the Princeton faculty that had the greatest influence on him were Wilbert Moore, an industrial sociologist, and Mel Tumin, an anti-functional theorist in sociology.

David's Master's thesis was an assessment of America's anarchist movement beginning with the Haymarket events to Emma Goldman. Much of his early graduate work had focused upon political and radical social movements and he planned to write his doctoral dissertation, under the direction of Wilbert Moore, on shifts in the American labor force in relation to the trade union movement.

During this period, David married and became a father. Moreover, just before he began his dissertation, Wilbert Moore went on leave from Princeton for a year. Moore's leave resulted in David being without a research assistantship to help support his family as well as a major professor. At this time, David met Gresham Sykes, a newly-hired assistant professor at Princeton. Sykes had just received a grant to study delinquency and offered David a one-year research assistantship that he readily accepted. This marked the beginnings of the Sykes and Matza professional collaboration and the formative beginning of David becoming a criminologist. Like so many careers, David becoming a criminologist clearly involved elements of serendipity.

David's initial research in criminology involved fieldwork in which he interviewed incarcerated boys at a state custodial institution. He recalls that he went into his work with delinquents with a very tolerant and appreciative view of delinquency, in part, because of his experiences in junior high school where he and his friends were routinely subjected to confrontations from older boys demanding their money through threats of violence. He recalled that he never really came to dislike the older boys and would merely comply with their demands by allowing them to search him for money without resistance.

Between 1957 and 1959, before he completed his dissertation, David took his first teaching job at Temple University and worked there with Negley Teeters. After completing his dissertation in 1960, David moved to the University of Chicago Law School for post-doctoral studies. His studies at Chicago were focused upon observations of juvenile courts. During this period, he began the preliminary research for his first book *Delinquency and Drift*. Before the publication of *Delinquency and Drift* in 1964, David published four criminological articles. These included "Techniques of Neutralization" (with Gresham Sykes, *American Sociological Review*, Volume 22, 1957), "The Extent of Delinquency in the United States" (with Negley Teeters, *The Journal of Negro Education*, Summer, 1959), "Subterranean Traditions of Youth" (*The Annals of the American Academy of Political and Social Science*, Volume 338, 1961), and "Juvenile Delinquency and Subterranean Values" (with Gresham Sykes, *American Sociological Review*, Volume 26, 1961). Emerging from these early publications and confirmed with the 1964 publication of *Delinquency and Drift*, was David's growing recognition as a criminological theorist with an ability to uniquely fit his theoretical conceptualizations with the known empirical patterns of juvenile delinquency and with existing theoretical formulations.

During 1960-1961 when David was completing his post-doctoral studies at Chicago, he decided not to return to Temple University. Specifically, he decided that he would pursue more independent research and writing and do less collaborative work. He then interviewed for several University faculty openings at Smith and at the University of Wisconsin at Madison. At this time, Reinhard Bendix, Chair of the Sociology Department at the University of California at Berkeley, visited Chicago and interviewed David for a faculty position. Bendix subsequently offered David a faculty position beginning in the Fall of 1961. David indicates that he was pleased to accept Bendix's offer and to be joining one of the very best sociology departments in the country with a truly distinguished faculty. As he recalls, it was a position that gave him professional pride and motivation.

Upon arriving at Berkeley, David taught a joint 500-student enrolled Introduction to Sociology course with Philip Selznick and William Kornhauser and a Social Problems course. As he remembers, there was confusion over his exact field of study. At one point, colleague Kingsley Davis asked David if he would be interested in a joint appointment with the School of Criminology but he was advised by other colleagues in sociology to decline the joint appointment, which he ultimately chose to do. During this time, David developed close bonds with colleagues Selznick, Kornhauser, and Bendix, as well as Erving Goffman with whom he co-taught several different courses.

While David remembers many positive experiences during his early years at Berkeley, there was considerable pressure to publish. As a result, *Delinquency and Drift* became the book that David "had to write," if he was to be promoted and tenured at Berkeley. During this period, there were several other rising scholars vying for a permanent position in the sociology department at Berkeley including Albert Cohen, Ernest Becker, and Jerry Skolnick. The Berkeley sociology faculty was comprised of a number of different academic orientations that included the extremes of humanism and positivism with a number of faculty falling somewhere in between. David did not easily fit within any of these faculty groupings given his criminological interests. Nonetheless, in 1964, with the publication of *Delinquency and Drift*, David was promoted to associate professor and awarded tenure. *Delinquency and Drift* received significant praise including a tremendously positive review by Edgar Friedenberg of the *New York Times Review of Books* making it's publication a positive and satisfying experience for David.

Following his promotion and award of tenure, David began teaching graduate courses and signed a contract for his next book, *Becoming Deviant*. David remembers thinking that he had another book in him because in *Delinquency and Drift* he had only covered a few authors and a more comprehensive and historically-informed review of delinquency was needed. His thinking about *Becoming Deviant* was also influenced by his experiences co-teaching the course Deviance and Social Control with Goffman. In the course, he lectured on the history of sociology and criminology. In discussions about his historical lectures on sociology and criminology with Neil Smelser, he was encouraged to write *Becoming Deviant*.

David recalls the period between 1964 and 1969, when his energies were focused upon writing *Becoming Deviant*, as a particularly chaotic and difficult period in his life both personally and professionally. Beginning in 1968, he was nearing the period where he needed to go up for promotion to professor and everything hinged upon the publication of and favorable reactions to *Becoming Deviant*. With these pressures and the book only half-written, David secured a Guggenheim grant to support him for a year at the London School of Economics (LSE) to finish writing *Becoming Deviant*.

At LSE, David met Stanley Cohen and David Downes who became friends and helpful colleagues. David was able to write despite the pressure the book was creating for him. His method of work was to write sections and then send them to

Sheldon (Shelly) Messinger at the Center for the Study of Law and Society at Berkeley for comments and suggestions. Shelly was a wonderfully-constructive critic and sophisticated sociological/criminological thinker who was well-recognized and respected by many prominent scholars and students for his uncanny ability to flesh out the intended argument(s) of writers and then point out what remained to be done in order to ultimately produce these intended argument(s). Shelly's often heard introduction following a review of a writer's work was "I think what you are trying to do is ... and here is what I believe is missing." David, like so many before and after him, benefited greatly from Shelly's help, which he eloquently articulated in the acknowledgements of *Becoming Deviant* as follows:

> I am especially indebted to Sheldon Messinger. During a few of the two thousand-odd days, he was a final though tenuous link with reality; on many others he was a critic, colleague and friend.

Toward the end of the year at LSE, Shelly recommended that David send a reduced version of the manuscript to his publisher that excluded two sections he had written on Gypsies and homosexuality. David agreed with Shelly's recommendation and sent the reduced version of the manuscript to the publisher where it was accepted for publication. In 1969, following the publication of *Becoming Deviant*, David went up for promotion to professor without a second university faculty offer which defied Berkeley's custom, but was promoted to professor nonetheless.

Criminological Contributions

In the preceding section, David's becoming a criminologist was described. In this section David's specific criminological contributions are identified and discussed. David's becoming a criminologist was largely a result of his meeting Gresham Sykes and agreeing to work with him on a delinquency research project. As a result of his research experiences with Sykes, David decided to write his dissertation on delinquency. The dissertation was titled "The Moral Code of Delinquents: A Study of Patterns of Neutralization." David explained in his dissertation that he found the existing theories of delinquency incomplete. Specifically, he concluded that the theories did not explain a number of the fundamental empirical features and nuances known to be associated with delinquency. This included the frequent cessation of delinquency at the onset of adulthood, the often conformist nature of delinquent behavior and the large numbers of non-delinquents in so-called "high-delinquency areas." David reasoned that most, though not all, delinquent behavior constituted relatively homogeneous phenomena that were developmental in character proceeding from trivial to more serious infractions. David believed that delinquent behavior represented youth's search for adventure that was accompanied by a withdrawal from conventional values and associated behavior. Very importantly, and what came to underlie David's subsequent criminological contributions was his emerging belief that many delinquents were not fully committed to a delinquent lifestyle.

To place his thoughts about delinquency into a theoretical framework, David turned to the notion of neutralization. As he explained in his dissertation the "ideology of neutralization is useful in the maintenance of a delinquent pattern because it renders ineffectual definitions favorable to conformity to the law." Neutralizing beliefs deflect rather than repudiate respectable values. These beliefs do not directly conflict with the dominant norms of behavior. They merely neutralize them.

To test his theoretical argument, he interviewed a number of incarcerated youth offenders at two institutions located in Jamesburg, New Jersey. David employed both structured questions and informal conversations in the interviews. David found that patterns of neutralization are, in fact, subculturally transmitted although in some cases they may originate in response to particular kinds of personality disorders. He also determined that a number of the delinquent youth exhibited and held neutralizing attitudes. He then categorized the modes of neutralization as a denial of responsibility, denial of injury, denial of the victim, an appeal to higher values (loyalty and honor), and cynicism.

Upon completion of the dissertation, David received a Post-Doctoral Fellowship for Behavioral Science and Law from the University of Chicago School of Law. During the course of the Fellowship, he began reading about juvenile law and conducting a series of observations of the Cook County Juvenile Court. Gresham Sykes had left Princeton and was at Northwestern University throughout the course of David's Fellowship at the University of Chicago. During this period, they worked together and wrote "Juvenile Delinquency and Subterranean Values," which, as noted above was published in the *American Sociological Review*.

Following his Fellowship, David accepted the faculty offer from the Department of Sociology at the University of California at Berkeley where he remained throughout his career. Upon his arrival at Berkeley, David joined Shelly Messinger and Philip Selznick who were in the process of organizing the Center for the Study of Law and Society and continued working on what was to become *Delinquency and Drift* as part of a curriculum development program funded by the President's Commission on Youth Crime and Juvenile Delinquency. In explaining the differences between *Delinquency and Drift* and his dissertation and the two ASR articles written with Sykes, David indicated that he intended to "institutionally contextualize the attitudes or techniques of neutralization." He explains that in the first ASR article "Techniques of Neutralization," they referred to the legal anchoring of the various rationalizations with little explanation. Moreover, his dissertation was primarily a study of incarcerated delinquent youth's attitudes. David elaborates that in *Delinquency and Drift*, he wanted to be able to place the "techniques" into a broader institutional or organizational context of the juvenile code and Juvenile Court. He further explains that in writing *Delinquency and Drift*, he was trying to develop a textbook on juvenile delinquency. Therefore, in the book, he attempted to integrate his readings and interpretations of various delinquency textbooks and articles.

David believed that *Delinquency and Drift* differed from mainstream delinquency texts, articles, and theories, which he felt were largely positivist while his book was more classical or neoclassical. He points out that he did not think that his theory was unique but rather old-fashioned in that he elaborated upon and refined the previous work of others. David does, however, acknowledge that his theory is neoclassical in its claim that delinquents do believe in mainstream values but often drift from mainstream behaviors. He elaborates that the average or modal juvenile delinquent (especially the "subcultural" or slum delinquent) was more integrated into the usual or semi-usual culture of American society than most writers of the time seemed to believe or infer from their data or observations. He concluded that delinquency was part of the functional mix of American society's "subterranean" youth culture.

With regard to the claim made by some control theorists that *Delinquency and Drift* supports their arguments, David responds that in the book's last chapter he made some control theory concessions to the view of delinquency as "action." He elaborates that he wrote that infants and little children can be observed cutting up things or hitting and acting out at others, so that humans can act badly, and thus live up to their image as portrayed in then existent versions of control theory. However, he points out that in the remaining part of the book's last chapter he goes back to stressing delinquency as an infraction. By the end of the book, he states that he was only in the "Control" camp in the sense that he was suggesting that to repeat the offense or go on to some greater offense, the practicing delinquent has to overcome the actual and anticipated incursions of the Controllers. David concludes that, "I guess that makes me perhaps an anti-control theorist. In both *Delinquency and Drift* and later in *Becoming Deviant*, I try theoretically and in Blumer's sense methodologically, to adapt the view of the subject. It is the subject's viewpoint and behavior I am trying to understand and explain. This can lead to some confusion since the subject is also the object of control theory."

As summarized by David in the preface of *Delinquency and Drift* (1964):

> In developing a conception of the classical delinquent—a delinquent seen in legal context—I have been led quite naturally, or so I would like to believe, to a portrayal that incorporates the associated assumptions of classical criminology. Thus, I have tried to convey the sense in which the precepts featured in a subculture of delinquency are only marginally different from those apparent in common sentiments of American life; and I have attempted to utilize the classic conception of a will to crime in order to maintain the eradicable element of choice and freedom inherent in the condition of delinquent drift.

Edgar Friedenberg's review in *The New York Review of Books* (1965) indicated that David achieved his purpose:

> *Delinquency and Drift* is elegant and light, precise and penetrating, wholly original, and so unsentimental that it can treat of misery to some coherent purpose, avoiding both disguise and despair. It is subtle, too intricate to summarize, yet very clear.

Following the 1964 publication of *Delinquency and Drift*, David began writing *Becoming Deviant*, which he intended to be different from *Delinquency and Drift*. David indicates that what he wanted to accomplish in his second book was to provide a sociological notion of how individuals become deviant without implying determinism. The idea of "becoming" was then popular in psychology and existentialism as a sufficiently general concept to allow the subject to be a part of the becoming deviant process.

Becoming Deviant provided a conceptualization of a sequential and open process that employed the concepts of affinity, affiliation, and signification. The sequential process allows for both non-re-offending and recidivism. David explains that the theoretical argument underlying the book came mainly from his undergraduate and graduate teaching between 1964 and 1969. In several courses that he co-taught with Goffman, he recalls trying to summarize the main themes in the sociology of deviance along with psychology. Ultimately, three "schools" of thought were integrated into the *Becoming Deviant* process, namely:

1. Affinity (i.e., Chicago School and functionalists: predispositions, subcultural, urban, class; Parks, Burgess, Shaw, McKay, and Thrasher.),
2. Affiliation (i.e., differential association and behavior system; Sutherland), and
3. Signification (i.e., labeling, selecting, framing; Goffman, Becker and Lemert).

David summarizes his *Becoming Deviant* argument as a process in which the subject sometimes moves from (1) an affinity to certain prohibited behaviors to (2) affiliation with circles and settings which include or sponsor the offenses to (3) the apprehension and signification of the offenses.

Following the 1969 publication of *Becoming Deviant*, David turned his scholarly attention back to his early graduate school interests in labor and social movements. This scholarly shift from criminology was shaped by the then changing social context of the times with the Vietnam War, strained race relations, and the prevailing crisis in the legitimacy of American institutions. This changing social context influenced a number of academics throughout the country to critically question and refocus their scholarly pursuits toward broader social, political, and economic concerns, particularly on the Berkeley campus.

Reflections on *Becoming Deviant*

With the publication of *Becoming Deviant* in 1969, David Matza provided a much anticipated sequel to his 1964 classic *Delinquency and Drift*. In *Becoming Deviant*, Matza has indicated that he intended to provide a conception of delinquency different from *Delinquency and Drift*. Specifically, he wanted to offer a sociological conception of how individuals become deviant without reliance upon notions of determinism. The intent was to acknowledge and elaborate upon the role of the subject in the process of becoming deviant.

Becoming Deviant was uniquely successful in changing the ways criminologists thought about crime and deviance. But exactly how did *Becoming Deviant* change criminological conceptions of crime and deviance and how does it continue to inform contemporary criminological theory? To address these questions, I surveyed a number of criminologists, many with careers that have spanned the period of *Becoming Deviant*'s original publication and subsequent rise to prominence. I asked the criminologists to share their view on *Becoming Deviant*'s major contributions to criminology in 1969 and its continuing contributions today. Among the early and continuing contributions of *Becoming Deviant* that were articulated are:

- "I'm sure you know quite well that I haven't been involved in the fields of deviance or criminology for a very long time.... Nevertheless, the part of the book that sticks with me most is the three vignettes illustrating the three processes of becoming deviant: affinity, affiliation, and signification," (Becker, 2009).
- "I think Matza is infused in the contemporary work of all of us, certainly in mine. I was particularly influenced by labeling as a social process, as a stigmatizing process, that could lead to denial and indeed a great variety of techniques that neutralize the social control projects of those who impose the label. I think there are clues in Matza to the contexts where labeling stigmatizes counterproductively that also become clues to where it can confront educatively. Understanding when acknowledging deviance increases it and when acknowledgment reduces it is the project put on the agenda by Matza and his community of scholars that I was interested in following up," (Braithwaite, 2009).
- "*Becoming Deviant* made a big impact at the time, as a tour de force which gave shape to the emergent sociology of deviance and control as a clear alternative to conventional criminology. Part 1 was, and remains, an utterly original analysis of the growth of 'naturalism' in sociological work on crime and deviance. The shift from correction to appreciation, simplicity to complexity, and pathology to diversity transcended the tendency—partly encouraged by Matza himself in *Delinquency and Drift*—for oversimplified histories of the field to view the subject as a battle between positivism (bad) and interactionism (good). For example, Matza gave functionalism, usually dismissed as irrelevant or stultifying, a key role, for its stress on irony—'good' things can flow from 'bad' causes—and complexity—the social is not simple. Perspectives on the Chicago School, functionalism and the neo-Chicagoans gained fresh life from this mode of conceptualizing their achievements. Part 2's examination of the three master paradigms in the explanation of the process of becoming deviant—affinity, affiliation, and signification—was a bold way of mastering the field. It was in the final chapters, on signification, that he made his most important contribution to understanding what is entailed in becoming deviant—for instance—the notions of gross and reasonable exclusion as extending and intensifying deviant identity," (Downes, 2009).
- "I was very influenced by *Becoming Deviant* when I read it. (1) The power of it, I thought was that by shifting the frame of reference or perspective,

one could reconstitute the object; (2) Made sociological thought relative; (3) Rejected conventional theories based upon values, norms and beliefs and tried to focus on meaning and action; (4) It moved away from a blame the deviant toward seeing such activity as orderly, meaningful, logical and collective. (5) It brought theoretical acuity to an area seen as a bit too "practical" for sociologists. (6) It bridged deviance and crime and moved away from mere textbook treatments. At the time, I thought it was one of the most subtle and complex books I had read in the field. I still do," (Manning, 2009).

- Identifying "the powerful hold of the conventional order on those who would violate even its most important rules. It is a much more sophisticated account than the idea of 'subculture' or 'street codes' of the complex process of normative detachment—always partial and contingent—that precedes or co-occurs with deviant action," (Rosenfeld, 2009).

- "The first section of *Becoming Deviant* is still required reading in my introductory graduate course on criminological theory. What I find most compelling about this book are the carefully crafted discussions of correction v. appreciation, pathology v. diversity, and simplicity v. complexity. What this amounts to is a subtle critique of the domain assumptions of positivism in criminology. Specifically it clarifies the assumptions that provide the warrant for inquiry that is mobilized to uncover the pathological differences that determine or at least cause criminal behavior. In the process, Matza illustrates the limitations and contradictions of those assumptions, and provides what I consider to be a most valuable critique of the dominant paradigm in the field," (Chiricos, 2009).

- "*Becoming Deviant* remains a brilliant critical analysis of how we think about and try to explain crime and deviance. It remains quite relevant as scholars circle back around to the issue of human agency and cognitive transformation in life-course offending. Today's scholars focus more on the role of human agency in desisting from crime, whereas Matza was concerned, in a sophisticated way, in how individuals used agency to become criminals. Regardless, his insights on human agency (which avoid a crude free-will perspective) would benefit anyone delving into this topic today," (Cullen, 2009).

- "David Matza's *Becoming Deviant,* which I first encountered during my first semester as a graduate student, was one of the two or three most important books published in criminology from, at least, the early 1960's to early 80's—the other two were Howard Becker's *The Outsiders* and Jack Douglas' *The Social Meanings of Suicide*. I think that *Becoming Deviant's* lasting importance derives from two main things. First, it represents the high point in the development of what was called the "Neo-Chicagoan" or labeling approach to the study and explanation of crime and deviance. Second, and, more importantly, it still provides a bugle call for criminologists to conduct studies on crime and deviance from an *appreciative naturalistic* approach. Although I have never considered myself an exponent of labeling theory, *Becoming Deviant* helped ignite the fire under me that first inspired my taking of an appreciative naturalistic approach in studying the problem of violent crime," (Athens, 2009).

- "When it first appeared in 1969, *Becoming Deviant* was a witty and intelligent commentary on the major theoretical tendencies in criminology and the sociology of deviance. It synthesized a mass of material and rendered comprehensible the history of the field in a lucid and compelling fashion," (Scull, 2009).
- "Among the key ideas in Matza's *Becoming Deviant* were the notion of provisional identity (identity is always more supposition than conclusion) and his rejection of the commonplace and unfortunate idea that categories like 'deviant,' 'delinquent,' or 'criminal' are ontological boxes into which humans can be neatly fit. Both of these are of course linked to his earlier work on *Drift*. These ideas have resonated in criminology for decades in everything from labeling theory to modern life-course criminology," (Warr, 2009).
- "By the end of the 1960s when *Becoming Deviant* was published, criminology was just beginning to see the rise of 'social control' theory and its emphasis on correctionalism, both of which were strong competitors to *Becoming Deviant* in the marketplace of ideas as well as the shifting social and political tastes of the public.... A perusal of criminology and criminal justice journals indicates—at least to me—that correctionalism holds sway once more—or still does—and it would be timely and important to the health and vigor of criminological theory and our failed attempts to incarcerate our way out of crime to re-issue *Becoming Deviant*," (Lilly, 2009).
- "The life-course of the field of criminology is one marked by growth generally, and both continuity and change in particular. Our young discipline has grown tremendously and quickly in its short life, and several instant-classic readings have emerged during this period. One of these is Matza's *Becoming Deviant*. As he states in his introduction, the theme of the first part of *Becoming Deviant* is growth, and he shows how major sociological viewpoints build off one another. Today, this framework is exemplified across many criminological theories, most notably developmental/life-course criminology, which seeks to incorporate ideas from various disciplines and continually build a more complete theory about the longitudinal patterning of criminal activity," (Piquero, 2009).

As these commentaries affirm, *Becoming Deviant* was and remains a criminological classic. What distinguished *Becoming Deviant* in 1969 and what continues to distinguish it from other theories of crime today is that it places the reader in the subjective realm and mind of the deviant subject. Rather than being on the outside looking in, *Becoming Deviant* places us on the inside looking out through the subjective lens, thoughts and actions of the deviant subject. Truly an important and illuminating perspective that begs for further theoretical refinement and empirical validation. I am pleased that Transaction is publishing the Second Edition of this unique work. Scholars and students from criminology, sociology, and related disciplines will find it to be invaluable in the ongoing effort to comprehend the complexities of criminal behavior and thereby to better inform what are far too often misguided efforts to reduce the pain and suffering of crime.

Thomas G. Blomberg

References

Athens, L. Survey via email. 2009

Becker, H. S. *Outsiders: Studies in the Sociology of Deviance.* New York: Free Press. 1963.

Becker, H. Survey via email. 2009.

Braithwaite, J. Survey via email. 2009.

Chiricos, T. Survey via email. 2009.

Cloward, R. A., & Ohlin, L. 1960. *Delinquency and Opportunity: A Theory of Delinquent Gangs.* Glencoe, IL: Free Press.

Cohen, A. K. 1955. *Delinquent Boys: The Culture of the Gang.* Glencoe, IL: Free Press.

Cullen, F. Survey via email. 2009.

Downes, D. Survey via email. 2009.

Friedenberg, E. "Dropping Out." *The New York Times Review of Books.* 1965.

Lemert, E. *Social Pathology.* McGraw-Hill, 1952.

Lilly, R. Survey via email. 2009.

Manning, P. Survey via email. 2009.

Matza, D. *Delinquency and Drift.* New York: Wiley, 1964.

Matza, D. *Becoming Deviant.* Englewood Cliffs, NJ: Prentice Hall, 1969.

Merton, R. K. 1938. Social Structure and Anomie. *American Sociological Review,* 3, 672–82.

Park, R. and E. Burgess. *Introduction to the Science of Sociology* (Second Edition). Chicago: University of Chicago Press, 1924

Piquero, A. Survey via email. 2009.

Rosenfeld, R. Survey via email. 2009.

Scull, A. Survey via email. 2009.

Shaw, C. R. *The Natural History of a Delinquent Career.* Chicago: University of Chicago Press, 1931.

Sutherland, E. *Principles of Criminology* (Third Edition). Philadelphia: J.B. Lippincot, 1939.

Warr, M. Survey via email. 2009.

Acknowledgments

The last thing one does before a book finally goes to press is to acknowledge the debts amassed with colleagues, helpers, families and foundations. An embarrassing consequence of so poorly-timed a project is to bring into stark relief the suppressed memory of how absurdly long it took to write so short a book. In about two thousand days, I wrote a little over two hundred pages—an abominable record of publication by American standards (and as good a reason as any for me to repudiate quantitative considerations). But thanks to the helpful interest and indulgence of a few, and to the sustained indifference of many, I have somehow managed not to perish—thus giving the lie to popular stereotypes regarding academic life generally, but Berkeley in particular.

For financial aid at various phases of the project, I am indebted to the President's Committee on Youth, Crime and Juvenile Delinquency (now defunct) and The Center for the Study of Law and Society (still struggling), also to The Guggenheim Foundation, for generously affording me a necessary year away from frenzied Berkeley in not-so-swinging London, and to the London School of Economics for kindly providing its facilities. For intellectual stimulation, collegial support and valuable criticism (too-rarely taken) I thank Erving Goffman, Howard Becker, Edwin Lemert, Jerome Skolnick, Philip Selznick and Phillipe Nonet. Also, I am indebted to Michael and Shirley Sanford, Forest Dill and Richard Wood-

xxiv   *Acknowledgments*

worth, graduate students at The Center for the Study of Law and Society, who occasionally took leave of their studies to provide invaluable instruction. Other students from whom I have learned include—at a minimum— Glen Lyons, Jerome Mandel, Norman Linton, Fred Templeton, John Irwin, Jacqueline Wiseman and Nancy Achilles. During my year in London, I received encouragement for which I am grateful from two remarkably unEnglish sociologists, David Downes and Stanley Cohen. For truly helpful assistance with the final phases of putting a manuscript together, I thank Anita Mitchell. And, like almost everyone connected with The Center for the Study of Law and Society, I am especially indebted to Sheldon Messinger. During a few of the two thousand-odd days, he was a final though tenuous link with reality; on many others he was a critic, colleague and friend.

Finally, for their capacity to put up with me through all these years, I am deeply grateful to Cynthia, Naomi and Karen—appearances notwithstanding.

David Matza

Berkeley, California

Becoming Deviant

University of Winchester
Tel: 01962 827306
E-Mail: libenquiries@winchester.ac.uk

Borrowed Items 10/12/2019 06:43
XXXX8537

Item Title	Due Date
* Becoming deviant	20/01/2020

* Indicates items borrowed today
Thank you for using this unit

www.bibliotheca.com

The aim of writing is to create coherence. The risk is that coherence will be imposed on an actual disorder and a forgery thus produced. No way of avoiding that risk exists since to write is to
take on the task of bringing together or organizing materials.
Thus the only legitimate question about a work is the measure of
imposition, or the amount of forgery, the only off-setting compensation
the possibility of entertainment or illumination.

In Becoming Deviant, I organize two kinds of material. In the
first part of the book, a perspective on deviant behavior is developed. I
call that perspective naturalism, and trace its main themes through three
major sociological viewpoints—the Chicago school, the functionalists,
and a contemporary neoChicagoan approach. In Part II, I turn to
the process of becoming deviant and consider the major ways in which
it has been conceived.

The theme of the first part is growth—something that should not
be lightly assumed in a discipline like sociology. I will show how each
viewpoint built on those of its predecessors and addressed itself to
many of the same issues and dilemmas. Since the allegation of intellectual
evolution or growth runs an especially high risk of forgery, the reader is
forewarned. Except that the posited growth is slight, I would not seriously
entertain so remote a possibility.

1

Natural Deviation

My aim in this introduction is to suggest a revised idea of naturalism and an elementary conception of deviation. The first—naturalism—refers to the perspective commended in this book; the second—deviation—to the general topic considered; thus, the title "natural deviation."

To assert the natural character of phenomena is the broadest meaning of naturalism, and, accordingly, the least useful. No contemporary view of human behavior—deviant or conventional—would deny its natural character. But the meaning of the term "natural" varies enormously among viewpoints, and correspondingly variable is the quality and measure of naturalist affirmation. To take viewpoints at their word may be misleading. We may be deceived into equating an idle and thus meaningless verbal affirmation with an abiding commitment. Only the latter warrants the designation "naturalism." Naturalism *is* a commitment, and to decide whether a given viewpoint is naturalist or not we must first answer the question: *to what* is naturalism committed?

The commitment of naturalism, as I conceive it, is *to phenomena and their nature; not* to Science or any other system of standards. Such a conception of naturalism differs somewhat from ordinary usage. Thus, I must defend and clarify this somewhat unorthodox conception.

Marvin Farber draws the typical contrast. Naturalism is the "philosophy based upon the findings and methods of the sciences." Subjectivism, its opposite, maintains "the primacy of experiencing being."[1] The tie between naturalism and science—the view that naturalism was committed *to* the *method* of science—is contained in Ralph Perry's definition of naturalism as "the philosophical generalization of science."[2] This usage is common, but misleading. A conception of naturalism as "the philosophical generalization of science" has confused accident with essence—something that philosophers, of all people, should not do. It has mistaken a superbly serviceable means for probing the nature of certain things for the more profound meaning of naturalism. It has transformed a means into an end. Perry's conception has transformed into naturalism itself a main method by which we might commit ourselves to certain phenomena and engage their nature.

This common conception of naturalism is familiar. Most often it has been expressed by philosophers of science or by social scientists who are concerned with philosophical issues.[3] With very few exceptions, the writers claiming jurisdiction over the term naturalism have forwarded this conception whether or not they favored the philosophic generalization of science. For instance, Natanson, a phenomenologist, is as taken by this conception of naturalism as those more positivist in spirit.[4] In the dominant conception, naturalism is equivalent to scientific philosophy, experimental method, a stress on objective, external, or observable features of phenomena, and, in general, positivism. In the same conception, naturalism's opposites are idealism, existentialism, phenomenology, and, in general, a stress on subjective experience and a corresponding reliance on intuition and insight rather than rigorous, replicable procedure.[5] Naturalism is counterposed to subjectivism. My thesis is that this conception and juxtaposition mistakes the nature of naturalism, and does so largely as a result of confusing tem-

---

[1] Marvin Farber, *Naturalism and Subjectivism* (Springfield, Ill.: Charles C Thomas, Publisher, 1959), p. vii.

[2] Ralph Barton Perry, *Present Philosophical Tendencies* (New York: Longmans, Green & Company, Ltd., 1916), p. 45. See also Perry, *Philosophy of the Recent Past* (New York: Charles Scribner's Sons, 1926), pp. 1–2 and p. 5.

[3] Representative statements may be found in William R. Dennes, "The Categories of Naturalism," pp. 270–294, Yervant H. Krikorian, "A Naturalist View of the Mind," pp. 242–269, and Thelma Z. Lavine, "Naturalism and the Sociological Analysis of Knowledge," pp. 40–64, all in Krikorian, *Naturalism and the Human Spirit* (New York: Columbia University Press, 1944). The same viewpoint is expressed in a later collection of essays including: Thelma Lavine, "Note to Naturalists on the Human Spirit" and "What is the Method of Naturalism?" pp. 250–261 and pp. 266–270 respectively, Maurice Natanson, "A Study in Philosophy and the Social Sciences," pp. 271–285, and Leon Goldstein, "The Phenomenological and the Naturalistic Approaches to the Social," pp. 286–301, all in Maurice Natanson, *Philosophy of the Social Sciences* (New York: Random House, Inc., 1963).

[4] See Maurice Natanson, "A Study in Philosophy and the Social Sciences," in Natanson, *op. cit.*, pp. 271–285.

[5] The most recent statement of the nature of naturalism and its antagonists, barely distinguishable from its predecessors, may be found in William Catton, *From Animistic to Naturalistic Sociology* (New York: McGraw-Hill Book Company, 1966).

poral or ephemeral features of naturalism with its lasting or persistent nature.

One writer, John Randall, Jr., has been sensitive to the error inherent in conceiving naturalism's commitment as being to the method of science.[6] Such a view would better be termed "scientism," and it has been so designated. Naturalism, as the very term implies, is the philosophical view that strives *to remain true to the nature of the phenomenon under study or scrutiny.* For naturalism, the phenomenon being scrutinized is to be considered object or subject depending on its nature—not on the philosophical preconceptions of a researcher. That specific nature commands the fidelity of naturalism. This does not mean that the nature of phenomena is readily apparent; their nature may sometimes be at issue. But the resolution of that issue must be based on experience or more rigorous empirical methods. How the phenomenon is conceived, as object or as subject, is henceforth to be guided by that empirical resolution rather than by convenience or the distinguished precedents set by other disciplines.

So conceived, naturalism stands against all forms of philosophical generalization. Its loyalty is *to the world* with whatever measure of variety or universality happens to inhere in it. Naturalism does not and cannot commit itself to eternal preconceptions regarding the nature of phenomena. Consequently, it does not and cannot commit itself to any single preferred method for engaging and scrutinizing phenomena. It stands for observation or engagement of course for that is implicit in fidelity to the natural world. But naturalistic observation may also include experience and introspection, the methods traditionally associated with subjectivism.

Randall suggests that the adversaries of naturalism were first supernaturalism and, more recently, reductionism. He says:

> The "new" or "contemporary" naturalism . . . stands in fundamental opposition not only to all forms of supernaturalism, but also to all types of reductionist thinking which up to this generation often arrogated to itself the adjective "naturalistic" and still is suggested by it to the popular mind. Second only to the unanimity with which these writers reject supernaturalism and acclaim scientific procedures is their agreement that the richness and variety of natural phenomena and human experience cannot be explained away and "reduced" to something else. The world is not really "nothing but" something other than it appears to be: it is what it is, in all its manifold variety, with all its distinctive kinds of activity. . . . Human life in particular displays characteristic ways of action which have no discoverable counterpart in the behavior of any other being. Man's searching intelligence, his problems of moral choice and obligation, his ideal enterprises of art, science, and religion are what they inescapably are. . . . Inquiry can find out much about them, about their conditions and consequences, their functions and values; but what it

[6] John H. Randall, Jr., "The Nature of Naturalism," in Krikorian, *op. cit.,* pp. 354–382.

finds is an addition to our knowledge of what they are, not the amazing discovery that they are not, or ought not to be.[7]

Given Randall's conception the aim of naturalism is to render the phenomenon cogently in a manner that maintains its integrity—not the integrity of any philosophic viewpoint. Once that is understood, it becomes possible to separate temporal from more essential and permanent features. The temporal features of naturalism were inherent in the philosophic viewpoint of science and were successful in comprehending certain phenomenal levels while maintaining the integrity of things existing at that level. The nature of phenomena existing at the level most vulnerable to the philosophy and method of science was itself complex. But one general feature was outstanding and of immediate relevance. These phenomena were, by nature, *objects*. Though in somewhat different terms, Gordon Allport asserts the subjectivity of being human. The *activity* of certain levels of being in contrast to the mere *reactivity* of other levels suggests the inadequacy of likening man to object:

> *We are told that every stone in the field is unique, every old shoe in the closet, every bar of iron, but that this ubiquitous individuality does not affect the operations or the progress of science. The geologist, the physicist, the cobbler, proceed to apply universal laws, and find the accident of uniqueness irrelevant to their work. The analogy is unconvincing. Stones, old shoes, bars of iron are purely reactive; they will not move unless they are manipulated. They are incapable of becoming. How is it then with uniqueness in the realm of biology where in addition to reactivity each plant manifests the capacities of self-repair, self-regulation, adaptation? One leaf of the tree is large, another small, one deformed, another healthy. Yet all obey the sure laws of metabolism and cell structure. . . . But here too the analogy is weak. Unlike plants and lower animals, man is not merely a creature of cell structure, tropism and instinct; he does not live his life by repeating, with trivial variation, the pattern of his species.*[8]

At first, it was proper for naturalists to conceive the phenomena scrutinized as objects. By and large, though variably, the phenomena scrutinized during this period *were* objects. The philosophical viewpoint of science was uniquely suited to the study of such phenomena. *Its* assumptions, with regard to being, happily coincided with the *nature* of phenomena it chose to scrutinize and analyze. Indeed, its assumptions were largely derived from the ascendant, and as it turned out, *truthful* view of the then controversial nature of certain realms of existence. Early naturalism inferred a truth—objectivity—from important and ubiquitous levels of existence. Its

---

[7] *Ibid.*, p. 361. For a recent and excellent statement of this view as it pertains to sociological analysis, see Herbert Blumer, "Sociological Implications of the Thought of George Herbert Mead," *American Journal of Sociology*, LXXI (March 1966), 535–547.

[8] Gordon Allport, *Becoming* (New Haven: Yale University Press, 1955), pp. 21–22.

followers then proceeded to generalize that truth and apply it to other realms of existence. The result was predictable—falsification.

The opposition to the methods of experience, intuition, and empathy that developed during the early growth of naturalism was understandable and legitimate. Fidelity to objective phenomena hardly necessitates these forms of scrutiny. Indeed, it was mandatory that the study of the physical and organic realms be purged of supernatural conceptions of phenomena. The objective, and especially the mechanistic view, opposed and more or less vanquished ideas of vitalism and teleology.[9]

Thus, the objective view of naturalism was positive and appropriate when the object of inquiry was in fact an object. The confusion arose when the spirit of naturalism turned to the study of man. The major result of that confusion was a longstanding misconception of man from which the disciplines purporting to comprehend him are only beginning to recover. The minor result was the one immediately relevant—a misconception of the meaning of naturalism.

The confusion began when primitive social scientists—many of whom are still vigorous—mistook the phenomenon under consideration—man—and conceived it as object instead of subject. That was a great mistake. Numerous theories appeared positing man as merely reactive and denying that he is the author of action, but none were convincing.

The misconception of man as object oscillated between two major forms: the first radical, the second heuristic. In the first, man *was* object. In the second, scientists deemed it heuristic merely to act *as if* man were object.[10] In both views, however, a similar consequence appeared. Irrespective of whether man was object or merely heuristically treated as object, the terms of analysis were set in a fashion that minimized man's causal capacity, his activity, his tendency to reflect on himself and his setting, and his periodic struggles to transcend rather than succumb to the circumstances that allegedly shaped and constrained him.[11]

[9] In recent years, many writers have argued that the mechanists went much too far, at least with respect to the organic realm. See Marjorie Grene, "Portmann's Thought," *Commentary*, XI, No. 5 (November 1965), 31–38. Also see, Adolf Portmann, *New Paths in Biology* (New York: Harper & Row, Publishers, 1964), pp. 32, 34.

[10] For a distinction between these different versions of determinism, hard and soft, see my *Delinquency and Drift* (New York: John Wiley & Sons, Inc., 1964), Chapter 1, pp. 1–32. In that discussion I more or less settle on a position of soft determinism. I suppose the present discussion moves even further away from an acceptance of any sort of determinism.

[11] The Meadian view is in large measure the sociological tradition that maintained the humanist stress on subjectivity. He was not alone in that endeavor but, perhaps, central in the United States. In his view, being objectified is important, whether it is the self treating itself as object or perceiving another in that way. But objectifying, in Meadian tradition, was viewed as a subjective capacity. It was an activity performed by the self on itself or on another. That is quite different from radically or heuristically conceiving man as object. The subject who views himself as object is still the author of action.

These minimizations of man persisted as presumptions which guided research and shaped operative theory. They were maintained despite classic repudiations of the objective view by Max Weber and George Herbert Mead and despite Robert MacIver's explicit and brilliant, but still unappreciated discussion of various existential realms and the distinctive features of each.[12] The initial mistake continues to plague sociology, as well as the other human disciplines. For instance, the opinion cited by Donald Cressey affirming the utility of mathematizing Sutherland's theory of differential association is not simply an act of disciplinary statesmanship or professional promotion. He who says "that the only difference between physical science and social science is a billion man-hours of work" simply continues to miss the fundamental point made by Weber, Mead, and MacIver.[13]

Man participates in *meaningful* activity. He creates his reality, and that of the world around him, actively and strenuously. Man *naturally*—not supernaturally—transcends the existential realms in which the conceptions of cause, force, and reactivity are easily applicable. Accordingly, a view that conceives man as object, methods that probe human behavior without concerning themselves with the meaning of behavior, cannot be regarded as naturalist. Such views and methods are the very *opposite* of naturalism because they have molested in advance the phenomenon to be studied. Naturalism when applied to the study of man has no choice but to conceive man as subject precisely because naturalism claims fidelity to the empirical world. In the empirical world, man is subject and not object, except when he is likened to one by himself or by another subject. Naturalism must choose the subjective view, and consequently it must combine the scientific method with the distinctive tools of humanism—experience, intuition, and empathy. Naturalism has no other choice because its philosophical commitment is neither to objectivity nor subjectivity, neither to scientific method nor humanist sensibility. Its only commitment is fidelity to the phenomenon under consideration. Thus, in the study of man, there is no antagonism between naturalism and a repudiation of the objective view, nor a contradiction between naturalism and the humane methods of experience, reason, intuition, and empathy. Naturalism in the study of man is a disciplined and rigorous humanism.

The fidelity of naturalism to the empirical world has created a certain stress on the mundane, the matter-of-fact—even the vulgar. Naturalism has therefore been an anti-philosophical philosophy in one key sense. The common view of being philosophical, of holding to a philosophy, emphasizes

[12] See Max Weber, *The Theory of Social and Economic Organization* (New York: Free Press of Glencoe, Inc., 1964), pp. 88–114; George Herbert Mead, *Mind, Self, and Society,* ed. Charles Morris (Chicago: University of Chicago Press, 1934); and Robert MacIver, *Social Causation* (Boston: Ginn and Company, 1942).

[13] Donald Cressey, "The Language of Set Theory and Differential Association," *Journal of Research in Crime and Delinquency,* III (January 1966), 26.

the precedence of abstraction, theory, or metaphysics over the world. That stereotype of philosophy has never been wholly incorrect; even naturalism, which began with a commitment to the world, turned away from the concrete and attached itself to the abstraction—science. But for naturalism at least, that attachment may be regarded as an infidelity, or so I have suggested. Moreover, the world was paid tribute, despite its being cuckolded. Though small consolation to its subject matter—for the cuckold there are no minor infidelities—the antagonism toward abstraction, formalism—toward what the common man means by philosophy—persisted and survived. A preference for concrete detail, an appreciation of density and variability, a dislike of the formal, the abstract, the artificial, served to unify what otherwise may seem disparate developments: the naturalism of plant and animal life, literary naturalism, and the emergent naturalism of sociology. Only through its differences with science has the unity of naturalism in art, journalism, literature, zoology, botany, ecology, and sociology become evident. That unity has been expressed in an anti-philosophical tendency.

But unfortunately, no philosophy can succeed in being anti-philosophical. A countertendency to abstract, classify, and generalize appeared partly because it was inevitable: the very act of writing or reporting commits the author to a *rendition* of the world, and a rendering is a sifting. Moreover, the naturalist could find in the world itself, especially among human subjects, a warrant for the countertendency: The human world itself was given to abstraction, generalization, and classification and thus it contained a measure of order and regularity. In this way, within the very spirit of naturalism, the anti-philosophic tendency met its opposite. But the anti-philosophy is worth noting nonetheless and should be kept in mind because it served to control and discipline the philosophical tendency. It is naturalism, and not science, that provokes students to disgustedly ask of their professors: "But what does that have to do with what goes on in the world?" Those who share the naturalist outlook differ on many points, says Harold Larrabee, but they "tend to begin with whatever confronts the human observer in his complete daily living and to endeavor to frame a satisfactory account of it in its own terms."[14] Thus, the attitude of naturalism grew in America, matter-of-fact, concrete, and committed to the world despite its long flirtation with science. Its aim is a faithful rendition of worldly activities. But being a *rendition* or summary of the world, it must be satisfied with a mere approximation of that ideal.

I have spent more time on philosophy than is perhaps appropriate, and it may appear to the reader that a great deal of effort has been expended merely to wrest a term from those who use it otherwise. My defense for this procedure has two bases: I believe the equation of naturalism with science to

[14] Harold Larrabee, "Naturalism in America," in Krikorian, *op. cit.*, p. 319.

be a misconception, and I need the idea of naturalism as an organizing principle for the developments described in the first part of this book. The growth of a sociological view of deviant phenomena involved, as major phases, the replacement of a correctional stance by an *appreciation* of the deviant subject, the tacit purging of a conception of pathology by new stress on human *diversity,* and the erosion of a simple distinction between deviant and conventional phenomena, resulting from more intimate familiarity with the world as it is, which yielded a more sophisticated view stressing *complexity*. These three—appreciation, diversity, and complexity—are the topics in Part I of the volume. Their relationship becomes clearer and their character more unified if we see each as part of the advent of naturalism. My thesis is that naturalism, in this sense, has illuminated the nature of deviant phenomena.

Deviation

One may make a fetish of definitions. Except when needing a term that has been used otherwise, I prefer to make little of them, at least in the beginning. In the final chapter, a slightly more elaborate conception will be presented. Now, a *nominal* definition will suffice.[15] A nominal definition is one that is not too outlandish, one that will facilitate and not hamper meaningful discourse. Since no further use, such as "generating propositions," is contemplated, premature elaboration or esoteric usage serves little purpose. Indeed, such elaboration or usage would discourage the reader because his capacity to survive conceptual discussion depends on whether he has first been exposed to the concrete.

According to any standard dictionary—still the best source of clearly stated nominal definitions—to deviate is to *stray,* as from a path or standard. If one delights in such a pursuit, he may classify the forms of straying according to a number of ready-made criteria: the clarity of the path, the distance from the path, the auspices under which the path is constructed or commended, whether one strays from the path in isolation or in company, the penalty, the motives commonly imputed for straying, or (what usually comes to the same thing) the academic discipline currently claiming learned jurisdiction over the souls of those who stray. But when all is said and done, we inevitably return to the wise observation that there are many kinds of deviation and that deviation is in some measure a matter of degree. At the

[15] Robert Bierstedt, "Nominal and Real Definitions in Sociological Theory," in Llewellyn Gross, *Symposium on Sociological Theory* (Evanston, Ill.: Row, Peterson & Co., 1959).

nominal level, nothing more can be said, though that much can be said in surprisingly extended detail.

Whatever the conception of standard or path, occasional phenomena existing at the border are readily observable. When these lie at the margin of deviant or conventional realms, the very designation, *deviant, is* dubious. Such uncertainty is troublesome for those who abhor sloppiness, but, in truth, the difficulty resides in the nature of society not in the conception of deviation. Cultural definitions, especially in contemporary society, tend toward ambiguity. Since standards shift, members of society may respond to marginal phenomena with open ambiguity, or, if there is reason to be guarded, with a certain shiftiness.

Students of society must tolerate such ambiguity. Finely drawn and strictly operational conceptions leaving no place for ambiguity may be a source of satisfaction for the analyst, but he will find that ordinary subjects of inquiry have the capacity to subvert such conceptions and render them useless. Whether the phenomenon personified, say, by a waitress in topless attire is deviant is a question that will yield a clear-cut answer if our conception of deviation is sufficiently rigorous and operational. But the clear-cut yes or no will be gained only by suppressing, and thus denying, the patent ambiguity of this novel phenomenon and the easily observable tentative, vacillating, and shifty responses to it. Accordingly, the cost of rigor may be deemed excessive since certainty in classifying the phenomenon as deviant or not is accomplished through the dubious expedient of restricting our view of compelling and relevant social facts—ambiguity and shift.

There is another aspect of this problem. In a pluralistic society, one man's deviation may be another's custom. Or as Talcott Parsons puts it:

> . . . *There is a certain relativity in the conceptions of conformity and deviance. . . . It is not possible to make a judgment of deviance . . . without specific reference to the system . . . to which it applies. The structure of normative patterns in any but the simplest sub-system is always intricate and usually far from fully integrated; hence singling out one such pattern without reference to its interconnections in a system of patterns can be very misleading . . .*[16]

Moreover, libertine and puritan traditions may divide even those segments of the population for whom the activity is not customary, yielding enormous differences in the level of toleration. In such societies, some phenomena will be sensed as morally complicated, defying easy classification. In short, there may be differences of opinion among ordinary members

[16] Talcott Parsons, *The Social System* (New York: The Free Press of Glencoe, Inc., 1951), pp. 250–251.

of society; that social fact affects even the most nominal of definitions. The social fact of pluralism, like that of ambiguity, must be lived with and appreciated. It cannot be evaded simply to expedite a rigorous definition of deviation. Shift, ambiguity, and pluralism are implicated in the very idea of deviation; their net effect is to make even our nominal conception inexact and blurred at the edges. The uncertainty cannot be liquidated; it can only be observed and reported.

When there is no authoritative resolution of differences regarding the moral status of a phenomenon, it is presumptuous, and perhaps even useless, to say anything more than that the point is moot. But often there *is* authoritative resolution. When there is, as in civil or criminal law, we may observe either laboriously or simply that the issue, the difference of opinion, has been painfully and tentatively resolved—though not to everyone's satisfaction. Thus, for instance, the moral status of waitresses in topless attire was tentatively and joyfully resolved in San Francisco, at least with respect to legality, but the ambiguity of the phenomenon remains, as do the plural and shifty responses to it. Both the authoritative resolution and the continuing disagreement are consequential and thus worth noting.

The appreciation of shift, ambiguity, and pluralism need hardly imply a wholesale repudiation of the idea of common morality. Such an inference is the mistake of a rampant and mindless relativism. Plural evaluation, shifting standards, and moral ambiguity may, and do, coexist with a phenomenal realm that is *commonly sensed* as deviant. The very meaning of pluralism, the very possibility of shift and ambiguity depend on a wider consensus, founded in common understandings, regarding the patently deviant nature of many nonetheless ordinary undertakings. Thus, the deviant nature of many phenomena is hardly problematic, the best evidence being that no operative member of society bothers to develop a position one way or the other. Except for those who conjure a path whenever they see a company of strayers, it is clear to everyone—including the strayers—that commonly understood and commonly held deviations have occurred. Thieves—except perhaps for Genet and He who sanctified him—do not believe in stealing, though they engage in it, defensively justify it, and even develop a measure of expertise and sense of craft. Bullies do not believe in assaulting people though they, too, may cultivate, justify, and develop their special skill. Bastards are frowned on and derogated despite the fact that they are regularly spawned and variably tolerated. Thus there is little need to choose abstractly between a common, and perhaps natural, human morality and what has come to be known as cultural relativism.

Beyond this brief consideration of a nominal and simple conception of deviation and the inevitable difficulties in applying it to empirically problematic phenomena, elaboration would be misleading. To labor long is to imply inadvertently that there is something mysterious and slippery about the concrete phenomena to which the nominal conception points—and that is precisely the stance I wish to avoid. Instead, I want to assume that deviant phenomena are common and natural. They are a normal and inevitable part of social life, as is their denunciation, regulation, and prohibition. Deviation is implicit in the moral character of society: "To give oneself laws and to create the possibility of disobeying them come to the same thing."[17]

That deviation is implicit in the idea of society was well-stated by Durkheim and has since been a matter of general consensus among sociologists. No matter what the measure of moral rectitude, deviation will occur. Moral improvement of a citizenry will not of itself diminish deviation since the very fact of moral uplift will suggest new and more demanding standards of conduct.

> *Imagine a society of saints, a perfect cloister of exemplary individuals. Crimes, properly so called, will there be unknown; but faults which appear venial to the laymen will create there the same scandal that the ordinary offense does in the ordinary consciousness. . . . For the same reason, the perfect and upright man judges his smallest failings with a severity that the majority reserves for acts more truly in the nature of an offense. Formerly, acts of violence against persons were more frequent than they are today, because respect for individual dignity was less strong. As this has increased, these crimes have become more rare; and also, many acts violating this sentiment have been introduced into the penal law which were not included there in primitive times (e.g., calumny, insults, slander, fraud, etc.).*[18]

Thus, according to Durkheim, deviation is implicit in social and moral organization. When specific deviations are brought under control and reduced or obliterated, the category of deviation nonetheless survives. The demise of the specific deviation is coincident with the general elevation of the standards it violated. Consequently, phenomena that are more refined violations of the same general standards will emerge as new deviations. Durkheim's point here is not merely the thesis of relativism. It is more subtle, and more universal. His thesis rests on a coincidence between the decline in the prevalence of gross violations of the sentiment of individual dignity and the heightened morality of a society experiencing that decline. A population experiencing heightened morality—a society of saints—will gradually come to see that insults and slander, too, are serious and actionable violations of individual dignity. Other precepts—minimality, for instance— may serve to limit or check the insatiable morality posted by Durkheim. But

[17] Jean Paul Sartre, *Saint Genet* (New York: New American Library, Inc. [Mentor], 1964), p. 35.
[18] Emile Durkheim, *The Rules of Sociological Method* (New York: The Free Press of Glencoe, Inc., 1938), pp. 68–69.

even if checked and hampered by others, the lifting of standards and the survival of categories of deviation are tendencies, nonetheless.

Since deviation is a common feature of society, since it is implicit in social and moral organization, it needs no extraordinary accounting. Straying from a path need be regarded as no less comprehensible nor more bewildering than walking it. Given the moral character of social life, both *naturally* happen, and thus are pondered and studied by sociologists and others.

2

Correction and Appreciation

During the past forty or fifty years, a fundamental aspect of naturalism emerged. It was a most rudimentary aspect, and thus hardly an occasion for great cheer or self-congratulation. Still, it was consequential. Though little more than a posture, a habit of mind—an attitude—it was prerequisite to future development. This posture is an essential element of naturalism whether the world to be engaged and comprehended was that of objects or subjects. It may be termed *appreciation*.

Appreciation is especially difficult when the subject of inquiry consists of enterprises that violate cherished and widely shared standards of conduct and morality. Almost by definition, such phenomena are commonly *unap-preciated*; indeed, they are condemned. Accordingly, the purpose of much research on deviation has been to assist established society ultimately to rid itself of such troublesome activities. The goal of ridding ourselves of the deviant phenomenon, however Utopian, stands in sharp contrast to an appreciative perspective and may be referred to as *correctional*.

A basic difficulty with a correctional perspective is that it systematically interferes with the capacity to empathize and thus comprehend the subject of inquiry. Only through appreciation can the texture of social patterns and the nuances of human engagement with those patterns be understood and analyzed. Without appreciation and empathy we may gather

15

surface facts regarding a phenomenon and criticize the enterprises connected with it, but we will fail to understand in depth its meaning to the subjects involved and its place in the wider society. In this respect, as in others, the study of subjects stands in marked contrast to the study of objects, though even in the latter case a fondness for the object of inquiry is far from unknown. The difference is that in the study of subjects, appreciation and empathy are essential tools of inquiry, a basic resource without which the enormous distance between analyst and subject remains. The correctional standpoint interferes with engaging the deviant phenomenon because it is informed and motivated by the purpose of ridding itself of it. Until recently, and still in large measure today, the study of deviant phenomena has been dominated by the correctional view.

As with naturalism generally, an appreciative view is flanked on both sides by attitudes that threaten it. The desire to liquidate the phenomenon is almost as inimical to the spirit of appreciation as the frequent tendency to suppress features of the phenomenon which by conventional standards are distasteful. Curiously enough, this romantic tendency sometimes appears within a predominantly correctional perspective, but most often it accompanies appreciation. But such appreciation is only a pale imitation since it is achieved at the cost of denying essential features of the deviant enterprise.

Paupers occasionally fleece the welfare system, robbers often brutalize or otherwise molest their victims, motorcycle gangs are a terrible nuisance to policemen, prostitutes sometimes roll their customers, drug addicts are engaged in a great deal of petty and grand theft, homosexuals are relatively promiscuous, Gypsies have been known to swindle Gentiles if a promising opportunity appears, Bohemians engage in what has been called "free love," and so on. These features—detestable by conventional standards—can hardly be denied or suppressed; they are part of what must be appreciated if one adheres to a naturalistic perspective, for they are a part of various deviant enterprises. This willingness to empathize with the deviant phenomenon in its full scope contrasts naturalism with the romanticism that superficially resembles it. The appreciative spirit was well expressed by George Borrow, the famous gypsiologist, whose writing in 1843 foreshadowed subsequent developments by eighty or ninety years. He said:

> *The cause of truth can scarcely be forwarded by enthusiasm, which is almost invariably the child of ignorance and error. The author is anxious to direct the attention of the public towards the Gypsies; but he hopes to be able to do so without any romantic appeals in their behalf, by concealing the truth, or by warping the truth until it becomes falsehood.*[1]

[1] George Borrow, *The Zincali, An Account of the Gypsies of Spain* (New York: G. P. Putnam's Sons, 3rd ed., 1843), I, xv.

Though romanticism has hindered the growth of naturalism, the main obstacle is implicit in the correctional perspective. The correctional perspective is reasonable enough, perhaps even commendable, except that it makes empathy and understanding difficult, and sometimes impossible. Correction reflects the easily appreciated social view that persons who have strayed from moral standards ought to be persuaded by a variety of means to return to the fold, and it argues that knowledge may be put to that service. To appreciate the variety of deviant enterprises requires a temporary or permanent suspension of conventional morality, and thus by usual standards inescapable elements of irresponsibility and absurdity are implicit in the appreciative stance. Deviant enterprises, and the persons who engage them, are almost by definition troublesome and disruptive. How silly and perhaps evil, therefore, seem the appreciative sentiments of those who have been guided by the naturalist spirit. These appreciative sentiments are easily summarized: We do not for a moment wish that we could rid ourselves of deviant phenomena. We are intrigued by them. They are an intrinsic, ineradicable, and vital part of human society.

The Correctional Perspective

When deviant phenomena are seen and studied from the correctional perspective, the possibility of "losing the phenomenon"—reducing it to that which it is not—is heightened. The purpose of ridding ourselves of the phenomenon manifests itself most clearly in an overwhelming contemporary concern with questions of causation, or "etiology." The phenomenon itself receives only cursory attention. The ultimate purpose of liquidation is reflected in this highly disproportionate division of attention between description and explanation. With the possible exception of Sutherland's stress on behavior systems and their detailed description, and Maurer's detailed ethnography, traditional studies of deviant behavior have been highly vague and shortwinded about the phenomena they presume to explain.[2] Why bother with detailed and subtle description? The task before us, in the correctional perspective, is to get at the root causes in order to remove them and their product.

Apart from their lack of attention to detail, another noticeable consequence of many sociologists' aversion to the phenomenon itself was their incapacity to separate standards of morality from actual description. The

[2] Edwin Sutherland and Donald Cressey, *Criminology* (New York: J. B. Lippincott Co., 6th ed., 1960), pp. 237–252. Also see David Maurer, *The Big Con* (Indianapolis: The Bobbs-Merrill Co., Inc., 1940); and Maurer, *Whiz Mob* (Gainesville, Fla.: American Dialect Society, 1955).

standards intrude to assure that the phenomenon will be viewed from the outside and so described. This posture may be illustrated by two exemplary studies, pervaded by the correctional spirit, and made during the period when that spirit was still dominant. An appreciation of the correctional spirit is best gained if we go back to the decade immediately preceding the first World War, when the correctional spirit was largely unquestioned in both England and America, and was institutionalized in strong alliances among sociology, social work, and social reform.[3]

The *West Side Studies* and the *Pittsburgh Survey* both were sponsored by the Russell Sage Foundation, which was then, and is still in some measure, an influential representative of the correctional spirit. These studies, important in their time, were excellent and definitive. In them we may observe the dominant correctional attitude; additionally, however, some of the naturalistic precepts that were to appear a few years later in the Chicago school are foreshadowed. Thus, a brief consideration of these studies yields a glimpse of the correctional perspective just before its assumptions and temper were brought into question—first, inadvertently by the Chicago school and then explicitly and intentionally by two later groups.

Differences between the spirit animating the Russell Sage studies and that guiding the Chicago school can be easily exaggerated. Though there were differences, they were of degree and nuance and not clear-cut. The attitude implicit in the Russell Sage studies was not wholly correctional, just as the sentiments of the Chicago school were not wholly appreciative. The West Side and Pittsburgh surveys were already engaged in what was to become the central contribution to naturalism of the Chicago school. They, too, entered the world of the deviant, but to a much lesser extent than the Chicagoans. Their main reliance was still on newspaper accounts, police folders, and reports of social investigators. Some of this emphasis persisted in the work of the Chicago school, but much greater reliance was placed on the deviant subject's *own story*. Appreciation of deviant phenomena requires a consideration of the subject's viewpoint. Though it hardly requires an acceptance of that viewpoint, it does assume empathy with it. In the Pittsburgh and West Side surveys, there is a glimmer—but no more—of the connected naturalist precepts of entering the subjective world of the deviant and empathizing with the viewpoint implicit in that world. Mainly, the attitude and frame of reference for these studies were those of respectable, conventional society. Though they entered the deviant world, they did so hesitantly and without adopting the subject's point of view; though they sym-

---

[3] For a discussion of early British sociology and the influence of social work, or "practical philanthropy," see Donald MacRae, *Ideology and Society* (New York: Free Press of Glencoe, Inc., 1962), p. 7. For a consideration of early American sociology and the great concern with pathology and its amelioration, see Jessie Bernard, "The History and Prospects of Sociology in the United States," in George Lundberg, Read Bain, and Nels Anderson (eds.), *Trends in American Sociology* (New York: Harper & Row, Publishers, 1929), pp. 1–71.

pathized with the plight of slum children, they hardly empathized with it; and instead of appreciating the character of the distinctive human enterprises they encountered, they condemned them and yearned for correction.

The conventional and correctional assumptions that pervade these surveys are well illustrated in the following description of deviant behavior on the West Side of New York. This description is fairly typical of the attitude conveyed in the study. Only the deviant phenomena under consideration is unusual. Consequently, the implicit attitude does not pass unnoticed; usually it does.

> *The two chief sports of the Middle West Side—baseball and boxing—are perennial. The former, played as it always is, with utter carelessness and disregard of surroundings, is theoretically intolerable, but it flourishes despite constant complaints and interference. The diamond is marked out in the roadway, the bases indicated by paving bricks, sticks, or newspapers. Frequently guards are placed at each end of the block to warn of the approach of police. One minute a game is in full swing; the next, a scout cries "cheese it." Balls, bats, and gloves disappear . . . and when the "cop" appears . . . the boys will be innocently strolling down the streets. Notwithstanding these precautions, as the juvenile court records show, they are constantly being caught. In a great majority of these . . . games too much police vigilance cannot be exercised, for a game between a dozen or more boys, of from fourteen to eighteen years of age, with a league ball, in a crowded street, with plate glass windows on either side, becomes a joke to no one but the participants. A foul ball stands innumerable chances of going through the third-story window of a tenement, or of making a bee line through the valuable plate glass window of a store on the street level, or of hitting one of the passersby. . . . When one sees the words "arrested for playing with a hard ball in a public street" written on a coldly impersonal record card in the children's court one is apt to become indignant. But when you see the same hard ball being batted through a window or into a group of little children on the same public street, the matter assumes an entirely different aspect. . . . Clearly from the community's point of view, the playing of baseball in the street is rightly a penal offense. It annoys citizens, injures persons and property, and interferes with traffic.*[4]

There is little doubt that the researchers have adopted the community viewpoint and not that of the deviant subject—in this case, hard-ball players. Though the correctional temper is evident in the discussion of baseball, it is even more apparent in the discussion of the second major sport of the West Side. With regard to boxing, the investigators said:

> *The West Side youngster sees very little of the real professional boxers who, from the very nature of their somewhat strenuous employment, must keep in good condition. . . . But of their brutalized hangers-on,*

[4] *West Side Studies* (New York: Russell Sage Foundation, 1914), I, 29–30.

the "bruisers," who frequent the saloons and street corners and pose as real fighters, he sees a great deal; consequently, as a whole, prize-fighting must be classed as one of the worst influences of the neighborhood. It is too closely allied with streetfighting, and too easily turned to criminal purposes.[5]

The conventional commitment of the correctional perspective, as manifested in *West Side Studies,* was pervasive. Moreover, the standards espoused by the investigators are especially striking because they were so highly puritanical—so boy-scoutish. It was not simply that the ordinary member of society was entrusted with the research function; instead, perhaps, the *most moral* members served in that capacity. Note the range of values commended and stressed in the following excerpt. Note also the steady interpenetration of analysis and correctional viewpoint. Little effort is made to separate the two.

The West Side gang is in its origin perfectly normal. . . . Its influence [on a boy] is strong and immediate. . . . Untrammelled by the perversion of special circumstances it might encourage his latent interests, train him to obedience and loyalty, show him the method and the saving of cooperation, and teach him the beauty of self-sacrifice.[6]

So pervasive and so implicit are the moral standards manifested in the correctional view of *West Side Studies* that ordinarily they are obscured from the readers notice. Occasionally, standards so demanding and so different from those of our own time emerge as dramatic manifestations of what is implicit in the entire effort. One example of this is to be found in yet another allegedly lamentable feature of slum life: "Father and children eat the same food, and the boy is accustomed to the stimulus of tea and coffee from childhood."[7]

A wholly dim view of slum life and of its close relation to diverse pathologies has been a staple of the correctional perspective, and this external perspective shaped the conclusion of the West Side investigators. "At the very outset," they suggested, "poverty destroys the possibilities of normal development."[8] In this perspective, the slum was no less—and no more —than a pathological growth in modern society. Not just crime or alcohol, but ordinary childhood activities apparent in the round of slum life—from hardball to sipping father's coffee—were, in their view, manifestations of pathology resulting in more pronounced forms of vice and evil. Many of the worse evils of the slum are to be found on the "street"; consequently a major

---

[5] *West Side Studies,* p. 36.
[6] *West Side Studies,* p. 40.
[7] *West Side Studies,* p. 75.
[8] *West Side Studies,* p. 61.

policy recommendation of these early students of metropolitan social life was the increased construction of playgrounds.

Despite the careful detail with which slum life is depicted, the picture emerging from these studies lacks credence and fidelity. Written from the viewpoint of the conventional citizenry, it rarely transcends the limitations incumbent on the outsider. Although the observers toured the world of the West Side and sympathized with its residents, they developed little appreciation for its integrity and thus its workings. Being outsiders—and never transforming themselves—the observers were barely able to describe or comprehend the moral and social life of their subjects. Indeed, the virtual absence of moral life is taken as a cardinal feature of the West Side. They said:

> *Boys start out on "crookin" expeditions, taking anything edible or vendible that they can lay their hands on. . . . Here [as in the case of stealing coal] . . . the boys have a definite point of view. They are quite non-moral and have never learned to consider the question of property. Their code is the primitive code of might and they look upon their booty as theirs by right of conquest. Further, the very pressure of poverty is an incentive to stealing for various ends. . . . When one is penniless and knows no moral code and sees one's elders acknowledging none, the temptation to adopt the tactics of the thief and the thug becomes almost irresistible.*[9]

The point is not whether this interpretation is valid or not. Cultural relativism may err in the opposite direction by assuming too uncritically the moral character of deviant phenomena. That is an empirical issue that must be resolved specifically for each case. The point is that the observers of the West Side simply failed to consider the complexity of the question of moral systems. It was obvious to them that West Siders lacked a moral system because they were acting in violation of conventional precepts.

The Pittsburgh survey was guided by the same correctional spirit as the West Side studies. Most striking about correctional analysis, in the Pittsburgh survey, is the simplicity of its formulations, the lack of any sense of paradox or irony. The correctional view was—and is—pedestrian: Bad things result from bad conditions. That is almost the entire theory. Moreover, there are no tricksters, no surprises in the natural world described by the Pittsburgh surveyors. As we will see, irony became a central feature of the naturalist view, especially as it was advanced by the functionalists.[10] The Pittsburgh surveyors usually felt that analysis was complete when they had succeeded in finding "some consequences of bad streets, unsanitary housing, trade acci-

[9] *West Side Studies*, pp. 142–143.
[10] See Chapter 4.

dents, and the race problem.[11] This tendency is illustrated in an assessment of conditions in Skunk Hollow, a rundown section of Pittsburgh, and the consequences of these conditions.

> *Do you wish to see the housing problem? You need only follow Ewing Street the length of a city block and observe. Here are rampant the conditions generated when families with feeble resources attempt to "live," as we say, on land rendered all but valueless because to natural disadvantages have been added artificial ones which wreck home life. . . . Do you wish to catch glimpses of the problem of recreation, of juvenile delinquency, of the race problem, of the social evil, of liquor laws broken, of non-employment, and incapacity due to industrial causes; you need only happen in at the Hollow, and see how disintegrating forces assert themselves, when progressive ones are shut off through civic lethargy and selfishness.*[12]

Of course, the authors of this study did not believe that bad conditions inevitably corrupt human nature. Here and there, families and persons could be found who withstood the corrupting influence of slum life. The surveyors were pleased to observe that "tucked in between disreputable families of the lowest type, here and there, are bright-faced thrifty Italians."[13]

The stress on the bad consequences of evil phenomena obscured the possibility of paradox and irony, obscured the possibility of evil arising from things deemed good and good from things deemed evil. Nonetheless, there was a certain advantage to such a simple perspective. It made perfectly clear that many deviant enterprises have victims. In some versions of later analysis—especially that of the functionalist—there was often a curious omission of any mention of the victims of deviant behavior. Let us briefly consider the assessments made by the Pittsburgh surveyors of the political machine, or-

[11] *The Pittsburgh Survey,* ed. Paul Kellog (New York: Survey Associates, Russell Sage Foundation, 1914), V, 127.

[12] Florence Lattimore, "Three Studies in Housing and Responsibility," in *The Pittsburgh Survey,* p. 124.

[13] *Pittsburgh Survey,* VI, 351. In Pittsburgh, apparently it was the Italians who were the aspiring and conscientious minority at the beginning of the twentieth century. East European Jews in the same city were rather disappointing. Many of the men were to be found pimping for the whoring members of their "race." The Pittsburgh investigators report: "On a lower level [of prostitution] were the two-and one-dollar houses. These were by far the most numerous and the more profitable. They were filled with young Jewesses, many of them American born, with Pennsylvania Dutch, . . . Irish and German, Canadians, and a few 'drifters' from wornout American stock. . . . In a majority of the [cheaper] brothels not operated by Negresses, the proprietresses were Jewesses, and the men who financed them were of the same race. And of the same race were a majority of the pimps or cadets who lived wholly or in part on the earnings of the women. . . ." (*Ibid.,* pp. 351, 360.) For a somewhat different picture of Jews and Italians see Jackson Toby, "Hoodlum or Business Man: An American Dilemma," in Marshall Sklare, *The Jews* (New York: Free Press of Glencoe, Inc., 1958).

ganized vice, and prostitution—phenomena which were to become the topics of functional analysis some years later.

The machine system and its political boss were given a rather negative assessment. The prime defects of the "aldermanic system" were well described. The system concentrated "appalling power" and could easily be used for oppression. Though connected with the institution of criminal proceedings, the boss's activities were unsupervised and unregulated. Moreover, it was a system in which most of the judicial officers "[were] not versed in the statutes, [were] sometimes uncouth and generally ignorant." Finally, the machine infused the judicial system with politics and thus corrupted it.[14] These points should be kept in mind when considering Robert Merton's analysis of the machine.[15]

Organized vice and the rackets are viewed even more dimly. Rooted in the "quick riches and easy spending of the successful," organized vice in Pittsburgh, the surveyors found, "attracted not only the anti-social, the unproductive and the parasitic," but also "caused a constant drift of the weak and rebellious away from the mills."[16] Those who were so tempted ceased their honest industry and joined the great mass of criminal followers. "They will live by crime, or starve serving crime."[17]

Organized crime, which preyed on human weakness, attracted not only the racketeers who administered the system, but also an "army of parasites who seek only a living—night bartenders in lawbreaking saloons, bouncers in cut-throat dives, lookouts, doormen, dealers and waiters."[18] Even more malicious were the "boosters, cappers and steerers, who work upon percentages, today the false bell-wethers to rustics at a county fair; tomorrow the fleecers of workmen."[19] Finally, Forbes pointed to the impact of the rackets on honest workmen, the sense in which the "underworld drags upon the workaday life about it."[20] He indicted, for instance, the "chuck-a-luck" machine or "wheel of fortune," which were "for many years, a favorite means for separating the workmen, especially the foreigner, from his pay. Worthless 'prizes' were given out to keep interest alive, and clever boosters . . . were employed who won the more valuable rewards."[21] This stress of victimization should be kept in mind when considering Daniel Bell's more sanguine analysis of the rackets.[22]

Prostitution, though part of the system of organized vice, was singled out for special discussion. Here too, emphasis was put on the seamy aspects

[14] *Pittsburgh Survey,* V, 155.
[15] To be discussed in Chapter 3.
[16] James Forbes, "The Reverse Side," in *Pittsburgh Survey,* VI, 307.
[17] *Ibid.,* p. 316.
[18] *Ibid.,* pp. 316–317.
[19] *Ibid.,* p. 317.
[20] *Ibid.,* p. 319.
[21] *Ibid.,* p. 319.
[22] See Chapters 3 and 4.

and sad consequences. Though alluding to the belief of workingmen that visiting a prostitute is part of having "one big Saturday night town," Forbes would not be deceived. In his external perspective, "there can hardly be a sadder picture than the 'parlor' in a disorderly house where sit the daughters of working people soliciting debauch at the hands of youths of their class."[23] So perturbed was Forbes that he appealed to a sense of working class solidarity. He chided the labor unions of Pittsburgh for not directing their efforts toward the amelioration of this social problem. "My belief," he concluded, "is that labor unions are delinquent is not engaging aggressively in efforts to educate in their members a class consciousness without offense. A broader, more inspiring propaganda, linked to that for higher wages, should be possible to such organizations as the United Mine Workers, The Amalgamated Association of Steel, Iron and Tin Workers, and the various railroad brotherhoods. It is surely time for us to hear the last of the 'mill men's houses,' 'railroader's houses,' and so on in Pittsburgh and elsewhere."[24] Forbes' assessment and his plea to organized labor should be kept in mind when considering Kingsley Davis's analysis of prostitution.[25]

With this brief discussion of the correctional view as it appeared before the first World War, we may now turn to consider the first major American contribution to the naturalistic study of deviant phenomena—the work of the Chicago school. This school began with many of the same views and attitudes as its correctional predecessors, and in some cases never transcended those views. But its entry into deviant worlds was too profound and too dedicated to be without lasting effect. Consequently, in America, it was the Chicagoans who inspired the naturalistic study of deviant phenomena—despite their initial correctional perspective.

Appreciation and the Subjective View

Appreciating a phenomenon is a fateful decision, for it eventually entails a commitment—to the phenomenon and to those exemplifying it—to render it with fidelity and without violating its integrity. Entering the world of the phenomenon is a radical and drastic method of appreciation, and is perhaps a necessity when the phenomenon is ordinarily condemned. Until appreciation is instituted *as an ordinary element of disciplinary method,* first-hand contact with a deviant world seems the surest way of avoiding reduction of the phenomenon to that which it is not, thus violating its integrity. Accordingly, in the first stages of sociological naturalism, entry into the

[23] *Ibid.,* p. 349.
[24] *Ibid.,* p. 349.
[25] See Chapter 4.

deviant worlds and appreciation of them were closely linked. Later in the development of sociological naturalism, as we will see, appreciation was essayed at a distance.

The decision to appreciate is fateful in another, perhaps more important way. It delivers the analyst into the arms of the subject who renders the phenomenon, and commits him, though not without regrets or qualifications, to the subject's definition of the situation. This does not mean the analyst always concurs with the subject's definition of the situation; rather, that his aim is to comprehend and to illuminate the subject's view and to interpret the world *as it appears to him.*[26]

The view of the phenomena yielded by this perspective is *interior,* in contrast to the external view yielded by a more objective perspective. The deviant phenomenon is seen from the inside. Consequently, many of the categories having their origin in evaluations made from the outside become difficult to maintain since they achieve little prominence in the interpretations and definitions of deviant subjects. Such was the fate of central theoretic ideas forwarded by the Chicagoans. The subversion and eventual decline of the conceptions of pathology and disorganization resulted partly from the dedicated entry into deviant worlds by the Chicagoans themselves.

Let us consider one of the peculiar worlds entered and described by researchers of the Chicago school. It will be profitable to do this for two reasons: first, because there is much of substance that may still be learned from the Chicagoans—some of their work has never been surpassed; secondly, and perhaps more important, to understand the process by which intimate knowledge of deviant worlds tends to subvert the correctional conception of pathology.

The Hobo as Subject

In the preface to Nels Anderson's book on homeless men, the reader is told that Anderson had long been interested in hobos, having travelled as

---

[26] As will become apparent later, a commitment to the subjective view has even more profound consequences for the direction and tenor of sociological analysis. A serious commitment to the subjective view cannot grudgingly stop with the appreciation of the subject's definition of his specific deviant predicament. It must also entail an appreciation of the ordinary subject's philosophical definition of his general predicament. Concretely, this means that the ordinary assumptions of members of society like the capacity to *transcend* circumstances, the capacity to *improvise,* the capacity to *intend* must be treated seriously and occupy a central place in the analysis of social life. The question of transcending circumstances, and the violation of this sense in primitive sociology will be discussed later. A limited discussion of intentionality and the violation of that sense in criminology appears in my *Delinquency and Drift,* Chapters 1 and 6.

one before developing a scholarly interest in the subject.[27] Immediately, therefore, we are alerted to the likelihood that the author will convey an inside, or interior view of the phenomenon. Through the thirties and before, hobos were considered a major social problem. Their world was not viewed as a romantic and esoteric one—as it tends to be now—and thus a correctional perspective on this phenomenon was prevalent. Indeed, Anderson's study, like most emanating from the Chicago school, was supported and partly financed by municipal agencies and commissions that were interested in ameliorating the grievous conditions associated with vice, alcohol, wandering, vagrancy, and begging. Thus, the mixture of naturalist and correctional sentiments was institutionally based as well as existing as an intellectual tension in the work of the Chicago school.

The conception of a peculiar *world,* albeit deviant, with its own logic and integrity is introduced early in Anderson's volume and occupies a fundamental place in the study. Significantly, the conception of a deviant world —unlike the looser current conception of subculture—is ecologically anchored. Deviant subjects are concentrated in a particular locale. This notion is the early and persistent link between what might appear as two disparate outgrowths of the Chicago school—ethnography and ecology. Actually, the two were closely connected. Anderson suggested the ecological segregation of the peculiar world of the hobo. Though only between one and two and a half per cent of Chicago's population consisted of homeless men, Anderson observed that they "are not distributed evenly throughout the city; they are concentrated, segregated . . . in three contiguous, narrow areas close to the center of transportation and trade."[28] Moreover, he based the development of "characteristic institutions" in the ecological concentration. "This segregation of tens of thousands of footloose, homeless . . . men is the fact fundamental to an understanding of the problem. Their concentration has created an isolated cultural area—Hobohemia. Here characteristic institutions have arisen."[29] The *isolated cultural area* was an excellent and useful conception of a peculiar world, though it perhaps posited an exact relation between ecological and moral facts about which we would be more hesitant today. Though ecological segregation facilitates the development of a peculiar world, it may not always be necessary.

The hobo's own perspective was prominent in Anderson's analysis, as he described how the ecological sectors the hobo inhabits appeared to him, and how they were utilized by him. Though pointing to the solidary features of such areas, Anderson did not romanticize the social bonds that appear. He said:

[27] Nels Anderson, *The Hobo* (Chicago: University of Chicago Press, 1923).
[28] *Ibid.,* p. 14.
[29] *Ibid.*

Every large city has its district into which these homeless types gravitate. . . . Such a section is known as the "stem" or the "main drag." To the homeless men it is home for there, no matter how sorry his lot, he can find those who will understand. The veteran of the road finds other veterans; the old man finds the aged; . . . the radical, the optimist, the inebriate, all find others here to tune in with them. The wanderer finds friends here or enemies, but, and that is at once a characteristic and pathetic feature of Hobohemia, they are friends and enemies only for the day. They meet and pass on.[30]

Note that in the final part of the passage just cited, Anderson asserted a characteristic *feature* of Hobohemia. The conception of a characteristic or essential feature is central to a naturalist approach, and simultaneously, indicates a basic tension within that approach. To locate or assert an essential feature of phenomena is a basic part of naturalist analysis, as basic perhaps as posing a relationship between two variables is in more conventional sociological analysis. For the naturalist, the location of essential features is crucial because it is an attempt to cogently assert what the phenomenon *is*. But to assert essential features is inevitably to choose selectively from the factual world; thus naturalism, though it is anti-philosophic in temper, can hardly avoid philosophy in the form of *analytic abstraction*. The assertion of essential features is nothing less than an *analytic summary* of the phenomenon. For Anderson, the feature of *transient relations* was essential in the phenomenal world of hobos.

But the tendency to summarize the phenomenon analytically is countered in naturalism by an opposite tendency toward sheer descriptive detail; thus a tension exists. The essential features of a phenomenon are not in the facts simply waiting to be seen and catalogued. Their perception demands intuition, cogent argument, and evidence. Those preferring analytic summary resolve the tension by suggesting that the *intuitive* assertion of essential features, buttressed by evidence whenever possible, is mandatory if we are to get on with the task of social analysis.[31] From the analytic perspective, a mass of unsorted detail leads nowhere.

The opposite tendency—more dedicatedly ethnographic—appears also in the naturalist tradition. This tendency is defended partly on the grounds that analytic summary is often premature, that it must patiently await the collection of a larger and more comparative volume of fact; partly ethnography is preferred for its own sake. Detailed ethnography, bereft of analytic summary, may be preferred because of the naturalist's traditional fascination with *his* phenomenon in all its aspects. One part of the naturalist wishes to

[30] *Ibid.*, p. 4.
[31] Max Weber, for instance, defends this position. His rendition of the conception, essential feature, is "ideal type." See, for instance, Max Weber, *The Protestant Ethic and the Spirit of Capitalism* (New York: Charles Scribner's Sons, 1930).

explore all the minute variations of the phenomenal realm which intrigues him. For *him*, analytic summary is tantamount to *reduction*, the high sin to naturalism. But for the analytic naturalist, *summary* is just a simplified rendition of a phenomenon in which its integrity *is not violated*.

There is no final resolution of this tension within naturalism. One need not abstractly choose between the two tendencies, and when a choice is made, it is probably a matter of personal preference. Thus, for instance, Paul Cressey in his volume on taxi-dance halls told us more about many different kinds of dance-halls[32] than I, at any rate, wish to know. But some have a higher tolerance for detail, or perhaps a more dedicated interest in dance-halls.

Whatever the threshold of tolerance, however, it is perhaps possible to agree that detailed description and classification at some point ceases to be useful. The detailed description of mundane human behavior—with virtually no attempt to assert its meaning or relevance—is the vice that attends naturalist virtue. This vice was classically summarized and assessed in Gauguin's barbed remark, directed toward the greatest of all literary naturalists. "Everyone shits," said Gauguin, "but only Zola bothers about it."

In both analytic summary and detailed ethnography, some classification or differentiation within the omnibus form is normally a feature of naturalist analysis. Such differentiation may be taken as evidence that the observer has entered the deviant world and has begun to appreciate its complexity. From the outside, deviant persons, like members of racial minorities, tend to look alike. From the inside, there is bound to be assortment and variety, observable, known, and usually designated by those who inhabit that world. Since the Chicagoans stressed the internal view of the deviant subject, it was characteristic of them to distinguish among the variable manifestations of what to the outsider seemed an omnibus form. Anderson, for instance, developed a classification of homeless men. He began with those already suggested by knowledgeable internal authorities and concluded with his own modification. Ben Reitman, a noted anarchist, intellectual, and hobo of the era, suggested that "There are three types of the genus vagrant: the hobo, the tramp and the bum. The hobo works and wanders, the tramp dreams and wanders and the bum drinks and wanders."[33]

St. John Tucker, a former President of the Hobo College in Chicago, suggested a different classification. "A hobo," he said, "is a migratory worker. A tramp is a migratory non-worker. A bum is a stationary non-worker."[34] Anderson himself accepted Tucker's distinctions but went on to distinguish between seasonal workers and hobos. The seasonal worker, he

---

[32] Paul Cressey, *The Taxi-Dance Hall* (Chicago: University of Chicago Press, 1932). See, for instance, p. 18.
[33] Anderson, *op. cit.*, p. 87.
[34] *Ibid.*

suggested, "has a particular kind of work that he follows somewhere at least part of the year. The hotels of Hobohemia are a winter resort for many of these seasonal workers whose schedule is relatively fixed and habitudinal."[35] But despite the fact that such workers live part of the year in the same areas, Anderson felt that they should not be confused with hobos, whose style and temperament were essentially different. The hobo adhered to no fixed specialty. "The hobo, proper, is a transient worker without a program. A hobo is a migratory worker in the strict sense of the word. He works at whatever is convenient in the mills, the shops, the mines, the harvests, or any of the numerous jobs that come his way without regard for the times or the seasons."[36] Though he might occasionally exploit other means of gaining livelihood, the hobo primarily worked for a living. "He may even be reduced to begging between jobs, but his living is primarily gained by work and that puts him in the hobo class."[37] Anderson added one more category to those suggested by Tucker, making a total of five classes of homeless men. The final class was termed the "home guard." "The home guard," says Anderson, "like the hobo is a casual laborer, but he works, often only by the day, now at one and again at another of the multitude of unskilled jobs in the city."[38] He estimated nearly half of the homeless men living in Hobohemia were stationary casual laborers, or home guard. Thus, in summary, the seasonal worker, the hobo, and the tramp were migratory; the bum and home guard relatively stationary; the bum and tramp were unwilling to work and lived mostly by begging and petty thieving. The seasonal worker, hobo, and home guard mainly worked for a living.

Of the five classes of homeless men described by Anderson, the home guard were most like conventional people. Yet they were viewed with contempt by the still-migratory hobo and tramp.[39] When younger, members of the home guard were frequently migratory. They had retired from wandering, but they still belonged to the world of migrants. Being migratory was highly regarded in the peculiar world of hobos and tramps, and here we have the hallmark of a moral system, however peculiar. If there are men who fall short of standards—however deviant the standards—a normative system is suggested. Anderson proceeded to describe in considerable detail the system of rules and precepts that guided hobo life. Here too, Anderson anchored the rules and regulations in an ecological base. He suggested the central role of "jungles" in the development and dissemination of hobo standards of conduct. Jungle was the name given to "places where the hobos congregate to pass their leisure time outside the urban centers."[40] These

[35] *Ibid.*, p. 90.
[36] *Ibid.*, pp. 90–91.
[37] *Ibid.*, p. 91.
[38] *Ibid.*, p. 96.
[39] *Ibid.*, pp. 6, 10, 96.
[40] *Ibid.*, p. 16.

sites were on the outskirts of cities, typically near railroad crossings. Anderson described the role of the jungle in the development of a hobo morality:

> *The part played by the jungles as an agency of discipline for the men of the road cannot be overestimated. Here hobo tradition and law are formulated and transmitted. It is the nursery of tramp lore. Here the fledgling learns to behave like an old-timer. . . . Every idea and ideal that finds lodgement in the tramp's fancy may be expressed here in the wayside forum.*[41]

Thus, stable traditions and regulations emerged despite the transiency of the men, and despite the absence of administration. Moreover, the traditions and regulations persisted despite shifting personnel who could hardly be thought of as an enduring group. Indeed, those who were most persistent, least transient, in their presence—"buzzards"—were held in lowest esteem in the jungle. Here was a world in which transiency was at a premium.

Because of the enforced transiency of the hobos no better demonstration of the key sociological thesis of the "exteriority" of norms—first made by Durkheim—can be imagined. The adherence of traditions and norms to *sites* and *situations* rather than groups was to become a central idea of the Chicago school.[42] Thus, the emergence of a hobo morality may be viewed as a most rigorous test for this central sociological idea. The transiency of personnel and the limited character of the social bonds among them were described by Anderson:

> *Jungle populations are ever changing. Every hour new faces appear to take the place of those that have passed on. . . . Every new member is of interest for the news he brings or the rumors that he spreads. . . . But with all the discussion [of the road, working conditions and police] there is seldom any effort to discuss personal relations and connections. Here is one place where every man's past is his own secret.*[43]

Despite the transiency and limited character of social bonds and communication, the situation and the site remain stable. Thus, according to sociological rule, regulations and traditions *naturally* emerge. An intentional breaking of jungle regulations was met by sanctions in the form of forced labor, physical punishment, or expulsion. Anderson summarized the regulations:

[41] *Ibid.*, pp. 25–26.
[42] Clifford Shaw and Henry McKay in *Juvenile Delinquency and Urban Areas* (Chicago: University of Chicago Press, 1942) demonstrate with great cogency the similar point that a delinquent tradition is anchored in certain neighborhoods irrespective of the shifting ethnic groups inhabiting them.
[43] *Ibid.*, pp. 19–20.

Jungle crimes include (1) making fire by night in jungles subject to raids; (2) "hi-jacking" or robbing men at night when sleeping in the jungles; (3) "buzzing" or making the jungle a permanent hangout for jungle "buzzards" who subsist on the leavings of meals; (4) wasting food or destroying it after eating . . . ; (5) leaving pots and other utensils dirty after using; (6) cooking without first hustling fuel; (7) destroying jungle equipment. In addition to these fixed offenses are other crimes which are dealt with as they arise.[44]

Thus, we see that the deviant world of hobos and tramps was socially organized. It contained differentiated *roles* which were ordered and stratified and explicit *rules* which were disseminated and enforced. Moreover, the Chicagoans stressed a third principle: Deviant worlds possessed their own peculiar satisfaction or *rewards* that were by no means limited aspects of the deviant enterprise. That deviant worlds have their own intrinsic—and to the outsider, esoteric—satisfactions was another thesis deriving from the internal, subjective view of naturalism. These satisfactions are known to the inhabitants of the deviant world and may be inferred by the perceptive observer. In Anderson's study, some of them were quite ordinary, others rather esoteric:

In the jungle, the hobo is his own housewife. He not only cooks . . . but has invented dishes that are peculiar to jungle life. Chief among these is "mulligan stew." [Moreover,] the art of telling a story is diligently cultivated by the "bos" in the assemblies about the fire. This vagabond existence tends to enrich the personality and long practice has developed in some of these men an art of personal narrative that has greatly declined elsewhere.[45]

Appreciation and Functionalism

The naturalist perspective on deviant phenomena and its appreciative attitude were carried forward in a sociological viewpoint that has come to be known as *functionalism*. This viewpoint has been the subject of considerable controversy. My intention here is not to enter that controversy, but merely to note the ways in which functionalism may be regarded as part of the advent of naturalism in sociology.

The main contribution of functionalism to naturalism was effectively to purge the conception of pathology. That will be discussed more fully in the next chapter. Now, I want to focus on the sense in which functionalism maintained and extended the appreciative attitude initiated by the Chi-

---

[44] *Ibid.*, pp. 20–21.
[45] *Ibid.*, pp. 18–19.

cagoans. The appreciation of functionalism was usually from a distance. Unlike the Chicagoans, for whom direct exploration of deviant worlds was the primary method of appreciation, the functionalists were mainly theorists who based their familiarity with the deviant world on secondary sources. The appreciation of functionalism was abstract, resting on the theoretical doctrine that persistent patterns of activity—deviant or conventional—survive in society because of their serviceable, or *functional,* character. Thus, deviant phenomena might be appreciated because of their alleged contribution to ongoing social order. Moreover, appreciation of a sort was an inevitable concommitant of the generally "affirmationist" posture of the functionalists—a posture which drew considerable attack from those sponsoring a more "critical" sociology. However, the appreciative attitude of functionalism was also internal, based on the idea that persistent phenomena were socially and psychically serviceable for the deviant subjects. To this extent, the appreciative attitude of functionalism depends on *the choice to adopt the subjective viewpoint.* Indeed, some functional analyses sound suspiciously like the justifications of phenomena rendered by the deviant subjects who exemplify and perpetrate them. Thus, the functionalists continued the internal perspective despite being, with a few notable exceptions, insiders-from-a-distance.

Of the three functionalists explicitly concerned with a variety of deviant phenomenon, only Daniel Bell will be discussed in this chapter. The other two—Robert Merton and Kingsley Davis—were less concerned with the detailed nuances of the phenomena they analyzed. They were more concerned with forwarding a theoretic view; Merton especially used empirical cases to illustrate the utility of the functionalist approach to social reality. Davis, in his essay on prostitution, stood between Merton and Bell, as he was primarily interested in developing a theory of the part played by a deviant phenomenon in organizing or ordering society; but he simultaneously exhibited considerable familiarity with the nuances of "the life." Though not as concerned with the phenomenon for its own sake as Daniel Bell or the Chicagoans, Davis clearly differed from Merton who introduced his analysis of the political boss and the machine system with a declaration of inexpertise. "Without presuming to enter into the variations of detail marking different political machines," said Merton, "we can briefly examine the functions more or less common to the political machine as a generic type of social organization."[46]

Since both Merton and Davis were primarily interested in developing a functionalist theory, their work will be discussed in later chapters. Now, I want to consider the way in which detailed familiarity with deviant worlds enhances the appreciative attitude, and thus forwards the view of naturalism.

[46] Robert Merton, *Social Theory and Social Structure* (New York: The Free Press of Glencoe, Inc., 1957), p. 72.

For that purpose, it will be useful to consider Daniel Bell's essays on the rackets.

When Daniel Bell wrote "Crime as an American Way of Life" and "The Racket-Ridden Longshoremen," he was writing as a high-level journalist. However, he was already well-known among professional sociologists, and well-acquainted with intellectual currents in sociology and related disciplines. Later, he became a *bona fide* sociologist. When writing these essays, Bell did not explicitly or self-consciously rely on systematic functionalist theory; consequently, his entry into the deviant underworld is a most striking aspect of his reports. Because his appreciation is based partly on the inside view of things axiomatic in good journalism and partly on a brand of functionalism, Bell provides an excellent link between the Chicago school and the functionalists. That Bell provides the best link is not so surprising. Like Robert Park, founder of the Chicago school, Bell as journalist was immersed in the concrete detail of the everyday life of his subjects.

The connection between good journalism and sociological naturalism is easy to see. Somewhat more obscure, but still interesting to consider, is the connection between functionalism and the muckraking tradition in journalism. The functionalist approach to deviant phenomena may be viewed as a sophisticated form of reverse muckraking which is knowledgeable about the existence of muck but adopts a more tolerant and appreciative view of its part in society. The strategy and logic of functionalism with regard to deviant phenomena is to comprehend the steady persistence of sin or evil instead of simply exposing or condemning it. Just as Bell was an appropriate person to maintain the insider perspective of the Chicagoans by his journalistic competence, so too he was well-fitted to give the description of deviant phenomena an appreciative functionalist tone—a viewpoint that in his case was not derived from the lofty theories of Talcott Parsons but more naturally from a circle of jaded intellectuals in New York City. He was appropriate because the attitude of muckraking or exposé must have seemed to him, as to most sophisticated journalists of the period, a glaring admission of naiveté and callow immaturity. Of course, things are corrupt, they might say; that is the way the world is. The task of sophisticated journalism was to understand the bases of sin or evil, and for that task appreciation was perhaps mandatory. Though the Chicagoans took a subjective view, appreciated the deviant phenomena and described it internally, they frequently did so in a studied and practiced way. For Bell, and even more so for the neoChicagoans, who will be discussed shortly, empathy with and appreciation of the deviant enterprise apparently involved little effort. Frequently, they give the appearance of identifying with the deviant subject as a matter of personal inclination as well as professional commitment. In this sense, Bell also furnishes a kind of temperamental link between the functionalists and the later neoChicagoans. The temperamental affinity between them is reflected nicely in Bell's article on the role of newspapers in creating the appearance of crime waves. The undependability of public or official estimates of crime and the construction and fabrication of rates of deviant behavior was also a favorite theme of the neoChicagoans.[47] Consequently, Bell may be considered a pivotal figure in the naturalist study of deviant phenomena, despite the fact that his primary writing was on labor and political events. Let us briefly consider his two essays.

In "Crime as an American Way of Life," Bell early in the essay chided the Kefauver committee for having been out of touch with the facts of American life generally and the attitude of Americans toward gambling specifically. Moreover, he suggested that the Kefauver committee, viewing the underworld from the outside, could hardly make the distinctions necessary to comprehend it.

> *Throughout the Kefauver hearings . . . there ran the presumption that all gamblers were invariably gangsters. That was true of Chicago's Accardo-Guzik combine, which in the past had its fingers in many kinds of rackets. It was not nearly so true of many large gamblers in America, most of whom had the feeling that they were satisfying a basic American urge for sport and looked upon their calling with no greater sense of guilt than did many bootleggers. . . . The S&G syndicate in Miami, for example, (led by Harold Salvey, Jules Levitt, Charles Friedman, Sam Cohen and Edward [Eddie Luckey] Rosenbaum) was simply a master pool of some two hundred bookies that arranged for telephone service, handled "protection," acted as bankers for those who needed ready cash on hard-hit books, and, in short, functioned somewhat analogously to the large factoring corporations in the textile fields or the credit companies in the auto industry. . . . Salvey . . . was an old-time bookie who told us that he had done nothing except engage in bookmaking or finance other bookmakers for twenty years. When, as a result of committee publicity and the newly found purity of the Miami police, the S&G syndicate went out of business it was, as the combine's lawyer told Kefauver, because the "boys" were weary of being painted "the worst monsters in the world." "It is true," Cohen acknowledged, "that they had been law violators." But they had never done anything worse than gambling and "to fight the world isn't worth it."[48]*

The impression conveyed by Bell is clear. The world, as it exists naturally, before being classified and stereotyped by congressional committees or moralistic scholars, is a very complicated place. Persons deemed deviant by outsiders may have conventional motives, goals, and self-

[47] Daniel Bell, "The Myth of Crime Waves," in *End of Ideology* (New York: The Free Press of Glencoe, Inc., 1960), Chapter 8. See also Howard Becker, *Outsiders* (New York: The Free Press of Glencoe, Inc., 1963), Chapter 2; John Kitsuse and Aaron Cicourel, "A Note on the Uses of Official Statistics," *Social Problems,* XI (Fall 1963), 131–139.

[48] Daniel Bell, "Crime as an American Way of Life," in *End of Ideology,* pp. 136–137.

conceptions. Moreover, specialization or division of labor may appear in deviant worlds, so that persons who are implicated by indirection in heinous projects may obscure from themselves and fail to sense their alleged connection with some wider sinister purpose. Finally, the sinister character of gambling is acknowledged by only part of the citizenry, the remainder either indulging or indulgent.

The inside perspective was conveyed even better in Bell's "Racket-Ridden Longshoremen." That he should have possessed inside knowledge is easily understandable since Bell spent many years as highly astute labor editor for *Fortune*. The question posed by Bell in this essay was why the rackets continued to dominate some unions, specifically the east coast longshoremen, after they had declined in most unions throughout the nation. While his argument was framed in functionalist terms, the most striking aspect of the analysis was the substantive knowledge Bell apparently possessed of the intricate details of New York's docks. The economic interpretation suggested by Bell is no mere application of a Marxian or Beardian abstraction to a concrete situation. Instead, it seems to grow naturally from an internal view of the world he explored. In that world—the reader senses —money talked, and thus an economic interpretation promoted rather than hampered an appreciation of the subject and his motives.

Bell's main thesis developed around "the distinctive economic matrix" of the port of New York, how that essential feature "shaped a pattern of accommodation between the shippers and racketeers and led to a continuation of the system" that had declined in other trades and industries.[49] Speaking, it would seem, to himself and to others who had cherished and then abandoned a Marxian view with its stress on economic determination, Bell suggested that "in our fascination these days with power and manipulation, we often ignore the economic fulcrum underneath."[50] But this time the "economic fulcrum underneath" was specified and located in a more concrete reality. It was not to be generalized into a philosophy applicable everywhere.

The deviant phenomena covered in Bell's analysis of longshoremen included the loading racket (by which monopolies on loading were gradually and violently asserted at each pier), the shape-up with subsequent kickbacks for jobs, and the emergence of concessions for bookmaking and loansharking. Bell placed these in a functional context. He suggested a natural setting for their emergence, and described in relatively detailed manner how the deviant forms were originally serviceable ways of meeting the special problems of the New York port. The loading racket, for instance, appeared in New York but not in other major American ports. Loading de-

---

[49] Daniel Bell, "The Racket-Ridden Longshoremen," Chapter 9 in *End of Ideology* (New York: The Free Press of Glencoe, Inc., 1960), p. 176.
[50] *Ibid.*

veloped special significance in the New York port. "The *spatial* arrangements of . . . other ports is such that loading never had a 'functional'
significance." Other major ports had "direct railroad connections to the
piers." Thus, "the transfer of cargoes . . . [was] easily and quickly accomplished."[51] Moreover, other features of the economic matrix were unsuited
for the flourishing of labor racketeering. "Nor is there in these [other] ports
the congested and choking narrow street patterns which in New York forced
the trucks to wait, piled up 'time charges,' or made for off-pier loading."[52]
Given these and other features of the economic matrix, described by Bell,
various persons gradually asserted a monopoly on loading at each pier.
These monopolies were violently contested. "Control of loading and its
lucrative revenues was the major prize over which the bloody pier wars
were fought on the New York docks for thirty years."[53]

The loading racket, the biggest prize, was the hub of other rackets.
It was "the key to criminal infiltration and baronial domination of the
International Longshoreman's Association."[54] Since it was a monopoly
asserted and maintained through force and violence, it was not simply a
business, though like a business services were performed: The work got done,
and by a labor force that, given its social character and background, remained amazingly docile, except for an occasional courageous wildcat
strike. The transition from service to extortion was described by Bell:

> At first they offered a service; later they began to enforce compulsory
> service; and, in the classic monopoly fashion, they began to charge, lit-
> erally, all the traffic would bear. . . . So the tollgate was established.
> Whether you needed a loader or not, you had to pay for the service."[55]

Even after the violent conflict ceased in the mid-thirties, the combine
that organized the various local pier monopolies continued the same racketeering tactics. The deviant phenomenon survived, according to Bell, because
of its original function. For our purposes, the truth of that assertion is not
the important point; instead, the very logic of such an interpretation implies
an appreciative posture toward the phenomenon and the setting that allegedly nurtured it. Viewing the phenomenon appreciatively facilitates a
careful consideration of its *adequacies* and *strengths*. This attitude was implicit in the very language selected by Bell: never did he convey a tone of
disgust though he certainly pointed to "the victimization and corruption
implicit in the loading racket." Instead he said: "The beauty of 'loading' was

51 *Ibid.*, p. 187.
52 *Ibid.*
53 *Ibid.*, p. 183.
54 *Ibid.*
55 *Ibid.*, p. 184.

that it provided a bland legal mask for extraordinary gain on almost no investment, other than muscle-men for intimidation, and that it provided a lucrative income, as regular as death and taxes, and subject only to the normal vagaries of the business cycle."[56] Indeed, as Bell indicated, there is *beauty* in so well-conceived and well-suited a racket. But it is a beauty that is completely missed from the correctional perspective. It is only from an interior view, only from the view of subjects who conceived and constructed it that we may glimpse the truth that loading is a beautiful racket. Such a truth is obviously partial, but it is necessary to begin there. Otherwise, the coherence, form, texture, and even utility of deviant phenomena cannot become evident.

The NeoChicagoans

Appreciation of deviant phenomena founded on taking the internal view of the subject was begun by the Chicago school and continued in the functionalist view. In some measure that appreciation has become institutionalized in contemporary sociology. But as usual, an institutionalized sentiment survives in routine form. The routinized form of appreciation is *neutrality,* which is another thing altogether. Neutrality, buttressed as it is by the philosophy of science, is the sentiment toward deviant phenomena commended by most contemporary sociologists. We are to empathize with neither the correctional enterprise nor its deviant subjects (though, according to disciplinary ethics we may, if we wish, contract with the former). Thus it would be untrue to suggest that the appreciative attitude of naturalism has simply become the stance of general sociology. To trace the continuation of the appreciative attitude, we must focus more narrowly on a smaller group: an assortment of sociologists who share a more or less similar viewpoint. Though probably premature, and perhaps even a disservice to these individual sociologists, such similarity and distinctiveness warrants saddling them with a name and conceiving them as something like a school of thought. I will call them neoChicagoans because they have revived the Chicago school's stress on direct observation and field work, have maintained and extended the relevance of the subject's view, and in a variety of other ways have indicated their appreciation of deviant phenomena and their connected enterprises. A theme that has more or less unified the neoChicagoans has been their emphasis on the *process of becoming deviant* and the part played by the official registrars of deviation in that process.[57] A small but increasing number of sociologists identify with this viewpoint. In this volume, the

[56] *Ibid.,* p. 187.
[57] This final theme will be discussed in Chapter 7, "Signification."

discussion will focus mainly on the contributions to this viewpoint of Edwin Lemert, Erving Goffman, and Howard Becker.

Howard Becker, in *Outsiders,* pointed to the importance of the subjective view immediately. It is, he suggested, relevant to the very conception of deviation. "Outsiders" has a double meaning. The first meaning is conventional: deviates are outsiders. The second meaning is its reverse: conventional folk are outsiders, from the perspective of those involved in illicit activities. Viewing the social scene *as it appears to the persons we are trying to comprehend,* Becker explained:

> *But the person who is thus labeled an outsider may have a different view of the matter. He may not accept the rule by which he is being judged and may not regard those who judge him as either competent or legitimately entitled to do so. Hence, a second meaning of the term emerges: the rule-breaker may feel his judges are* outsiders.[58]

No inference of a complete division of opinion or a complete withdrawal of legitimacy need be drawn from Becker's statement. Its point is that we must factually ascertain the measure of consent or dissent, and to do that we must maintain the perspective of the deviant subject. A stress on the correctional perspective would be just as appropriate if the subject of inquiry were the correctors. Moreover, Becker's subjective stress need not mean that the assessments and views of deviant persons are to be taken at face value. Deviant persons may consciously attempt to mislead observers or other outsiders; they may unwittingly deceive themselves or otherwise mistake their predicament. The presenting of fronts is consistent with the capacity of subjects to use themselves in relating to their environment and the persons who compose it. The front is part of managing interaction, a conception that receives considerable attention among the neoChicagoans.[59] Just as the naturalist view avoids suppressing features of phenomena that are detestable by conventional standards, it avoids equating the subjective view with gullibility. Presenting a front, putting people on, and telling prepared sad tales are features of social life, deviant or conventional.

The misleading of the observer may be especially troublesome in the study of deviant phenomena. Since authority may frequently intervene to counteract or arrest the deviant tendency, deviant persons must frequently be devious. They are not alone in this respect, though by definition being devious seems senseless without being deviant. As a matter of degree, at

---

[58] Howard Becker, *Outsiders* (New York: The Free Press of Glencoe, Inc., 1963), pp. 1–2.

[59] See, for instance, Erving Goffman, *Presentation of Self in Everyday Life* (Garden City, N.Y.: Doubleday and Co. [Anchor] 1959) and *Stigma* (Englewood Cliffs, N.J.: Prentice-Hall, Inc., 1963). Also see Sheldon Messinger, Harold Sampson, and Robert Towne, "Life as Theatre," *Sociometry,* March 1962.

any rate, conventional persons have less reason to be devious. They may *be* devious, and somtimes are, but in that case our definition rescues us—they are merely being senseless. Conversely, being devious in the presence of outsiders may be counted a normal feature of persons participating in deviant phenomena.[60] Edwin Lemert suggested that sad tales are usually told by prostitutes to clients and researchers. Less obviously, he argued that much of the literature on white-slave traffic was premised on myths emanating from the sad tales told by prostitutes.[61]

Sophisticated disbelief is not inconsistent with an appreciation of the internal view of phenomena; nor is the appreciation of the devious an insuperable obstacle to social research. Being devious is based on the fear of apprehension, the sense that others expect a justification for what is commonly regarded as a sorry lot, and the intrinsic satisfactions associated with making fools of persons ordinarily bestowed with dignity or wisdom. If those are the bases, it is primarily the outsider who will be misled. Thus, the researcher may overcome this obstacle if he is defined as a courtesy insider or if he disguises his true identity and passes.

Self-deception is more complicated than the intentional deception of outsiders, but the exploration of that possibility, too, is essential in naturalist description and consistent with the subjective view. To view phenomena internally is to stress the way they seem, or appear, to the subjects experiencing them. That appearance is relevant and consequential. But the stress on appearance in no way precludes the observation that subjects may be so situated as to glimpse the phenomenon in a special, peculiar, or distorted fashion. Their relations may be so structured as to obscure aspects of the world surrounding them. From a phenomenal standpoint, the appearance *is* a reality; but so too is distortion or refraction. Thus, for instance, juvenile delinquents may believe that others in their company are committed to the performance of delinquent acts, but partly that is because public discussion of delinquency is severely inhibited by status anxiety.[62] The subject's perspective must be comprehended and illuminated, not enshrined. The angle of vision and consequent refraction must be considered as well as the substance of what is seen. .

Besides a commitment to the subjective view, qualified by an appreciation of deception, the neoChicagoans followed their predecessors in commending detailed description of the deviant phenomenon itself; correspondingly, they are probably less concerned with locating the social or personal

---

[60] In certain forms of sexual deviation, such as voyeurism, there are no insiders. Thus, being devious marks the voyeur even in the interaction with his unwitting victim.

[61] Edwin Lemert, *Social Pathology* (New York: McGraw-Hill Book Company, 1951), p. 255.

[62] See my *Delinquency and Drift* (New York: John Wiley & Sons, Inc., 1964), pp. 50–59.

factors allegedly leading persons to deviation than most sociologists. Indeed, as will be suggested later, there is less faith in the causal efficacy of such factors. The neoChicagoan view was well summarized by Howard Becker. Though there are a great many studies of delinquency, he observed:

> *Very few tell us in detail what a juvenile delinquent does in his daily round of activity and what he thinks about himself, society, and his activities. . . . One consequence [of this insufficiency] is the construction of faulty or inadequate theories. Just as we need precise anatomical description of animals before we can begin to theorize and experiment with their physiological and biochemical functioning, just so we need precise and detailed descriptions of social anatomy before we know just what phenomena are present to be theorized about. . . . We do not . . . [then] have enough studies of deviant behavior . . . [or of] enough kinds of deviant behavior. Above all, we do not have enough studies in which the person doing the research has achieved close contact with those he studies, so that he can become aware of the complex and manifold character of the deviant activity. . . . If . . . [the researcher] . . . is to get an accurate and complete account of what deviants do . . . he must spend at least some time observing them in their natural habitat as they go about their ordinary activities.*[63]

Once observed in their natural habitat, once their nefarious activities are put in proper context, once the subject is fully appreciated, the deviant person comes into proper, human focus. In what follows, we will see that the naturalist's stress on appreciation helped subvert the theoretical preconceptions that informed—or misinformed—the correctional study of deviant phenomena.

[63] Becker, *op. cit.*, pp. 166–170.

3

Pathology and Diversity

As it developed in the study of plant and animal life, naturalism forwarded a conception of pathology. Health and illness, growth and decay, maturation and degeneration, anabolism and catabolism, life and death were useful ideas in organizing and comprehending observable organic phenomena. In literary naturalism, too, the imagery of growth and decay, vivacity and morbidity was common. But the transfer of these conceptions, useful and legitimate in conceiving and organizing the organic realm, to a disciplined study of social life was yet another manifestation of the mistaken view that naturalism was "the philosophical generalization of science." This transfer was easily made because man is simultaneously organism and subject. Thus, the legitimate use of a conception of pathology—when considering man as organism—was extended. Man's subjective existence, too, was to be conceived in the organic terms of health and illness. Obviously, the transfer was easiest and made most sense during the vogue of biological determinism—the era when men deemed themselves bound by physiological and genetic circumstance. Once established, the transfer of conceptions across existential realms could survive the demise of biological determinism. Organismic pathologies were hardly necessary; hence personal and social pathologies appeared.

The question, of course, could never be: are there actually pathologies at the level of subjective existence? Pathologies exist only in the conceptual realm, and the only sensible question is whether the concept illuminates actual happenings. That question is still at issue; and, while, increasingly, doubt is cast on its capacity to illuminate, many sociologists continue to use a conception of pathology implicitly or explicitly.[1]

Just as the objective view was generalized from the science of the physical realm, a conception of pathology was generalized from the science of the organic. The idea of pathology has little currency below the organic realm—the level of merely physical existence. Thus, we may take issue with its capacity to illuminate phenomena that transcend the merely organic. Given its commitment to the integrity of phenomena, and given its appreciation of subjective existence, the basic tendency of the naturalist study of social life has been to question and criticize a conception of pathology, and, increasingly, to purge it from the discipline of sociology. This tendency has persisted despite the vacillation and uncertainty emanating from the mistaken idea of naturalism as the "philosophical generalization of science," from the correctional tendency to equate morality with health, and from an understandable and humane regret about the unfortunate lives frequently experienced by the subjects studied.

If the vacillation regarding a concept of pathology was caused by science, morality, and humane sympathy, the opposition to such a concept was founded essentially in the stress on the subject's internal view of phenomena. A pathology is an *untenable* variant or change. It is untenable in the sense of being a morbid and, by extension, mortal condition. It is not simply untenable in the sense of being annoying, troublesome, or disturbing.[2] Thus, an appreciation of the subject's view of the deviant phenomenon casts doubt on the untenability of his enterprise. To those participating, the enterprise seemed tenable enough, though not without weaknesses, problems, and dissatisfactions. And even to those manning the correctional establishment—from police or social worker to the tenders of the poorhouse, prison, or asylum—the vocabulary of morbidity, though it flourished, patently coexisted with a matter-of-fact accommodation. Though for decades, correctional personnel promised to treat their clientele, for the most part they remained discontentedly accustomed merely to patrolling and supervising their domains. But the main source of doubt continued to be the seemingly tenable character of deviant enterprises—as seen from the perspective of the deviant subjects.

The attempt to salvage the idea of pathology by suggesting that deviant phenomena made society—though not the deviant subject—untenable was never terribly convincing, though often stated. That attempt, first of all,

[1] For a recent explicit defense of the utility of a conception of pathology, see Harold Fallding, "Functional Analysis in Sociology," *American Sociological Review,* XXVIII, No. 1 (February 1963), 5–13.

[2] Garden weeds are troublesome and annoying, but they are certainly not conceived as pathological by botanists or wise gardeners.

confused pathology with parasitology, thus betraying a certain clumsiness in generalizing the philosophy of science; second, it flew in the face of the eternal, patent, and tenable coexistence of society and deviation; third, when forced to the hoary Hobbesian fear of the war of all against all, it hopelessly confused Hobbes with Kant, whose categorical imperative was a foundation for ethical imperatives and not an assertion of untenability. To ask the categorical question, "what would happen if everyone did that?" is to imply a *moral* directive. We ask it precisely because we know the behavior *is* tenable. Thus, the idea of pathology, whether at the personal or social level, always had certain difficulties. But despite the difficulties, it enjoyed a vogue that in some measure still persists.

The idea of diversity contested pathology. Diversity is a *tenable* variant or change. Deviation, the emergent conception, simply recognizes that some variants, while tenable, are proscribed, regulated, or controlled. Both conceptions may be rendered in a romantic way and this romanticizing is worth noting because it sometimes passes for naturalism. As suggested earlier, the idea of deviation is romanticized when the responses of certain deviant subjects are taken at face value and interpreted as purely customary, and not deviant at all from their own perspective. This is occasionally true to the phenomenon—and thus not romanticizing—but, most often, common morality is acknowledged even in its breach. More pertinent is the way in which the idea of diversity may be romanticized.

Check-forging is a tenable enterprise; and, so too, is a household full of bickering headed by a constant woman and shifting men. But the observation that they are tenable does not mean that check-forging is as tenable a method of larceny as others, that larceny is as tenable as labor, that irregularly composed households are as tenable as those that are more domestic. Phenomena may be tenable, but nonetheless harbor inherent weaknesses and dissatisfactions.[3] Thus, the repudiation of a conception of pathology hardly necessitates going to the opposite extreme and romanticizing. If persons are miserable, they may be so designated, and the quality of that misery described. Nothing but confusion is added by rendering that misery a pathology. But at the same time much that is essential to the phenomenon may be lost by neglecting to mention the misery. Thus, for instance, conceiving complicated families full of turmoil, distrust, and fighting as an instance of the well-known primitive system of "serial monogamy with a female-based household" is fundamentally to romanticize and thus falsify

[3] For a discussion of the inherent weaknesses of check-forging, see Edwin Lemert, "The Behavior of the Systematic Check-Forger," *Social Problems*, VI, No. 2 (Fall 1958), 141–149. For a similar discussion of homosexuality that, unfortunately, infers pathology from what is only inherent stress, see Hervey Cleckley, *The Caricature of Love* (New York: The Ronald Press Co., 1957). And, for a general consideration of the *variable* tenability of cultural and subcultural forms, see Gertrude Jaeger and Philip Selznick, "A Normative Theory of Culture," *American Sociological Review*, XXIX, No. 5 (October 1964), 653–669.

the lot of those living in that condition.[4] The very conception "serial monogamy with a female-based household" magically endows the phenomenon to which it presumably points with a form, intention, and regularity hardly evident in the world. It comes close to making a silk purse of a sow's ear. The basic defect of pathology and of its romantic opposite is that both yield concepts that are *untrue to the phenomenon* and which thus fail to illuminate it. Pathology reckons without the patent tenability and durability of deviant enterprise, and without the subjective capacity of man to create novelty and manage diversity.[5] Romance, as always, obscures the seamier and more mundane aspects of the world. It obscures the stress that may underlie resilience.

Though the naturalists sought to avoid romance, their main effort was to rid the study of man of the conception of pathology. Instead of pathology, the ideas of natural variation, cultural diversity, and normative deviation gradually emerged. The relation between the concept of deviation and that of variation or diversity deserves recognition. Otherwise, the term deviation is seen as having derogatory implications, as being linked to the correctional tradition. Such a view is misleading because it misses the broader intellectual context that nurtures a conception of deviation—a context antagonistic to the presumptions and goals of the correctional perspective and its establishment.

Embedded in the naturalist view was a certain moral innocence manifest in both functionalist and neoChicagoan analysis. The Chicagoans seemed far more committed to conventional morality and, as a consequence, were caught in a dilemma between the ideas of pathology and diversity. For functionalists and neoChicagoans, the sources of moral innocence were many and complicated. These sources included a cultural relativism originating in the anthropological study of primitive societies, an ethical neutrality implicit and increasingly explicit in the professional aspiration to scientific status. A moral libertinism grounded in avant garde intellectual circles, and an aficionado's appreciation fostered by the intense familiarity with deviant phenomena inherent in the serious pursuit of research were also important sources. Scientific aspiration was neither the only nor the most important justification and impetus; indeed, the professional aspiration to scientific status could and did manifest itself in an espousal of the conception of pathology before providing one of the bases for questioning that conception.

---

[4] See William Kvaraceus, *Delinquent Behavior: Culture and the Individual* (Washington, D.C.: National Education Association, 1959), pp. 94–97.

[5] For earlier and more systematic critiques of the conception of pathology, see Kingsley Davis, "Mental Hygiene and the Class Structure," *Psychiatry*, I (February 1938), 55–65; and C. Wright Mills, "The Professional Ideology of Social Pathologists," *American Journal of Sociology*, XLIX (September 1943), 165–180.

Let us consider the idea of pathology in the naturalist tradition, and, in the process, observe the gradual emergence of the antithetical view—diversity.

The Chicago Dilemma

How describe the fact of diversity in urban America yet maintain the idea of pathology? That was the Chicago dilemma. The Chicagoans never resolved it, though they came closer than their critics imagine. Moreover, the tension introduced by this unresolved dilemma was not altogether unproductive. The simple expedient taken by later viewpoints—especially the neoChicagoan—of resolving the dilemma by removing a horn may turn out to have its own defects.

The operative resolution of the dilemma was found in a conception of social disorganization. Rejecting *personal* pathology—but not entirely—recognizing the facts of diversity—but only begrudgingly—the Chicagoans based their resolution on the ubiquity of social organization. Society was composed of rules and roles that were organized or welded into coherent and usable form. Despite their familiarity with deviant roles and eccentric rules, they clung to the idea that social organization was equivalent to more or less *conventional* social organization. Thus the main part of the resolution was only apparent; substantially, it was no resolution at all. To the extent that social disorganization was the operative idea, the Chicagoans had suppressed the facts of diversity. Their intimate familiarity with these facts was not reflected in the theoretical conceptions developed and bestowed on the following generation of sociologists. Pathology remained secure; it was merely moved a bit from its personal lodging and relocated at the social level.

When the conventional rules and roles that organize social life and bind us to it are rendered inoperative, man appears dangerous and unrestrained. Under those conditions, brought about by dislocations like rapid social change, urbanization, immigration, economic or wartime crisis, the mixing of peoples, men disclose their baser selves. One of the Chicagoans, Norman Hayner, put it characteristically:

Released from the bonds of restraint operative in smaller and more intimate circles, the individual tends to act in accordance with his impulses rather than after the pattern of the ideals and standards of his group. Among the heavy offenders for stealing hotel property are listed men and women who in their own communities command respect, but who on going to a hotel, take a "moral holiday."[6]

Thus, the deviation—stealing hotel property—was conceived as resulting from a breakdown—in this case a mere interruption—in the organization of communal life. Community and social organization insured the restraint of impulse. But the facts of diversity with which the Chicagoans were familiar could intrude. Deviant organization could occur—and did—and such organization was described by the Chicagoans themselves. Tacitly, such organization was conceived as a response to the failure of conventional social organization. The metropolis came to be viewed as a setting in which social organization was sometimes thwarted and handicapped. The paucity, fragility, and segmented character of urban social relations contributed, it was held, to social disorganization and subsequent lessening of control over impulses. Thus, John Madge was partially right in suggesting the caricature of urban life perpetrated by the Chicagoans. Partially, though, Madge was himself guilty of caricaturing the Chicagoans since they distinguished among various sections of metropolis according to the measure of social organization. Nonetheless, the fragmented character of social relations was an important source of social disorganization, and that, in turn, contributed to the formation of deviant worlds. "In the village," suggested Madge, "which the Chicago school are constantly idealizing," almost everyone "has some economic and cultural relationship with everybody else. In the city such relationships no longer occur in the local community, and social distance consequently increases."[7]

Since the Chicagoans were intimate enough with their subjects to observe and describe the social organization of deviant life, and since they conceived of peculiar worlds, a question regarding the possibility of the integrity and autonomy of such worlds must have arisen. But to face such a question would have amounted to grappling with and actually resolving the choice between pathology and diversity. By conceiving of social disorganization, the Chicagoans avoided a resolution.[8]

[6] Norman Hayner, "Hotel Life and Personality," in Ernest W. Burgess, *Personality and the Social Group* (Chicago: University of Chicago Press, 1929), p. 116.

[7] John Madge, *The Origins of Scientific Sociology* (New York: The Free Press of Glencoe, Inc., 1962), p. 112.

[8] The dilemma posed by the contrasting ideas of pathology and diversity still remains largely unresolved. The radical diversity assumed by Walter Miller with respect to a delinquent subculture, and to a somewhat lesser extent by Lloyd Ohlin and Richard Cloward simply chooses diversity. Similarly, the view of mental illness developed by Erving Goffman is not a resolution but a choice of radical diversity, and risks a sacrifice of features of the phenomenon that were intuited but obscured by the conception of illness. Albert Cohen approximates a resolution by maintaining stress and ambivalence as inherent features of a delinquent subculture that nonetheless possesses integrity. But even there, it is not quite pathology and diversity that are synthesized; rather, middle- and lower-class sentiments. See Walter Miller,

Thus, the net effect of the conception of social disorganization was to relocate pathology; it was moved from the personal to the social plane. However, no blanket denial of personal pathology occurred. Like most subsequent sociologists, the Chicagoans begrudgingly admitted the existence of personality and its disorders. But since the admission was begrudging, personal pathologies had no secure place in the conceptual system. Like social diversity, personal eccentricity was acknowledged and described. And like diversity, it was neglected in the conceptual systems that were to summarize and reflect the world. The simultaneous admission and minimization of the personal is well illustrated in Anderson's discussion of the hobo. Not only was Anderson's discussion characteristic of the Chicagoans; it foreshadowed the usual way in which sociologists were to handle the matter of personal pathology: *gingerly*. Anderson said:

> *Psychological and sociological studies of vagabondage in France, Italy and Germany have led to the conclusion that the vagabond is primarily a psychopathic type. The findings of European psychopathologists are, of course, the result of case-studies of beggars and wanderers in these countries and cannot without reservation be accepted for the United States. Undoubtedly there are large numbers of individuals with defects of personalities among American hobos and tramps, but there are also large numbers of normal individuals. The American tradition of pioneering, wanderlust, seasonal employment, attract into the group of wanderers and migratory workers a great many energetic and venturesome normal boys and young men.*[9]

Later, Anderson suggested some of the processes leading to "economic and social degradation" implicit in the hobo's venture. "Unemployment and seasonal work disorganize the routine of life . . . and destroy regular habits of work but at the same time thousands of boys and men moved by wanderlust are eager to escape the monotony of stable and settled existence."[10] Still, Anderson did not contemplate the denial of personal pathology. "No matter how perfect a social and economic system may yet be devised," he said, "there will always remain certain 'misfits,' the industrially

---

"Lower Class Culture as A Generating Milieu of Gang Delinquency," *Journal of Social Issues*, XIV, No. 3 (1958), 5–19; Richard Cloward, *Delinquency and Opportunity* (New York: The Free Press of Glencoe, Inc., 1960); Erving Goffman, *Asylums* (New York: Doubleday and Company, Inc. [Anchor], 1961); Albert Cohen, *Delinquent Boys* (New York: The Free Press of Glencoe, Inc., 1955). For a general discussion of the conflict between a conception of disorganization and that of diversity, see Ruth Kornhauser, "Theoretical Issues in the Sociological Study of Juvenile Delinquency" (Berkeley: Center for the Study of Law and Society), unpublished manuscript.

[9] Nels Anderson, *The Hobo*, p. 70.

[10] *Ibid.*, p. 85.

inadequate, the unstable, and egocentric, who will ever tend to conflict with constituted authority in industry, society and government."[11]

Vagabondage is an "escape from reality"[12] even though Anderson, himself, described in classic fashion the hobo reality. My point is not that the existence of a hobo reality is necessarily inconsistent with the relevance of a reality escaped from; merely that the idea of diversity harbored in the hobo reality must be synthesized with the idea of pathology harbored in the escape from conventional reality. Because Anderson and other Chicagoans were content with simply sharing the plentiful pathology with their psychiatric colleagues, there was little impetus to square the facts of diversity with their master conception of social disorganization. Thus, the antithetical ideas persisted side by side. The tension between them never resolved, a neat division emerged: pathology was conceived and diversity described. The taxi-dance hall, say, was described in infinite detail, but the reality of that phenomenon was cast in a moral framework that rendered it pathological. "Among the recreational institutions of the American city none perhaps reveals with as much clarity as many of the perplexing problems which make difficult the wholesome expression of human nature in the urban setting as does the public dance hall."[13]

Though the Chicagoans conceived disorganization, they described diversity, and thus the possibility of choosing diversity became more readily available to subsequent students of social life.[14] To a greater extent than in the Russell Sage studies, ethnographic description was separated from theoretical preconception. Though the separation can be exaggerated, it was sufficient to provide subsequent sociologists with the sense that a choice could be made. In terms of the feasibility of choice, and thus in terms of future consequence, it is perhaps fair to assert that Harvey Zorbaugh's *Gold Coast and the Slum* was the most influential contribution of the Chicago school. In this study of contiguous areas in Chicago, the facts of diversity fly in the reader's face. Zorbaugh documented in a manner still unsurpassed the variation in customary behavior as it occurred within several areas in one small part of Chicago. Zorbaugh achieved the aspiration of Robert Park. It was as if an anthropologist let loose in Chicago had discovered urban America in its full diversity. But the conception of pathology remained, unconnected with the reality of diversity despite the idea that was

---

[11] *Ibid.*

[12] *Ibid.*, p. 230.

[13] Paul Cressey, *The Taxi-Dance Hall*, p. vii.

[14] This choice was made quite explicitly by early critics of the Chicago school. See August Hollingshead, "Behavior Systems as a Field of Research," *American Sociological Review*, IV, No. 6 (December 1939), 816–822; William F. Whyte, *Street Corner Society* (Chicago: University of Chicago Press, 1943); and more generally in the work of Edwin Sutherland.

implicit in the work of the Chicago school—an idea that might be capable of uniting the still disparate ideas, if properly conceived.

Pathos

Pathology is very likely a misconception when applied to the realm of subjective existence. But, like many misconceptions, it reflects a partial truth.[15] It is presumptuous and hardly useful to depict those who conceived of personal and social pathology as simple fools. Partly, as suggested thus far, the idea of pathology was transferred to the study of man as part of the generalization of science. Partly, however, something in the reality of human experience, something in the concrete phenomenal world, *invited,* even seduced, that transfer. The conception of pathos points to that reality, and simultaneously, is capable of synthesizing in subjective, human terms the ideas of pathology and diversity. Why is a synthesis between the two necessary?

An unalloyed conception of diversity tends to romanticism. This tendency may be guarded against; thus an appreciation of diversity has not always been romantic. To guard against the romantic rendition of diversity implicit, say, in the view that "mental illness" has little or no reality aside from the imputation of outsiders requires an appreciation of features of the phenomenon that warrantedly elicit pathos. Diversity in its romantic rendition is not unlike pathology. Both minimize the depths of subjective experience: pathology by casting the experience in terms having little to do with the subjective realm, romantic diversity by omitting mention of pathetic features.

The Chicago school noticed and described the pathetic features of phenomena studied, especially as they were disclosed in modern urban life. These features appeared most notably in Norman Hayner's "Hotel Life and Personality," Paul Cressey's *Taxi-Dance Hall,* and in sections of Harvey Zorbaugh's *Gold Coast and Slum.* Loneliness, anonymity, ennui are subjec-

[15] The process by which language forwards proper conceptions of phenomena which are then lost through the mindless or routinized use of language is relevant here. A conception of *disease* would have been applicable to the realms of subjective existence if its original meaning had been maintained. Originally, as the word itself implies the conception pointed to a state of dis-ease. Such a conception does no violence to the subjective realm. But the very meaning of the term—and even pronunciation—is transformed as the original and commonplace rendering is forgotten. Disease becomes morbidity and not simply a sense of dis-ease. In this rendition, the concept is applicable to the organic realm; its relevance to subjective existence is dubious. For a reminder of the wisdom of this much abused conception, I am grateful to Philip Rieff, *The Triumph of the Therapeutic* (New York: Harper & Row, Publishers, 1966), p. 3.

tive experiences that may be essential features of specific sections or social circles. The shortcoming of the Chicago school was that it never coherently organized these experiences into humane conceptions. Instead, it tried to fit them into prevalent ideas of pathology or social disorganization.

By describing loneliness, despair, and misery, the Chicagoans had laid a groundwork on which subsequent sociologists could develop a conception of diversity that appreciated the *variable quality* and the *variable tenability* of different styles of life. Instead of grasping this opportunity, the mainstream of sociology took a different path. In rejecting pathology, it neglected to retain pathos. Accordingly, sociologists not only questioned the utility of the idea of social disorganization; they accused the Chicagoans of distorting the nature of city life. It has become part of the oral as well as the written tradition of contemporary sociology that the Chicagoans greatly exaggerated the pathetic features of the subjects they studied and underestimated solidary and satisfying aspects.[16]

There was a tendency among some of the Chicagoans to exaggerate pathetic features, but not so great as that of subsequent sociologists to exaggerate the Chicago tendency. Many of the Chicagoans were careful to specify the situations and locate the segments of city life harboring loneliness, ennui, and other pathetic features. It will be useful to consider these briefly. My purpose is not simply to defend the Chicago school against unjust criticisms; more important, the particular phenomenon selected to exemplify pathetic existence—and its virtual neglect in recent sociology—will help reveal how some naturalists in sociology came close to losing the reality of pathos.

For the Chicagoans, the rooming-house dweller and the world he inhabited exemplified the pathetic potentiality of urban life. As such, it was a negative ideal—a nadir—of civil life. Like Weber's ideal conception of bureaucracy or Michels' "law" of oligarchy, it indicated a tendency. Zorbaugh and other Chicagoans used the rooming house and its inhabitants to illuminate a tendency in the lower reaches of society, and that tendency can only be regarded as pathetic. They had no intention of uncritically generalizing the predicament of the rooming-house dweller to the rest of the metropolis, but they did conceive of its impact on the great city. The metropolis was to be drawn by the tendencies emanating from its nadir as well as those originating at the zenith. "Such complete anonymity," said Zorbaugh, "could be found nowhere but in the city of today, and nowhere in the city save in the rooming-house."[17] Unless we appreciate the theoretical

---

[16] See, for instance, William F. Whyte, "A Slum Sex Code," *American Journal of Sociology*, XLIX (July 1943), 24–31; Whyte, *Street Corner Society* (*op. cit.*); and Madge, *op. cit.*

[17] Harvey Zorbaugh, *The Gold Coast and the Slum* (Chicago: University of Chicago Press, 1929), p. 75.

use made of the rooming-house, we fundamentally misinterpret the portrait of the metropolis drawn by the Chicago school. We imagine that when Zorbaugh said, "this is the world of furnished rooms, a world of strangely unconventional customs and people, one of the most characteristic of the worlds that go to make up the life of the great city," he meant to imply that this world was *characteristic* in a modal or statistical sense.[18] Many sociologists imagined that and, on the basis of that supposition, criticized the Chicagoans for exaggerating misery. But, unquestionably, Zorbaugh meant characteristic in another sense—that of nadir or negative ideal. One has only to read the rest of *Gold Coast and Slum* to confirm this interpretation. In the boarding-houses, which were another thing altogether, the ghettoes, the wealthy residential areas described in other chapters, he stressed different features, noticeably less pathetic. Indeed, the basic theme of this classic work was the diversity and pluralism of the great city—and the diversity stressed by Zorbaugh pertains to the measure of pathos as well as to the extent of disorganization or the differences in customary behavior.[19]

Though a tendency in the wider metropolis was speculatively suggested, the main assertion of spreading loneliness and anonymity was securely grounded in the shift from boarding- to rooming-house. In this shift occurring at the nadir of society, Zorbaugh perceived, perhaps mistakenly, a microcosm of more general yet less discernible trends. He drew a contrast between the two living arrangements with respect to the quality of life experienced:

> *The rooming-house which has replaced the boarding house is a very different sort of place to live. It has no dining room, no parlor, no common meeting place. Few acquaintances spring up in a rooming-house. . . . The rooming-house is a place of anonymous relationships. One knows no one, and is known by no one. One comes and goes as one wishes, does very much as one pleases, and as long as one disturbs no one else, no questions are asked.*[20]

Norman Hayner noted a similar tendency and related it to the depersonalization implicit in bureaucratic organization. He said:

> *In the metropolitan hotel the guest is only a number. His mark of identification is a key and his relation to the host is completely depersonalized. His status, insofar as he has any, is almost entirely a matter of outward appearance and "front." . . . He meets his neighbors, perhaps, but does not know them. One may be ill and die without producing a ripple on*

18 *Ibid.*, p. 69.
19 *Ibid.*, p. 159.
20 *Ibid.*, pp. 73, 75.

the surface of the common life. One loses his identity as if a numbered patient in a hospital or a criminal in a prison.[21]

Their description of the pathetic life in furnished rooms is limited to that special situation. Notice, however, in the following, how familiar and *au courant* the assertions are:

Such is the world of furnished rooms—a mobile anonymous, individual world, a world of thwarted wishes, of unsatisfied longings, of constant restlessness. . . . It is a world of atomized individuals, of spiritual nomads.[22]

The words used by Zorbaugh are almost exactly those current in descriptions of the "mass society." One may assert the tendency toward a mass society[23] or rebut it. But, whether the tendency is deemed general or not we may still grant, with Zorbaugh and Hayner, that it is pronounced in limited segments. Those segments—however widespread—can hardly be described in naturalist terms *without* stressing pathetic features. Moreover, to stress the pathos of rooming-houses or mental illness or prostitution is not to impute states of being from the outside in terms that are unfamiliar to those experiencing the life. Unlike pathology, sadness, loneliness, misery, and thwarted wishes are experienced in the lives of persons who, nonetheless, become accustomed to their arrangements. A young woman—and not a sociologist—who had recently entered the world of rooming-houses anticipated her future existence:

It was at the "Y" that I had my first acquaintance with that most pitiful figure of the rooming-house world—the old and unmarried woman who works. They were conspicuous in either the cafeteria or the upstairs sitting-room, because of their loneliness—eating lunch at the solitary table, sitting by themselves knitting, with shabby and unbecoming clothes, care-worn faces, and toil-worn hands. I was to learn later some of the tragedies their mute lips harbored.[24]

Similarly, it was a mad woman, and not a psychiatrist, who, as if directing her remarks to those trivializing mental illness by simply conceiving it as either pathology or diversity, said:

[21] *Op. cit.,* p. 113.
[22] Zorbaugh, *op. cit.,* p. 86.
[23] See Jules Henry, *Culture Against Man* (New York: Random House, Inc., 1963); Edgar Friedenberg, *The Vanishing Adolescent* (Boston: Beacon Press, Inc., 1959); Arthur Vidich and Joseph Bensman, *Small Town in Mass Society* (Garden City, N.Y.: Doubleday & Company [Anchor], 1960); and William Kornhauser, *The Politics of Mass Society* (New York: The Free Press of Glencoe, Inc., 1963).
[24] Zorbaugh, *op. cit.,* p. 77.

I who stand on the other side of this phenomenon called madness would like to stretch a hand across to those whom may some day, go through it. Or (may God spare them) stand by someone they love and watch the barrier rising; see the gulf, more grim than death, across which there is no reaching. They learn what real loss is by learning that the loss which has to do with shrouds, coffins and the calm finality of soft earth falling is preferable.[25]

Thus, the Chicagoans provided a basis for the development of a conception—pathos—that could maintain and heighten the sensitivity to misery and despair implicit in the idea of pathology but could avoid its minimization of subjective experience and capacity. Instead of grasping this opportunity, some of those who forwarded the idea of diversity seemingly, at least, avoided the idea that life at the nadir of society was demonstrably pathetic though manageable, tenuous though tenable. There was no explicit movement in this direction, simply an omission of major concepts that could point to the pathetic features of some social realms. Others more or less dissipated the idea of pathos by indiscriminately spreading it across the whole of modern society.[26]

Functionalism and Pathology

The Chicagoans left the idea of pathology in a tenuous state. While maintaining it in their concept of social disorganization, they weakened it by the attention they devoted to the facts of diversity, especially the social organization of deviant life. The idea of pathology and the framework for analysis it provided was so weakened that it could be blown over by a doctrine equally abstract, equally removed from the concrete reality of the world. And so it was.

It is fitting and just that the task of finally purging the idea of pathology from the study of social life was left for the functionalists. Pathology in the study of human affairs was, after all, just a framework—an analogy originating in organic science. The deviant phenomena that were deemed pathological hardly died or declined, and those exemplifying the phenomenon survived at about the same rate as anyone else involved in a dangerous pursuit. What better way to purge a mere framework based on an organic analogy than to substitute another?

To study pathology is to focus on the inherent deficiencies of the body

[25] From the *Autobiography of Lara Jefferson,* reprinted in ed. Bert Kaplan, *The Inner World of Mental Illness* (New York: Harper & Row, Publishers, 1964), p. 31.

[26] A good example of this latter tendency may be found in Arthur Vidich and Joseph Bensman, *op. cit.*

which lead ultimately to its demise. The body, and phenomena likened to it, may also be studied with a focus on its wisdom. The latter was the basic strategy of functionalism.[27] The organism, in this view, has self-corrective capacities; bodily states which at first seem unpleasant are reconstituted and conceived as part of the method by which defeat or demise is avoided. The functionalist stress need not contradict pathology; indeed, the concept of dysfunction is more or less equivalent to pathology. The concept of dysfunction, similar as it was, led some writers in the naturalist tradition to consider functionalism a latter-day version of pathology. Howard Becker, for instance, took that view. A consideration of his thesis will help introduce the discussion of *how* functionalism purged pathology from the study of social life.

Becker pointed to the similarities between the functional view and the conception of pathology:

> *Some sociologists . . . use a model of deviance based essentially on the medical notions of health and disease. They look at a society, or some part of a society, and ask whether there are processes going on in it that tend to reduce its stability, thus lessening its chances for survival. They label such processes deviant or identify them as symptoms of social disorganization. They discriminate between those features of society which promote stability (and thus are "functional") and those which disrupt stability (and thus are "dysfunctional"). Such a view has the great virtue of pointing to areas of possible trouble in a society of which people may not be aware. But it is harder in practice than it appears to be in theory to specify what is functional and what is dysfunctional for a society or social group. . . . Factions within the group disagree and maneuver to have their own definition of the group's function accepted. The function of the group or organization, then, is decided in political conflict, not given in the nature of the organization. . . . It is likewise true that the question of what rules are to be enforced, what behavior regarded as deviant, and which people are labeled as outsiders must also be regarded as political. The functional view of deviance, by ignoring the political aspect of the phenomenon, limits our understanding.[28]*

Everything Becker said about functionalism is more or less accurate.[29] It *is* based on an organismic analogy, it *is* difficult to assess what is functional or dysfunctional, and there *is* a tendency for factional viewpoints to pass as consensual judgments. The trouble lies in what Becker did not say. Though, in theory, functionalism *could have* merely continued the concep-

[27] Walter Cannon, *The Wisdom of the Body* (New York: W. W. Norton and Company, Inc., 1939).

[28] Howard Becker, *Outsiders* (New York: The Free Press of Glencoe, Inc., 1963), p. 7.

[29] Moreover, it is affirmed at the empirical level in the recent essay by Harold Fallding, "Functional Analysis in Sociology," *op. cit.*

tion of pathology in new guise, in practice, it did just the opposite. The meaningful question is not what the functionalists could have said about deviant phenomena; rather, what they did say. Moreover, the point at issue is not whether the assessments they made were valid, invalid, or even subject to the canons of empirical verification; the narrow issue before us is whether the doctrine of functionalism itself forwarded or subverted the doctrine of pathology. I wish to assert that functionalism had the latter effect and in that measure served the cause of naturalism. Beyond that, its validity or utility in the analysis of social phenomenon—deviant or conventional—is debatable. Accordingly, its value has been endlessly debated.

What did functionalists actually write about deviant phenomena? Overwhelmingly, they stressed the functions—not dysfunctions—of deviant forms. The dysfunctions were hastily acknowledged in a first paragraph. The actual analysis ignored them, took them for granted, viewed them as something everyone already knew about. The dysfunctions were *manifest*. Their reiteration was deemed neither a contribution to knowledge nor a sign of acuity. The important and remembered contributions to functionalist theory always contained an element of surprise—the functions of inequality, of ignorance, of deviance, of crime, of prostitution, of the political boss, of organized gambling, of labor racketeering, of youthful rebelliousness. Only Melvin Tumin, a dedicated critic of the dominant tendency in functionalism consistently pointed to the dysfunctions of social inequality and social mobility.

Despite Merton's commendation of its use, the functionalists—and Merton himself—made very little use of the concept of dysfunction. They made especially little use of that concept when considering deviant phenomena. *Written* functionalism, spoken functionalism were overwhelmingly concerned with *latent* functions—consequences of patterns that were allegedly unintended and unrecognized. To the recitation or publication of manifest functions, the obvious response is yawning acknowledgment. Thus the actual work of most functionalists focused on the latent contributions of previously maligned phenomena to society. In this they followed Cannon by emphasizing the body's wisdom and eschewing its stupidity, even though, theoretically, both were to be considered.[30] It is precisely on this account that the functionalists have been persistently criticized as conservative, unduly affirmationist, or Panglossian. The criticism has emanated from many

[30] Robert Merton, for instance, commends Dickinson W. Richards for complementing Cannon's stress in an essay relating to the stupidity of the body entitled "Homeostasis Versus Hyperexis: or Saint George and the Dragon," *The Scientific Monthly*, LXXVII, No. 6 (December 1953), 289–294. For a discussion of this balanced perspective, see Robert Merton, "Social Problems and Sociological Theory" in *Contemporary Social Problems*, eds. Robert Merton and Robert Nisbet (New York: Harcourt, Brace & World, Inc., 2nd ed., 1966), pp. 817–823. For an equally balanced earlier statement, see Robert Merton, "Manifest and Latent Functions," *Social Theory and Social Structure*, Part II, pp. 19–84.

-sources but particularly from those who dislike surprise and novelty and thus fail to see the social purpose of swamps.[31] This criticism has been slightly unfair, since the functionalists have paid some attention to dysfunction. My point here is that with regard to *deviant phenomena,* the tendency of functionalism was to assert *latent functions*—hardly a development that could foster the equation of deviation and pathology.

Indeed, one may observe a curious relation between the discovery of latent functions and the consideration of a phenomenon as deviant by sociologists. The sub-fields of sociology are constantly shifting and from time to time concrete phenomena are relocated. Mental illness, for instance, was traditionally the domain of sociologists who specialized in social psychology or medical sociology. Increasingly, however, students of deviant phenomena have focused on mental illness. With that shift has come an increasing consideration of the functions of mental illness—for families, for professionals, and for maintaining social order.[32]

Because of that shift, a slight change must be made in Melvin Tumin's acute and sardonic observation. Mental illness must be relocated and joined with "such phenomena as delinquency, divorce, adultery, prostitution, and crime. . . ." With that modification, Tumin's is a fair statement of functionalist tendency.

> *Mental illness, racial discrimination, and poverty have no positive functions for anyone, judging by most sociological writings; or, if they do, then clearly the persons or interest blocs who do profit from these problems are villainous. Above all, no good can be identified for the system as a whole. By contrast, . . . in considering such phenomena as delinquency, divorce, adultery, prostitution, and crime, we have become very adroit at identifying positive functions for actors, interest blocs, and the society as a whole.*[33]

[31] For a delightful discussion of the Jeffersonian circle and its belief in the "wisdom of nature," see Daniel Boorstin, *The Lost World of Thomas Jefferson* (New York: Holt, Rinehart and Winston, Inc., 1948), pp. 44–53. Boorstin credits the theory of the function of swamps and marshes to the philosopher Adam Seybert who reasoned that marshes were "very necessary to keep the atmosphere in a *proper degree* of purity, for it is not only the impure atmosphere which kills animals, but the too pure also; and . . . animals live too fast in atmospheres overcharged with oxygen gas." (*Ibid.,* p. 45) Seybert concluded by expressing the opinion that "ere long marshes will be looked upon by mankind as gifts from Heaven to prolong the life and happiness of the greatest portion of the animal kingdom." The phrase "social purpose of swamps" is Lon Fuller's, *The Morality of Law* (New Haven: Yale University Press, 1964), p. 146.

[32] See Harold Sampson, Sheldon L. Messinger, *et al.,* "The Mental Hospital and Marital Family Ties," in *The Other Side,* edited by Howard Becker (New York: The Free Press of Glencoe, Inc., 1964); Erving Goffman, *Asylums* (New York: Doubleday & Company [Anchor], 1961); and Thomas Scheff, *Being Mentally Ill* (Chicago: Aldine Publishing Co., 1966).

[33] Melvin Tumin, "The Functionalist Approach to Social Problems," *Social Problems,* XII (Spring 1965), 384.

Thus functionalism, with its eye for the wisdom of the body and its taste for latent consequences, freed naturalism from the idea of pathology in spite of a theoretical doctrine that *could have* maintained a place for it. The reason pathology did not survive functionalism has already been suggested: The functionalists had no eye for stupidity and no taste for patency.

Functionalism assessed the consequences of social phenomena, but its stance encouraged seemingly odd or peculiar evaluations. Unlike the conceivers of social pathology, who had tended to equate conventional morality with health, functionalists frequently saw conventional morality as a repository of ignorance, bias, or ethnocentrism. No longer, argued the functionalists, could the conventionally assumed foundations and consequences of social phenomena, especially deviant, be echoed in sociological theory. The foundations and consequences of deviant phenomena, and thus their very nature, were to be newly discovered.

Robert Merton signaled the assault on the common sense, calling for its replacement by an uncovering of latent functions. He said:

> *The discovery of latent functions . . . introduces a* qualitatively different increment in the previous state of knowledge. . . . [It] precludes the substitution of naive moral judgments for sociological analysis. . . . *We should be prepared to find that analysis in terms of latent functions at times runs counter to prevailing moral evaluations. For it does not follow that the latent functions will operate in the same fashion as the manifest functions which are ordinarily the basis of these* [naive moral] *judgments.*[34]

Merton proceeded to illustrate this point by suggesting that though "in large sectors of the American population, the political machine or the 'political racket' are judged as unequivocally 'bad' and 'undesirable,'" the same phenomena can be conceived in terms of their unnoticed contributions —their latent functions.[35] His repudiation of conventional morality began innocently; indeed, his rejection of the correctional perspective was never unequivocal. That rejection was a strategy by which we could better achieve correctional aims. The functional view was commended (to correctors, I suppose) because in the long run it promised a better chance of liquidating what was conventionally deemed evil:

> *To adopt an* exclusively *moral attitude toward the "corrupt political machine" is to lose sight of the very structural conditions which generate the "evil" that is so bitterly attacked. To adopt a functional outlook is to*

[34] Robert Merton, *Social Theory and Social Structure* (New York: The Free Press of Glencoe, Inc., 1957), pp. 70–71.
[35] *Ibid.*

provide not an apologia for the political machine but a more solid basis for modifying or eliminating the machine, providing specific structural arrangements are introduced either for eliminating these effective de-mands . . . or . . . of satisfying these demands through alternative means.[36]

However, this promissory note tendered to those sponsoring correction need not be taken seriously, since it figured neither in actual functional analysis nor in the account systems of those sponsoring social research. Then, it was an expression of good will and intention—no more and no less. To utter it now would be an expression of bad faith. As naturalism continued to develop, it became increasingly clear that its descriptions, conceptions, and frameworks were intended neither to provide apologia nor to create a more solid basis for correction. Its purpose was only to illuminate phe-nomena. The latent or manifest functions of these sociological views on policy-makers and others is another question altogether. With regard to that question, many views have been expressed, all unsubstantiated. My own view—equally unsubstantiated—is that the functionalist perspective has had little public consequence. It has neither bolstered the social order nor sub-verted it. Except among a few thousand sociologists it has passed unnoticed.

After placating the correctional impulse, Merton considered the latent functions of the political machine. He introduced that consideration by won-dering how machines survive considering the customary and legal opposition they must withstand: "In view of the manifold respects in which political machines, in varying degrees, run counter to the mores and at times to the law, it becomes pertinent to inquire how they manage to continue in opera-tion."[37] The preference of functional analysis for latency and the disdain for patency appeared in the very next sentence: "The familiar 'explanations' for the continuance of the political machine," said Merton, "are not here in point."[38] This is a remarkable sentence and is central to an understanding of how functionalism purged pathology, while it could theoretically have harbored that conception.

In that sentence, we may glimpse the cavalier spirit with which pathol-ogy was eliminated. The older views regarding the nature of the political ma-chine are never directly assaulted; instead they are merely discounted. Three methods of derogation, none addressing the issue of validity, are used in a single sentence: the term explanation is encircled by quotation marks, im-plying that they are really not explanations but avoiding the necessity of direct confrontation; they are "familiar," which is to say they are manifest, patent, or old hat; and they are "not here in point," implying that the author

[36] *Ibid.,* p. 76.
[37] *Ibid.,* p. 71.
[38] *Ibid.*

is not about to bother considering them seriously. In short, pathology is spoofed out of existence. Though illicit by scholarly standards, such a procedure was just—in the poetic sense—since the conception of pathology itself, when applied to social life, was founded on an equally unsubstantial base. Pathology was a spook, and spooks need not be treated fairly.

The same spirit was evident in Merton's treatment of the common sense—the source of knowledge regarding manifest functions. He discredited the patent reasons for the rise of the political machine by archly considering the solutions to the problem implicit in the common sense. Never are these patent reasons for the machine seriously discussed, never are we told why civic virtue and good citizenship are, by implication, impractical. The patent reasons and the patent solutions, being familiar "explanations" are simply "not here in point." Merton observed:

> To be sure, it may well be that if "respectable citizenry" would live up to their political obligations, if the electorate were to be alert and enlightened; if the number of elective officials were substantially reduced . . . ; —if these and a plethora of similar changes in political structure were introduced, perhaps the "evils" of the political machine would indeed be exorcized.[39]

Having thus dismissed the familiar explanations, Merton proceeded to a "serious" analysis of the political machine. He began with an assumption that is more or less common in the functional view of deviant phenomena. Merton maintained the assumption even though his discussion of anthropological functionalism included a specific criticism of it. Thus, Merton assumed what in the doctrine of functionalism we are not permitted to assume—that persistence is evidence of function. There is no better evidence of the basic differences between functionalist theory and practice. The latter, *practice,* with its assumption that persistence is evidence of function, has been featured in the actual analysis of deviant phenomena by this school of thought. The *doctrine,* restricting this assumption, has mainly been used against critics as evidence that functionalism need not be obtuse about the stupidity of the body. The actual practice and the theoretical doctrine were joined by Merton; but, doctrine, as usual, was parenthetic and practice pervasive. He said:

> Proceeding from the functional view . . . that we should ordinarily (not invariably) expect persistent social patterns and social structures to perform positive functions which are at the time not adequately fulfilled by other existing patterns and structures, the thought occurs that perhaps this publicly maligned organization is, under present conditions, satisfying basic latent functions.[40]

[39] *Ibid.,* p. 71.
[40] *Ibid.,* pp. 71–72.

Thus, since the political machine has persisted, we can expect that it performs positive functions despite the doctrinal restraint. The functional argument is of dubious validity; nonetheless, it turned the table on the equally dubious perspective of pathology. The political machine was no longer to be conceived as a cancer; rather it was a blessing in disguise. The latter view replaced the former, and since the credibility of the functional view was always suspect among men endowed with good sense and reason, it did not seriously interfere with the substantive aim of naturalism. Thus, subsequent naturalist sociologists were to view, describe, and analyze similar phenomena in neither terms, but, instead, in terms more congenial to those engaged in and affected by the projects. Not a cancer, not a blessing in disguise, the political machine could be seen for what it unalterably *is:* a pretty good racket.

Not especially impressed by the phenomenon on its own terms—a pretty good racket—Merton rapidly proceeded to the functions performed by the political machine, organizing his discussion around the "boss." Two related topics were then considered. Together, they suggested the general principles of functional analysis.[41] To understand the contribution of the boss and the political machine he personifies, suggested Merton, we must focus on "the structural context which makes it difficult, if not impossible, for morally approved structures to fulfill essential functions" and, subsequently, we must locate and specify "the subgroups whose distinctive needs are left unsatisfied, except for the latent functions which the morally disapproved machine in fact fulfills."[42] The structural context suggested is the "dispersion of power" through the political organization. The contribution of the boss "is to organize, centralize and maintain in good working condition 'the scattered fragments of power.' "[43] Without a conducive structural context, there would be no occasion for the emergence of a political boss. Thus, the context is suggested:

> The constitutional dispersion of power not only makes for difficulty of effective decision and action but when action does occur it is defined and hemmed in by legalistic considerations. [In consequence, there developed] a much more human system of partisan government, whose chief object soon became the circumvention of government by law. . . . The lawlessness of the extra-official democracy was merely the counterpoise of the legalism of the official democracy. The lawyer having been permitted to subordinate democracy to the law, the Boss had to be called in to extri-

[41] These general principles are further developed in Merton's "Social Structure and Anomie," *op. cit.,* pp. 131–160.
[42] Merton, "Manifest and Latent Functions," *op. cit.,* p. 72.
[43] *Ibid.*

cate the victim, which he did after a fashion and for a consideration.
. . . The functional deficiencies of the official structure generate an alternative (unofficial) structure to fulfill existing needs somewhat more effectively.[44]

Whose needs are served by the unofficial, alternative system? Merton suggested a number of "subgroups" whose "needs" would be left largely unsatisfied were it not for the latent functions fulfilled by the machine. Though he was not terribly specific in pointing to actual subgroups and not especially justified in using the term "need"—"want" would have been preferable—Merton did suggest in a general way who benefits from the machine system. Those in need of "all manner of assistance" are aided in a personal and human way by the machine through its local agents.[45] Being a particularistic method of assistance, the machine avoids the formalism, red tape, and officious character of bureaucratic and even-handed service. The machine provides windfall assistance for citizens, businessmen, politicians, and others affiliated with it.[46] Graft, payoffs, uncontested contracts for construction and other public works are also part of the machine's operation. Finally, the machine contributes, according to Merton, to the American dream of opportunity and advancement through the class system by providing channels of social mobility for those excluded from conventional avenues of advancement.[47] Here too, the machine operates particularistically, offsetting the formal and painstaking avenue for mobility provided by the educational system. Though the school system, too, may harbor a particularism in the form of middle-class bias, waspish leanings, or merely prissy standards, the machine, with its local ties and sentiments, its ethnic and ·racial bonds and, above all, its lubrication of personal payoffs and favors, represented the more profound particularism. Thus, as in the case of assistance and gains, it is fair to say that the machine provided not just another avenue for social mobility, but a channel for windfall mobility: opportunity for advancement over and above one's due.

By stressing the assistance, gains, and social mobility provided, Merton specified the serviceable character of the machine, and enlightened us with respect to its possible latent functions. But by omitting to mention the windfall character of the assistance, gains, and mobility provided and, consequently, by remaining disinterested in the location of "subgroups" *at whose expense* these windfalls are provided, Merton obscured a basic fact. The machine was a pretty good racket that, if anything, exploited the vast majority of the ethnic poor along with the more fortunate good citizens to pro-

[44] *Ibid.,* p. 73.
[45] *Ibid.,* p. 74.
[46] *Ibid.,* p. 75.
[47] *Ibid.,* p. 76.

vide windfall assistance, gains, and mobility for a favored few. The question "who benefits"—Merton's second topic—really makes little sense unless we simultaneously ask "at whose expense." By not linking the two in practice as well as doctrine, we blind ourselves to the occasional stupidity of social arrangements and the pathos frequently implicit in the lives of those subjected to them.

Despite these omissions in the functional view, it *was* an advance. It routed the conception of pathology, though doctrinally it granted the possibility of dysfunctions. But, more important, it created a climate conducive to the further growth of naturalism by sponsoring a moral innocence that fostered the study of the *actual workings* of deviant phenomena. The naturalist's interest in what actually happens in the realm he chooses to study was encouraged. Merton was explicit on this point:

> *The basic sociological role of the machine . . . can be more fully appreciated only if one temporarily abandons attitudes of moral indignation, to examine in all moral innocence the actual workings of the organization.*[48]

But Merton's moral innocence was too limited. Indignation was to be temporarily abandoned, presumably so that with the resources of "social science" we could, by and by, more effectively liquidate what now we were impotently indignant about. Moreover, when viewed in terms of subsequent developments in naturalism, his conception of "actual workings" of a deviant phenomenon was too extensive. Insufficient attention was paid to internal workings and the main focus put on external workings, or wider social consequences. In the work of the neoChicagoans and of Daniel Bell that balance is reversed. Description of structure, or anatomy, takes precedence over the inference of function. And, not surprisingly, this reversal is accompanied by a moral innocence surpassing anything apparently contemplated by Merton.

Pathology and the NeoChicagoans

The designation of phenomena as pathological, the equation of deviation with pathology, the signification of persons as deviant are themes that pervade the writings of the neoChicagoans. But between the correctional manner of developing these themes and the neoChicagoans is a vast difference. From the correctional standpoint, designation of phenomenon as

[48] *Ibid.*, p. 78. See also Eric McKitrick, "The Study of Corruption," *Political Science Quarterly*, LXXII, No. 14 (Dec. 1957), 502–514.

pathological, the equation of deviation with pathology, and the signification of persons as deviant are *operations performed by the scientific analyst.* From the neoChicagoan view, designation, equation, and signification are ordinary social operations performed by common men. These processes are consequential and implicated in the process of becoming deviant, but they are not thereby transformed into useful assertions, defensible assessments, or abiding truths. The neoChicagoans strongly opposed the idea that pathological imputations are ever warranted or useful. They occur in the world, and thus their consequences must be pondered. In considering the consequences of imputing pathology, the neoChicagoans go beyond most of the functionalists. Sensitive, perhaps hypersensitive, to the impact of labeling and stigmatizing, they incorporated their critique of the idea of pathology into a theory of the process of becoming deviant that distinguished theirs from other contemporary sociological accounts. Their account of the natural process of becoming deviant will be considered, along with others, below. Now, I limit myself to the narrower question of how the concept of pathology fared in neoChicagoan hands. Even more than the functionalists, and much more directly, they repudiated its utility.

Edwin Lemert, the earliest contributor to this viewpoint, suggested that little would be lost by divesting pathology of its traditional implications. Though not averse to maintaining the term, Lemert fundamentally reconceived its meaning. Lemert said:

> We may pertinently ask at this juncture whether the time has not come to break abruptly with the traditions of older social pathologists and abandon once and for all the archaic and medicinal idea that human beings can be divided into normal and pathological, or at least, if such a division must be made, to divest the term "pathological" of its moralistic, unscientific overtones. As a step in this direction, the writer suggests that the concepts of social differentiation and individuation be rescued from the limbo of the older textbooks on sociology, . . . perhaps being supplemented and given statistical meaning with the perfectly usable concept of deviation. . . . [But since] some method must be found to distinguish that portion of differentiation which can be designated appropriately as falling within the field of social pathology, the second necessary postulate is that there is a space-time limited societal awareness and reaction to deviation, ranging from strong approval through indifference to strong disapproval. Thus, by further definition, sociopathic phenomena simply become differentiated behavior which, at a given time and in a given place, is socially disapproved, though the same behavior may be socially approved at other times and at other places, and for our society as a whole there may be no consensus as to whether the behavior is desirable or undesirable.[49]

[49] Edwin Lemert, "Some Aspects of a General Theory of Sociopathic Behavior," *Proceedings of the Pacific Sociological Society* (State College of Washington Research Studies, 1948), XVI, No. 1, 24–25.

Lemert's revision of the conception of social pathology was tantamount to its repudiation. Only the term itself was to survive. Sociopathic phenomena were simply differentiated patterns eliciting disapproval. The repudiation of the idea of pathology was, for Lemert, justified by the term's unscientific and moralistic overtones. There was no way of cogently conceiving a phenomenon pathological. Erving Goffman, writing specifically about mental illness, but intending the point more generally, suggested some of the main defects in the idea of social pathology and the medical analogy on which it is founded. In considering the applicability of the concept of pathology in mental institutions, Goffman said:

> *Ordinarily the pathology which first draws attention to the patient's condition is conduct that is "inappropriate in the situation." But the decision as to whether a given act is appropriate or inappropriate must often necessarily be a lay decision, simply because we have no technical mapping of the various behavioral subcultures in our society, let alone the standards of conduct prevailing in each of them. Diagnostic decisions, except for extreme symptoms, can become ethnocentric, the server judging from his own culture's point of view individuals' conduct that can really be judged only from the perspective of the group from which they derive. Further, since inappropriate behavior is typically behavior that someone does not like and finds extremely troublesome, decisions concerning it tend to be political, in the sense of expressing the special interests of some particular faction of persons rather than interests that can be said to be above the concerns of any particular grouping as in the case of physical pathology.*[50]

Goffman's skepticism regarding a conception of social pathology was founded on two connected features of social life: variation in standards of behavior and a factionalism involving vested interests in particular standards over others. What is deemed pathological by the professional server in the mental institution may seem normal enough in the client's subculture. The server, having a vested interest in order and career, may be motivated to regard behavior troublesome *to him* as a symptom of the client's illness. Moreover, suggested Goffman, behavior that seems odd or inappropriate to the client may sometimes seem healthy enough to the professional. He observed that "perception of losing one's mind is based on culturally derived and socially ingrained stereotypes of symptoms such as hearing voices, losing temporal and spatial orientation, and sensing that one is being followed."[51] However significant and spectacular such events are to the layman,

[50] Erving Goffman, *op. cit.*, pp. 363–364.
[51] *Ibid.*, p. 132.

they may on occasion "psychiatrically signify merely a temporary emotional upset in a stressful situation."[52]

Thus, even in dealing with the most patently bizarre human conduct, Goffman questioned the capacity to impute pathology. In so doing, he forwarded, more explicitly than the functionalists, an idea antithetical to pathology—diversity. The concept of pathology assumed a basic normal system. In social affairs, Goffman contended, normality is an appropriate response to a situation. The very idea of normality flounders, according to him, because there is "no technical mapping of the various behavioral subcultures." Where such a mapping does not exist, the conception of pathology—in addition to its other difficulties—simply has no moorings.

Howard Becker went even further in repudiating the validity or utility of a concept of pathology. Moreover, he suggested that this notion, and the correctional stance with which it has been so closely linked, still dominates much sociological research and theory. Becker pointed to the difficulties of applying an idea of health to the realm of social existence:

> This [pathological] view rests, obviously, on a medical analogy. The human organism, when it is working efficiently, and experiencing no discomfort, is said to be "healthy." When it does not work efficiently, a disease is present. The organ or function that has become deranged is said to be pathological. Of course, there is little disagreement about what constitutes a healthy state of the organism. But there is much less agreement when one uses the notion of pathology, analogically, to describe kinds of behavior that are regarded as deviant. For people do not agree on what constitutes healthy behavior.[53]

In the work of the neoChicagoans the attitudes of appreciation and diversity are linked. Moreover, the older Chicago methods of close contact with the subjects of research and field observation are connected to the possibility of finally purging the lingering suspicions of pathology and believing —instead of temporarily pretending to believe—that in social existence there is only diversity. Both Goffman and Becker contended that close observation of deviant subjects was the best safeguard against the pathological implications of the correctional view. Goffman made this point as radically as possible:

> As has been repeatedly shown in the study of non-literate societies, the awesomeness, distastefulness, and barbarity of a foreign culture can de-

[52] *Ibid.* See also the discussion of folk conceptions of going "loco" in Lloyd Rogler and August Hollingshead, *Trapped: Families and Schizophrenia* (New York: John Wiley & Sons, Inc., 1965), Chapter 10.

[53] Howard Becker, *Outsiders* (New York: The Free Press of Glencoe, Inc., 1963), p. 5.

crease to the degree that the student becomes familiar with the point of view to life taken by his subjects. Similarly, the student of mental hospitals can discover that the craziness or "sick behavior" claimed for the mental patient is by and large a product of the claimant's social distance from the situation that the patient is in, and is not primarily a product of mental illness. Whatever the refinements of the various patients' psychiatric diagnoses, and whatever the special ways in which social life on the "inside" is unique, the researcher can find that he is participating in a community not significantly different from any other he has studied. Of course, while restricting himself to the off-ward grounds community of paroled patients, he may feel, as some patients do, that life in the locked wards is bizarre; and while on a locked admissions or convalescent ward, he may feel that chronic "back" wards are socially crazy places. But he need only to move his sphere of sympathetic participation to the "worst" ward in the hospital, and this, too, can come into social focus as a place with a livable and continuously meaningful world. This in no way denies that he will find a minority in any ward or patient group that continues to seem quite beyond the capacity to follow rules of social organization, or that the orderly fulfillment of normative expectations in patient society is partly made possible by strategic measures that have somehow come to be institutionalized in mental hospitals.[54]

Thus, even with "crazy" persons, an interior view stressing the subject's own perspective is inimical to a conception of pathology. In the same spirit, and in a manner that hopefully left ample opportunity for an appreciation of pathos, Becker concluded his volume:

We ought not to view it [deviant behavior] as something special, as depraved or in some magical way better than other kinds of behavior. We ought to see it simply as a kind of behavior some disapprove of and others value, studying the processes by which either or both perspectives are built up and maintained. Perhaps the best surety against either extreme is close contact with the people we study.[55]

The appreciation of the subject and a stress on his own perspective of the enterprise engaging him subverted the assumptions of pathology. Naturalism, guided by this antagonism to correctional assumptions, developed the idea of diversity, even to the extent of omitting mention of pathetic features of deviant phenomena. Another tendency emergent in naturalism was to break down any simple distinction between deviant and conventional realms. In the next chapter, we turn to that development.

[54] Goffman, *op. cit.*, p. 130.
[55] Becker, *op. cit.*, p. 176.

4

Simplicity and Complexity

Vision, in contrast to mere sight, is the capacity to see things unconventionally and more profoundly than others, partly by possessing a wider visual span. Seeing phenomena in relation to others, or within some wider context, is the very meaning of sociological vision and a certain mode of vision emerged as part of the naturalist perspective.

The general vision of sociology stresses the perception of discrete phenomena in a wider context. Putting the individual in a group context, the group in communal, historical, or societal contexts are prime projects of sociologists, and such placement requires the naive or trained capacity to see things in that way. Sociological imagination, according to C. W. Mills, for instance, was the capacity to see the relation between personal troubles and social structure.[1] Earlier, this general vision of sociology was formulated by Durkheim in terms never surpassed. Durkheim placed the supreme act of social renunciation—suicide—in societal context.[2]

Though basic to sociology, this kind of vision is too general to inform us of the path taken by emergent naturalism. The vision of naturalism in sociology was narrower and more constrained. Attracted as they were by

[1] C. W. Mills, *The Sociological Imagination* (New York: Oxford University Press, 1959).
[2] Emile Durkheim, *Suicide* (New York: The Free Press of Glencoe, Inc., 1951).

mundane features of social life and guided by an antagonism to correctional presumptions, naturalists challenged the simplistically clear distinction between conventional and deviant phenomena, between good and evil, and finally, between cause and effect.[3]

From the concreteness of the naturalist standpoint, clear-cut and simple distinctions were features of the world of reified abstraction—a world naturalists rejected, though inevitably one they periodically revisited. But at the very least their abstractions were bound to the social world as it apparently was. In that world, the distinction between deviant and conventional phenomena was blurred, complicated, and sometimes devious. The subtlety of relation among phenomena that appeared alongside, interpenetrated, and shaped each other was not merely to be noted; rather, it emerged as a basic social fact.

Two ideas summarize the emergent appreciation of the complicated relations among deviant and conventional phenomena. The first conception may be termed *overlap;* the second *irony.* Both depend on the capacity to see phenomena as they appear alongside one another. The social facts, allegedly apparent in the world, yielded implicit conceptions in the writings of naturalist sociologists. My aim here is to make these explicit.

Overlap refers to the stress put on two closely related themes: the marginal rather than gross differentiation between deviant and conventional folk and the considerable though variable interpenetration of deviant and conventional culture. Both themes sensitize us to the regular exchange, traffic, and flow—of persons as well as styles and precepts—that occur among deviant and conventional worlds. Thus, the conceptual distinction between deviation and convention, necessary as it may be, is rendered in a manner that recognizes the process of movement between the two realms. The sensitivity to overlap is illustrated in Durkheim's perceptive discussion of phenomena that neighbor on suicide. Because suicide has been a phenomenon virtually unstudied by sociologists with a naturalist bent, Durkheim's acute observation had little explicit impact on subsequent studies. For Durkheim, however, the principle of overlap was a key social fact, and a main though neglected source of his theory concerning the foundations of suicide. He said:

> *Suicides do not form, as might be thought, a wholly distinct group, an isolated class of monstrous phenomena, unrelated to other forms of conduct, but rather are related to them by a continuous series of intermediate cases. They are merely the exaggerated form of common practices. . . . A man exposing himself knowingly for another's sake but without the certainty of fatal result, . . . the daredevil who intentionally toys with death while seeking to avoid it, . . . the man of apathetic temperament*

[3] Their critique of the final separation between cause and effect will be discussed in Chapter 7.

*who, having no vital interest in anything, takes no care of health . . .
are not radically distinct from true suicide. They result from similar
states of mind, since they also entail mortal risks not unknown to the
agent, and the prospect of these is no deterrent; the sole difference is a
lesser chance of death. . . . All such facts form a sort of embryonic suicide, and though it is not methodologically sound to confuse them with
complete and full suicide, their close relation to it must not be neglected.
For suicide appears quite another matter, once its unbroken connection is
recognized with acts, on the one hand, of courage and devotion, on the
other, of imprudence and clear neglect.*[4]

In the final sentence of the passage, Durkheim made the key point:
our whole conception of the phenomenon shifts—it "appears quite another
matter"—when we recognize its "unbroken connection" with other social
realms. By seeing the obscured similarities among phenomena that at the
surface appear grossly different, our vision of them is fundamentally altered.
The dense barrier between deviation and convention is broken down, and
the human quality of each realm thereby enriched. More specifically, the
connection of suicide to acts "of courage and devotion" suggests the motive,
altruism, while its connection with "imprudence and clear neglect" suggests
those of egoism and anomie.

The idea of irony grows easily from that of overlap. Once the distinction between good and evil is made problematic, once their interpenetration
is stressed, a similar insight may develop with respect to the relations between phenomena and their purported causes. Whereas overlap refers to the
complicated relations among good and evil *phenomena,* irony refers to the
complicated—and surprising—relations between good and evil in *sequence.*
Irony is a state of affairs or a result opposite to, and as if in mockery of, the
appropriate result. Accordingly, a stress on irony may be taken as a self-
conscious reversal of the earlier correctional view that bad things were
caused by bad conditions. Given the ironic tendency of naturalism, bad
things could result from highly treasured and revered aspects of social life,
and good could be born of what was conventionally deemed evil.

Reinhold Niebuhr defined irony as "apparently fortuitous incongruities
in life which are discovered, upon closer examination, to be not merely
fortuitous."[5] This discovery is central in Niebuhr's conception and distinguishes irony from mere comedy. He elaborated the distinction:

*Ironic contrasts and incongruities have an element of the comic in them
insofar as they exhibit absurd juxtapositions of strength and weakness;
of wisdom through foolishness; or foolishness as the fruit of wisdom; of*

[4] Emile Durkheim, *op. cit.,* pp. 45–46.
[5] Reinhold Niebuhr, *The Irony of American History* (New York: Charles
Scribner's Sons, 1952), p. viii.

guilt arising from the pretensions of innocency; or innocency hiding be-
hind ostensible guilt. Yet contrasts are ironic only if they are not merely
absurd, but have a hidden meaning. They must elicit not merely laughter
but a knowing smile. The hidden meaning is supplied by the fact that
the juxtapositions and contrasts are not merely fortuitous. They are
related to each other by some foible of the person who is involved
in both. The powerful person who is proved to be really weak is involved
in an ironic contrast only if his weakness is due to some pretension of
strength. . . . There is no irony in a purely fortuitous escape of a guilty
man from punishment. But it is ironic if those who are despised by their
fellowmen achieve recognition and justification in some higher court
through the very qualities which brought about their original condemna-
tion; or when the naiveté of babes or simpletons becomes the source of
wisdom withheld from the wise.[6]

Thus a key element of irony is latency—inherent qualities of phenomena that, despite their hidden nature, culminate in outcomes that mock
the expected result. Irony is natural trick depending on a feature common to
all tricks—something being hidden from view that appears only at the culmination. Latency occurs in overlap, too, which stresses the good that may
be obscured in evil, and the vice that lurks in virtue. Let us consider the
idea of irony—and overlap—as they developed in the three phases of naturalism. Taken together, the two ideas express the fundamental vision of the
relation between society and deviation proposed by each school of thought.

The Chicago School

Entering deviant worlds was the major contribution of the Chicago
school to emergent naturalism. Chicagoans prepared the way for a repudiation of the concept of pathology, but did not themselves explicitly participate
in purging sociology of that idea. Similarly, while the Chicagoans occasionally noted the existence of overlap, and developed a characteristic irony in
accounting for modern pathologies, they were not accomplished in either
endeavor. Their appreciation of overlap was minimal. They exaggerated
the separation between deviant and conventional worlds, drawing barriers
too densely. Their insensitivity to the flow of ideas and persons among different social worlds resulted partly from a dedicated focus on the details of
each world taken separately. A certain blindness to overlap and connection
thus was the vice attending their ethnographic virtue. The naturalist may become so immersed in the distinctive projects of *his* people that the flow between them and others is sometimes obscured.

A stress on moral isolation or subcultural autonomy was a useful and

[6] *Ibid.,* p. 154.

perhaps even necessary corrective to the older view that denied morali\
and culture to primitives, deviant persons, and the lower orders.[7] To establish that the worlds of hobos and taxi-dancers, for instance, had their own
rules, regulations, and rewards, the Chicagoans and subsequent sociologists
tended to minimize the importance of the fact that, *unlike primitives,* most
deviant groups existed in the context of conventional America, drew sustenance from that milieu, dispensed services to it, recruited persons from it,
and frequently delivered repentant deviators back to it. This exaggeration of
dense separation and moral isolation was reinforced in many ways: the
uncritical transfer of anthropological ideas derived from the study of primitive tribes to modern society; the presumption, before the empirical study
of social mobility, that movement to and from the lower orders was extremely rare; and a rather static view of deviant worlds that failed to consider the relevance of frequent turnover in the membership that composed
them. All were in turn reinforced by a mistaken conception of the subjective
view, a conception that granted too much credence, was too greatly reliant
on the subject's own story. To conceive oneself as cut off from the conventional world, as permanently unsuited for—or uninterested in—participation, is a meaningful subjective state. To stress the subject's perspective
commits us to taking such states seriously, but it does not compel us to
equate those states with the reality they purport to represent.

Taxi-dancers, studied by Paul Cressey, for instance, were very impressed with how different their lives were from those of conventional girls.[8]
This sense of moral peculiarity or isolation deriving from the subject became part of the conceptual rendition of sociologists. The separation of
peculiar worlds, and later of subcultures, came to dominate the conceptual
systems to such an extent that the ordinary facts of *transiency* hardly seemed
worthy of account. In Cressey's own study of taxi-dancers, many girls left
their deviant world, settled down, and married. Like most juvenile delinquents, they became ex-members of deviant worlds. Transient membership is
an ordinary fact of many deviant enterprises; but, because of the tendency
to classify "types" of deviation, to separate them from others and from conventional behavior, and to view them statically, there is little impulse to account for transiency. The subject of inquiry may be forgiven for viewing as
permanent what is only temporary; he may fail to see himself in full complexity or in process. But the student of social life must have a fuller view
of the intricate careers of actual persons. Often, both style and substance
change during a life-cycle.

Nevertheless, connections among various deviant worlds were occasionally noted by writers of the Chicago school; they were not always deemed
worlds unto themselves. Anderson, for instance, observed that "Bohemia

[7] Jaeger and Selznick, *op. cit.*
[8] Paul Cressey, *The Taxi-Dance Hall,* pp. 32–33.

and Hobohemia meet at 'Bughouse Square.' " There one could find a scattering of tramps, hobos, free-lance propagandists, dreamers, fakers, bootleggers, dope-fiends, vagabond poets, and artists.[9] More important, perhaps, was the growing recognition that hobos were similar in character and disposition to persons who, in another social context, might be praiseworthy. In his introduction to *The Hobo,* Robert Park observed:

> *The man whose restless disposition made him a pioneer on the frontier tends to become a "homeless man"—a hobo and a vagrant—in the modern city. From the point of view of their biological predispositions, the pioneer and the hobo are perhaps the same temperamental type; from the point of view of their socially acquired traits, they are something quite different.*[10]

Though aspects and instances of overlap were noted by the Chicagoans, they were of little importance in the Chicago rendition of deviant phenomena. Overlap was acknowledged, but that social fact had no prominence in their summary of the world.

Since the appreciation of irony is so related to that of overlap, neither was it well developed among the Chicagoans. There was an irony in the causal theories of the Chicagoans, in the ways deviant phenomena were accounted for, but it was one which long since had become trite and worn. From Colonial times in America, and even earlier in Europe, intellectuals, statesmen, and publicists shared with the common man a deep distrust of urban life. Robert Park, and his followers in the Chicago school, held this distrust and echoed the timeworn irony implicit in it. Beneath the surface gloss and strength of metropolis lay sorrow and weakness; and that latency would, as if in mockery of urbane virtue, reveal itself in vice, corruption, and pathology.[11] The attraction of cities—freedom, mobility, and stimulation —masked their danger and potential decay. The irony chosen by the Chicagoans was already part of the conventional wisdom of American intellectuals. The city was both attractive and destructive, "like the attraction of the flame for the moth."[12]

The fact that a central irony is worn does not mean that it is untrue or misleading; it may be credible and useful but *as irony* it lacks potency. Such an irony fails to elicit a knowing smile (the test, as Niebuhr suggests); in-

[9] Anderson, *The Hobo,* pp. 8–9.

[10] *Ibid.,* p. v.

[11] For a lucid treatment of the long tradition of anti-urbanism among American intellectuals and, more specifically, of the place Robert Park occupied in that tradition, see Morton and Lucia White, *The Intellectual Versus the City* (Cambridge: Harvard University Press and M.I.T. Press, 1962).

[12] White and White, *op. cit.,* p. 159 and Robert Park, *Human Communities* (New York: The Free Press of Glencoe, Inc., 1952), pp. 47–48.

stead it elicits a jaded yawn. Accordingly, the Chicagoans cannot be considered important in forwarding the naturalist vision of the relation between deviation and society. They visualized such a relationship, but mainly cast it in traditional terms hardly inconsistent with correctional assumptions. To forward the vision of symbiotic relation, the overlap between deviant and conventional phenomena had to be more pronounced, and the irony more potent, surprising, and specific.

Functionalism

Perhaps because they did not focus as sharply as the Chicagoans on their deviant subjects, perhaps because of the stress on latency, and perhaps because they could build upon the observations of predecessors, the functionalists were more accomplished in sociological vision and more adept in the peripheral perception on which it is based. Not only was overlap noted, and irony cultivated, but both were prominent in the conceptual rendition of deviant worlds and their relation to the wider social context.

As long as correctional presumptions lingered, the intricate relations among conventional and deviant phenomena could not attain conceptual or theoretical prominence. Connections could be noted, and the hypocrisy or corruption of allegedly conventional persons exposed or condemned, but a conceptual block separating disparate worlds would remain. Eric McKitrick, the political scientist, commented on the removal of that conceptual block in considering the contribution of functional theory:

> The most fascinating changes, . . . and by far the most complex and difficult to trace down, are those connected with . . . social mobility . . . [and] . . . the underworld. One of the most remarkable of recent discoveries in the social sciences has been the manner in which these two areas are related. . . . Somewhere along the way a conceptual block has been removed, and we are now able to see that not only do the values of mobility, status and respectability operate in the underworld in a way precisely analogous to their workings in the "upperworld," but also, that the extent to which the two worlds overlap . . . is considerable.[13]

Until the conceptual block was removed, the visible similarity between deviant and conventional phenomena was obscured. To illuminate the similarities did not imply a dismissal of differences, but it minimized them.

[13] Eric McKitrick, "The Study of Corruption," *Political Science Quarterly,* LXXII (1957), reprinted in S. M. Lipset and N. J. Smelser (eds.) *Sociology: The Progress of a Decade* (Englewood Cliffs, N.J.: Prentice-Hall, Inc., 1961), pp. 454–455.

Part of the motive for pointing out similarities between deviant and conventional phenomena was to distinguish them more carefully. For instance, Kingsley Davis specified important similarities between prostitution and conventional sexual exchange in order to locate the essential difference. By separating similarities from differences, Davis attempted to locate the reason for social condemnation of prostitution.

> *Prostitution is condemned in contemporary . . . societies mainly because it involves a high degree of sexual promiscuity which fulfills no publicly recognized societal goal. . . . The norms of every society tend to harness and control the sexual appetite, and one of the ways of doing this is to link the sexual act to some stable, or potentially stable, social relationship.*[14]

It is not the trading of sexual favors, Davis suggested, that elicits widespread condemnation of the prostitute, nor even her feeling of emotional indifference toward the sexual act.[15] Married women trade sexual favors, unmarried women may withhold them in exchange for marriage, and both may submit dutifully as well as joyfully to sexual relations. Thus, Davis concluded that "so long as the bargain struck is one that achieves for the woman a stable relationship with a man, especially a relationship like marriage where reproduction is officially sanctioned, the mores offer praise rather than condemnation for the exchange of feminine sexual favors."[16] The difference between prostitution and conventional sexual trading becomes clear, according to Davis, only after we point to their similarities. The condemnation of prostitution and the approval of ordinary feminine manipulation are based on the *manner* in which the prostitute trades. "The prostitute's affront is that she trades promiscuously. She takes money or other valuables for each act of intercourse. She is indifferent not only to sexual pleasure but also to the partner. Her 'selling' and her indifference therefore reflect a pure commercialization of the sexual relation."[17] Davis' point about the relation between prostitution and conventional feminine manipulation is reminiscent of Durkheim's observation regarding suicide and other flirtations with death. In each case, there is a basic continuity which cannot be obscured merely because the difference is also relevant.

Of all the functional discussions of deviant phenomena, Daniel Bell's essay on "Crime as an American Way of Life" is the most explicit and sustained in its concern with overlap.[18] As the very title conveys, overlap is the

---

[14] Kingsley Davis, "Prostitution," in Merton and Nisbet, *Contemporary Social Problems* (New York: Harcourt, Brace & World, Inc., 1961), p. 264.

[15] *Ibid.*, pp. 264–265.

[16] *Ibid.*, p. 265.

[17] *Ibid.*

[18] Daniel Bell, "Crime as an American Way of Life," Chapter 3 in *End of Ideology* (New York: The Free Press of Glencoe, Inc., rev. ed., 1962).

organizing idea of Bell's analysis of organized crime. His central and imaginative thesis is suggested almost immediately:

> *Crime, in many ways, is a Coney Island mirror, caricaturing the morals and manners of a society. The jungle quality of the American business community, particularly at the turn of the century, was reflected in the mode of "business" practiced by the coarse gangster elements, most of them from new immigrant families, who were "getting ahead" just as Horatio Alger had urged.*[19]

For Bell, this assertion was no mere literary flourish, as it had been for many others. He intended it seriously and used the insight to inform his consideration of organized crime. Crime, he suggested, can hardly be understood or appreciated unless seen in a wider context—a view that reveals its profound connection with conventional concerns and ordinary elements of American life. The general relation between crime and convention is among Bell's basic themes:

> *The desires satisfied in extra-legal fashion were more than a hunger for the "forbidden fruits" of conventional morality. They also involved, in the complex and ever shifting structure of group, class, and ethnic stratification, which is the warp and woof of America's "open" society, such "normal" goals as independence through a business of one's own, and such "moral" aspirations as the desire for social advancement and social prestige. For crime, . . . has a "functional" role in the society, and the urban rackets—the illicit activity organized for continuing profit, rather than individual illegal acts—is one of the queer ladders of social mobility in American life. Indeed, it is not too much to say that the whole question of organized crime in America cannot be understood unless one appreciates (1) the distinctive role of organized gambling as a function of a mass-consumption economy; (2) the specific role of various immigrant groups as they, one after another, became involved in marginal business and crime; and (3) the relation of crime to the changing character of the urban political machines.*[20]

So connected are they that changes in the structure of conventional enterprise are reflected in shifts in the character of criminal organization. In lagging fashion, suggested Bell, the style with which organized crime is perpetrated follows the manner of business. "As American society became more 'organized,' as the American businessman became more 'civilized' and less 'buccaneering' so did the American racketeer."[21] Moreover, criminal insti-

[19] *Ibid.,* p. 128.
[20] *Ibid.,* p. 129.
[21] *Ibid.*

tutions became modernized reflecting the rationalization experienced in ordinary business. The decline of feudal organization and its retrograde forms was most apparent in gambling—the racket whose enormity increasingly dwarfed its erstwhile competitors. With the decline of prohibition, of prostitution (which also underwent a process of decentralization), the passing of industrial racketeering, and the minimal financial importance of drugs, gambling emerged in the '40s as the main commodity of organized crime.[22] As if in parody of Marx's contention regarding the key role of advanced or progressive industry, gambling, the vanguard of illicit production, spawned a technology and organization that would engulf and defeat earlier retrograde methods. Gambling, like all vanguard industry, would revolutionize the methods of underworld activity:

> *As a multi-billion-dollar business, gambling underwent a transition parallel to the changes in American enterprise as a whole. This parallel was exemplified in many ways: in gambling's industrial organization (e.g., the growth of a complex technology such as the national racing-wire service and the minimization of risk by such techniques as lay-off betting); in its respectability, as was evidenced in the opening of smart and popular gambling casinos in resort towns and in "satellite" adjuncts to metropolitan areas; in its functional role in a mass-consumption economy (for sheer volume of money changing hands, nothing has ever surpassed this feverish activity of fifty million American adults); in the social acceptance of the gamblers in the important status world of sport and entertainment, i.e., "cafe society."* [23]

Bell stressed the overlap between institutions, their substantive and stylistic similarities, despite their acknowledged differences in aim. Correspondingly, he showed the personal response to gambling and other deviant commodities to be mixed, shifty, or ambivalent. Official condemnation encountered toleration, license, and indulgence. Thus, overlap had its final manifestation in the uncertainty and division with which public opinion morally conceived the phenomenon. Bell pointed to the lack of consensus and the personal ambivalence:

> *While Americans made gambling illegal, they did not in their hearts think of it as wicked—even the churches benefited from the bingo and lottery crazes. So they gambled—and gamblers flourished. Against this open canvas, the indignant tones of Senator Wiley and the shocked righteousness of Senator Tobey during the Kefauver investigation rang oddly. . . . Probably, this . . . tone of surprise . . . gave the activity of the*

---

[22] Also see the excellent and authoritative Massachusetts Senate Commission Report: Commonwealth of Massachusetts, Special Commission Revived and Continued for the Purpose of Investigating Organized Crime and Other Related Matters, *Report,* No. 107 (May 1957).

[23] Bell, *op. cit.*, p. 130.

Kefauver committee its piquant quality. Here were some Senators who seemingly did not know the facts of life, as most Americans did.[24]

Though the functionalists were sensitive to overlap, its implications, except in Bell's essay, were not pursued as assiduously as those of irony. The latter was a central feature of functional analysis. Implicit in the conception of latent function and frequently the concrete manifestation of the body's wisdom, irony became an organizing intuition of functionalism. Dependent as it is on an appreciation of latency, the clear and simple relation between the surface, or patent, morality of cause and effect was undermined by the use of irony. Features of worthy phenomena far beneath the surface and thus hidden from view could yield immorality, and latent features of unworthy phenomena could improve society. By the idea of irony, the functionalists revealed social process as *devious* and thus increasingly complex.

The devious relation between virtue and vice was suggested by Merton. Given certain circumstances, "a cardinal American virtue, 'ambition' promotes a cardinal American vice, 'deviant behavior.' "[25] The circumstance or setting for such an irony is to be found "in the lower reaches of the social structure."[26] There, the virtue, ambition, harbors a weakness. Those in the lower classes are subjected to incompatible demands. "On the one hand, they are asked to orient their conduct toward the prospect of large wealth . . . and on the other, they are largely denied effective opportunities to do so institutionally."[27] Thus, the irony of a virtue, ambition, promoting a vice, deviant behavior, contains an ellipsis. Ambition promotes deviation when it is institutionally frustrated. The latent feature of ambition that will yield a reversal and mock its virtue is the reality of class barriers and restrictions on social mobility. Such barriers and restrictions inhere in the very idea of ambition; by definition its only possible aim is to overcome them. Thus, ambition contains within itself the seed of institutional frustration.

A similar construction appears in Davis' essay on prostitution. He began by observing—and the contention has been supported by Kinsey's findings—"that what the male has lost in frequency of intercourse with prostitutes he has gained in frequency with non-prostitutes."[28] From that observation, Davis developed an irony:

If we reverse the proposition that increased sex freedom among women of all classes reduces the role of prostitution, we find ourselves admitting that increased prostitution may reduce the sexual irregularities of respect-

[24] *Ibid.*, p. 136.
[25] Robert Merton, *Social Theory and Social Structure* (New York: The Free Press of Glencoe, Inc., 1949), p. 137.
[26] *Ibid.*
[27] *Ibid.*
[28] Davis, *op. cit.*, p. 283.

able women. This, in fact, has been the ancient justification for tolerated prostitution—that it "protected" the family and kept the wives and daughters of the respectable citizenry pure. . . . Such a view strikes us as paradoxical, because in popular discourse an evil such as prostitution cannot cause a good such as feminine virtue, or vice versa. Yet, as our analysis has implied throughout, there is a close connection between prostitution and the structure of the family.[29]

The same irony, put in reverse form, guides Bell's analysis of organized crime. Organized crime provided a means of attaining respectable social status. As Bell put it, organized crime was a "queer ladder" of social mobility. The vice harbored a latent virtue that would later reveal itself. Bell described the predicament of Italian immigrants and suggested the part played by racketeers in providing a basis for political power and subsequent entry into respectable sectors of American life:

The Italians found the more obvious big-city paths from rags to riches pre-empted. In part this was due to the character of the early Italian immigrant. Most of them were unskilled and from rural stock. . . . [They] found jobs as ditch-diggers, on the railroads as section hands, along the docks, in the service occupations, as shoemakers, barbers, garment workers, and stayed there. Many were fleeced by the "padrone" system; a few achieved wealth from truck farming, winegrowing and marketing produce; but this "marginal wealth" was not the source of coherent and stable political power. . . . The children of the immigrants, the second and third generation, became wise in the ways of the urban slums. Excluded from the political ladder—in the early thirties there were almost no Italians on the city payroll in top jobs, nor . . . can one find discussion of Italian political leaders—and finding few open routes to wealth, some turned to illicit ways. . . . It was oddly enough, the quondam racketeer, seeking to become respectable, who provided one of the major supports for the drive to win a political voice for Italians in the power structure of the urban political machines.[30]

Frank Costello exemplified racketeers who functioned in this way. Originally in bootlegging, later in slot machines and real estate, "Costello's political opportunity came when a money-hungry Tammany, starved by

[29] *Ibid.*, pp. 283–284. Lest the reader be confused by Davis' reference to paradox and mine to irony, let me clarify. There are two meanings of paradox—the general and the technical. The general meaning of paradox—a tenet contrary to common sense or received opinion—is not the same as irony but in no way precludes it. In the general meaning of paradox, something can be both paradox—a tenet contrary to received opinion—and irony—an outcome of events that mocks the fitness of things. In this passage, Davis intends paradox in the general and not the technical sense of an apparent internal contradiction. Thus, he may call it paradox and I, irony. The definitions stated above may be found in any standard dictionary.

[30] Bell, *op. cit.*, pp. 142–143.

lack of patronage from Roosevelt and LaGuardia, turned to him for financial support."[31] The support was forthcoming. But in exchange, Italian politicians were granted entry into the urban machine and the positions and perquisites it traditionally controlled. Obviously, this was not the only factor in the Italian ascent, but it did contribute.

Similarly, Bell pointed to the services performed by industrial racketeers in organizing and stabilizing previously chaotic and cut-throat industries. In this respect, Bell followed Merton. The use of latent function as an ironic device consistently points to the existence of *blessings in disguise.* Bell said:

> *Rothstein's chief successors, Lepke Buchalter and Gurrah Shapiro, were able, in the early thirties to dominate sections of the men's and women's clothing industries, of painting, fur dressing, flour trucking, and other fields. In a highly chaotic and cut-throat industry such as clothing, the racketeer, paradoxically, played a stabilizing role by regulating competition and fixing prices.[32]*

However, Bell continually complicated the situation, sensing the shift in the nature of phenomena that accompanies a changing context. "When the NRA came in and assumed this [stabilizing] function, the businessman found that what had once been a quasi-economic service was now pure extortion, and he began to demand police action."[33] Thus, with a shifting context—the introduction of governmental stabilization—the irony of racketeers contributing to orderly business vanishes. They revert to extortion, pure and simple.

Moreover, Bell—still an outsider to academic sociology when writing "The Racket-Ridden Longshoremen"—could not resist taking a swipe at doctrinal functionalism, in which he captured a major weakness of the functionalist view. "Industrial racketeering," he said, "performs the function—*at a high price*—which other agencies cannot do, of stabilizing a chaotic market and establishing an order and structure in the industry."[34] Thus, Bell recognized that a double irony had existed even before the legalized price-fixing and other regulatory devices instituted during the New Deal. When virtue came to depend on evil for the performance of necessary services, it was doubly mocked. Not only was virtue morally compromised by such dependence, but it was fleeced too. The body's wisdom, when based on such make-shift arrangements, turns out to be partly spurious after all. It contains an element of stupidity, and it was that stupidity that Bell—and not

---

[31] *Ibid.,* p. 144.
[32] *Ibid.,* p. 131.
[33] *Ibid.*
[34] Daniel Bell, "The Racket-Ridden Longshoremen" in *End of Ideology, op. cit.,* p. 176. My italics.

the academic functionalist—glimpsed in the exhorbitant price paid for services or functions so indiscriminately procured. The irony of good emanating from evil is compounded; the very process, and the possibilities it harbors, is itself mocked by the price paid for it.

The sense of irony developed by the functionalists was not profound, but neither was it superficial or hackneyed. Compared to the central irony of the Chicago school it was fresh and, equally important, more specific. When too highly extolled and too difficult to maintain, particular methods of improvement and uplift—and not modernization in general—left in their wake latent weaknesses that would return to haunt society. Subsequent developments in the naturalistic study of deviant phenomena continued this tendency. For the neoChicagoans, irony was even more highly specified, its element of surprise even more enormous. Moreover, their central irony suggested the main contours of a distinctive causal theory.

The NeoChicagoan Vision

Because the neoChicagoan irony—signification—was so central to their rendition of the very process by which persons become deviant, its extended discussion is best left for the portion of the volume concerned with that general topic.[35] As with their critique of the idea of pathology, the neoChicagoan irony is merged with the concept of deviation and their theory as to how persons come to be that way. Their irony, stated simply, is that systems of control and the agents that man them are implicated in the process by which others become deviant. The very effort to prevent, intervene, arrest, and "cure" persons of their alleged pathologies may, according to the neoChicagoan view, precipitate or seriously aggravate the tendency society wishes to guard against.

One illustration of the neoChicagoan irony will be useful. It pertains to the process of becoming mentally ill, and points out that professionals may inadvertently contribute to the process. Their own self-conception as fullfledged professionals may depend on possessing a clientele with suitable symptoms, manifesting the kind of behavior befitting their expertise. This possibility is put succinctly by Erving Goffman:

> *I am suggesting that the patient's nature is redefined so that, in effect if not by intention, the patient becomes the kind of object upon which a psychiatric service can be performed. To be made a patient is to be remade into a serviceable object, the irony being that so little service is available once this is done.*[36]

[35] See Chapter 7.
[36] Erving Goffman, *Asylums* (Garden City, N.Y.: Doubleday & Company [Anchor], 1961), p. 379.

Goffman's explicit reference to the irony of the professional's being of little service after having redefined the patient's character should not obscure the more profound irony implicit in the first portion of the passage. There, Goffman captures the central neoChicagoan irony: the contribution conventional persons, especially professionals and other officials, make to the process by which others are defined as, and subsequently become, deviant.

In Chapter 7, I will suggest that through use of this irony, the neoChicagoans rounded out a previously incomplete system for comprehending the process of becoming deviant. Perhaps exaggerating its importance, the neoChicagoans have continually stressed the central part played by institutions and organizations in shaping the lives of those they regulate. Thus the general environment that produced personal character stressed by traditional sociology came finally to include the specific institutions devoted to deviation itself.

If the institutions devoted to deviation are seriously implicated in the process by which their charges become deviant, it follows that until one has been put through the whole process he is only marginally different from those remaining unserved and even then he may not be so very different. Thus, the specific irony of the neoChicagoans is especially congenial with an appreciation of the considerable overlap between deviation and convention. Accordingly, overlap and its implications is a prominent theme in the writings of neoChicagoans.

To stress overlap is to magnify the awareness that persons with conventional public reputations participate, either frequently or occasionally, in deviant activity. Moreover, such a stress is reflected in the conceptual rendition of the world instead of remaining a casual or side observation. In the nature of social organization, the opportunity for surreptitious deviation— taken in a context of public reputability—derives from the defective nature of human surveillance. Systems of surveillance are eternally ineffective, and always in some measure incomplete. From the subject's viewpoint, such institutional shortcomings provide a basis for *subterfuge*. Arguing from the most extreme of situations, Goffman affirmed man's irrevocable capacity for unacknowledged deviation. In prison camps men wear overcoats, he observed, and that apparel, like any other, may be used to disguise or hide. "Since an overcoat *can* conceal clear evidence of migration, and since a personal front involving clothing accompanies our participation in every organization, we must appreciate that *any* figure cut by *any* person *may* conceal evidence of spiritual leave-taking."[37]

To note the possibility of concealed deviation, or "spiritual leave-taking," is of itself no extraordinary statement of the thesis of overlap. A departure from the ordinary statement of that thesis occurs only when the possibility is elevated to a central place in the conceptual rendition of happenings in the world. Since the neoChicagoans attempted just such an ele-

[37] *Ibid.,* p. 188.

vation, it may be fairly said that their vision of overlap was more acute than that of previous schools. Convinced of the importance of publicizing deviation, labelling or stigmatizing persons, the neoChicagoans followed Lemert in stressing "secondary deviation"—the situation "when the person begins to employ his deviant behavior or a role based on it *as a means of defense, attack, or adjustment to the* . . . *problems created by the societal reaction to it.*"[38] But precisely because they stressed the symbolic transformation of character and act attending publicity and societal reaction, the neoChicagoans developed an unprecedented appreciation for the ubiquity and commonplace character of deviations that symbolically continue to be defined "as adjuncts or accessories of socially acceptable roles."[39] Until societal reaction, deviation may be managed without being conceived as deviant. Lemert, and the neoChicagoans after him, referred to this condition as "primary deviation."[40] Deviation takes its place within a mainly conventional context and is so deemed by self and others. In the neoChicagoan view, as will be elaborated later, primary deviation abounds in society. Becoming deviant, in their view, pertained mainly to *secondary* deviation—organizing a life around deviations that have been disclosed and signified. Their stress on selection and signification makes little sense unless one assumes, as they did, that unacknowledged deviation—deviation that remains unsignified or undisclosed—is common and widespread.

But to assume that unacknowledged deviation—in Lemert's terms, "primary deviation"—is common need not imply that it exists invariably, or evenly, across sections of society or among persons of different disposition or temperament. It assumes only that deviation commonly exists within contexts that are deemed conventional. Though such existence is actual— indeed, it is common knowledge—deviation also exists as impulse or fantasy. "There is no reason," suggested Howard Becker, "to assume that only those who finally commit a deviant act actually have the impulse to do so. It is much more likely that most people experience deviant impulses frequently. At least in fantasy, people are much more deviant than they appear."[41]

Since unacknowledged deviation existed in the rendition of the neoChicagoans as well as in the world it purported to reflect, little credence was given official statistics on the volume and distribution of crime, delinquency, mental illness, and other deviant forms. To believe and use such estimates would have betrayed a lack of faith in the central place of unacknowledged deviation. Instead of using official estimates of volume and distribution as a basis for a fitting theory of deviation, the neoChicagoans used the estimates

[38] Edwin Lemert, "Some Aspects of a General Theory of Sociopathic Behavior," *op. cit.*, p. 28.

[39] *Ibid.*

[40] *Ibid.*

[41] Howard Becker, *Outsiders* (New York: The Free Press of Glencoe, Inc., 1963), p. 26.

themselves as a topic for speculation and explanation.[42] Such a reversal is quite consistent with the neoChicagoan irony; moreover, it reveals again the institutionalist tendency of this school of thought. The character and features of the institutions entrusted with the regulation and registration of deviation become a key topic of inquiry. In the neoChicagoan view, the explanation for the official estimates of the volume and distribution of deviation are to be found in the methods and presumptions of registrars as well as in the conditions that nurture deviation.

To recapitulate, an appreciation of overlap is expressed by the neo-Chicagoans in the prime place given unacknowledged deviation. Deviation exists in conventional context, obscured by our tendency to overlook or to define generously until a societal reaction takes place.[43] After societal reaction, character and activity become reconstituted, according to neoChicago precept. When that happens, the social tendency is reversed: we overlook the conventional elements harbored in a deviant context. "The deviant identification becomes the controlling one."[44] To appreciate overlap in this context is to recall knowledge and restore attention to the conventional aspects of deviant enterprises and the conventional interludes in deviant lives.[45]

In another example of overlap, Lemert directed our attention to the similarities between femininity, or other forms of sex appeal, and prostitution. Building on Davis' earlier observations on the continuity between ordinary sexual exchange and prostitution, Lemert suggested:

> *A strong case may be made that our culture normally disposes women to utilize sex for many purposes outside of the marriage relationship. . . . As one writer [Kingsley Davis] has cogently and realistically put it, there are elements of prostitution in the behavior of most women in our culture. . . . This is perceived in . . . the salesgirl who "charms" a male customer into purchasing goods, . . . the sale of war bonds with kisses by actresses, . . . the sexual submission of a secretary to her boss in order to hold her job.*[46]

Moreover, in a gem of a definition, Lemert hinted at a more profound and more disconcerting overlap between deviant and conventional realms.

[42] Howard Becker, *ibid.,* pp. 19–20. Also see John Kitsuse and Aaron Cicourel, "A Note on the Uses of Official Statistics," *Social Problems,* XI (Fall 1963), 131–139.

[43] An early statement of this view is implicit in Edwin Sutherland, *White Collar Crime* (New York: Holt, Rinehart and Winston, Inc., 1949).

[44] Howard Becker, *op. cit.,* p. 34.

[45] *Ibid.,* pp. 33–35; also, see my *Delinquency and Drift* (New York: John Wiley & Sons, Inc., 1964); "Subterranean Traditions of Youth," *The Annals* (November, 1961); and Mary Owen Cameron, *The Booster and the Snitch* (New York: The Free Press of Glencoe, Inc., 1964).

[46] Lemert, *Social Pathology,* p. 246.

By prostitution, Lemert means the coincidence of three features: an exchange of sexual favor for material return; more or less indiscriminate indulgence with many persons; and a dissociation of deeper feelings from the physical act.[47] If one omits the reference to the sexual act—the special province of prostitution—the elements of Lemert's conception suggest a similarity not limited to feminine activity. The rendering of a service for fee, the absence of discrimination in the choice of clientele (universalism), and a dissociation of deeper feelings from the service rendered (affective neutrality), are among the key elements of what is mainly a masculine activity —profession. There should be nothing surprising about this similarity: Prostitution is among the oldest of professions, and professionals always fear prostituting themselves.

The vision of naturalism strives to illuminate the world as it is. Since being in the world is rather complicated, fidelity requires a rendition maintaining that complexity. The naturalist tradition, especially in its functionalist and neoChicagoan phase, was sensitive to overlap and irony, and in that sense contributed to a complicated picture of deviant phenomena.[48] The two phases were linked by Albert Cohen after considering the ways in which deviations may cluster and provide a favorable habitat for one another. He added:

> *But this is not to say that the sources of deviant behavior are always to be found in the abnormal, the pathological, and the deplorable. They may also be found in the institutionally expected and the sacred. Implicit in the very idea of a system is the fact that whatever is found in it is a function of its total structure. The consequences of any particular feature of a system for deviant behavior or conformity depend not on its moral or hygienic status but on its context. The same strains which help to produce deviant behavior also help to produce the behavior we most admire and applaud. For example, the characteristic American belief that a man should "make something of himself" encourages hard work, self-discipline, and productivity . . . ; at the same time, it makes failure all the more . . . humiliating and . . . helps to motivate delinquent subcultures in American society. If Kingsley Davis is correct, the sanctity of the marriage institution and the high value placed upon female chastity help to explain prostitution as well as sexual continence. If Chein and Rosenfeld are correct, teen-age drug use may result from the impact upon a certain kind of personality of age-graded expectations which motivate other young people to assume the responsibilities of adulthood. Furthermore, much that is deviant can be largely attributed to efforts, some of them nobly motivated, to control deviant behavior . . . . In short, that*

[47] *Ibid.*, p. 238.

[48] To contend that being in the world is complicated is in no way inconsistent with the observation that men commonly attempt to simplify being in the world through stereotype and reification. Indeed, the complexity may be viewed as the reason for the frequency of human attempts to simplify. That process of simplification is stressed by the neoChicagoans and will be discussed in Chapter 7.

which we deplore and that which we cherish are not only part of the same seamless web; they are actually woven of the same fibers.[49]

Cohen's statement linked the functionalist and neoChicagoan irony. Furthermore, by considering them along with the clustering of deviation resulting from social disorganization, Cohen put the two in proper context. The latter phases of naturalism emanate from the Chicago school, and are indebted to it. Had the heritage been understood and appreciated instead of repudiated, its real limitations might have been transcended, its imagined defects never conjured.

[49] Albert Cohen, "The Study of Social Disorganization and Deviant Behavior," in eds. Robert Merton, Leonard Broom, and Leonard Cottrell, *Sociology Today* (New York: Basic Books, Inc., 1959), pp. 473–474. For his elaboration of the functionalist irony with respect to delinquency, see Albert Cohen, *Delinquent Boys* (New York: The Free Press of Glencoe, Inc., 1955). For a somewhat longer statement of the effects of social efforts to control deviation, see Albert Cohen, "The Sociology of the Deviant Act," *American Sociological Review*, XXX, No. 1 (February 1965), 5–14.

II

Almost all students of deviation have been concerned with the ways in which persons are joined with existing deviant phenomena or develop them anew. This association of persons with deviation is most commonly referred to as causal explanation or etiology, and has been the dominant question for students of deviant phenomena, especially those focusing on crime, delinquency and mental illness. Other aspects of deviant phenomena have received little attention. One reason for the overwhelming stress on etiology and the neglect of the phenomena themselves seems patent: etiology is more pertinent to the widespread aims of correction, whether it be restoration, reform or rehabilitation. Given the understandable dominance of the correctional perspective in the study of deviation, concern with the nuances and character of the phenomenon itself seemed idle, literary or even romantic. But whatever the reasons for the prominence of etiology, and however we judge this expenditure of ingenuity, few would challenge its intrinsic legitimacy or worth. Certainly I would not, though I do think we have given it too much emphasis. Be that as it may, the topic before us is the variety of ways in which etiology—or less pretensiously, becoming deviant—has been conceived in naturalist inquiry.

I suggest that three relevant master conceptions have emerged in naturalist inquiry; that the three are differentially suitable to our subject matter, man; and that they require reconceiving, though in varying measure, if they are to illuminate the process by which subjects become deviant. The master conceptions may be introduced through considering three fables, those of Elizabeth, Liz, and Betty.

Elizabeth[1]

Elizabeth was a bright, attractive 15 year old who had grown up in a house crowded with in-laws, brothers, sisters, nieces and nephews. Her parents both worked and were rarely at home. Her older brothers and sisters also worked, leaving their youngsters to manage for themselves. No one particularly cared whether Elizabeth, or any of the other children, got to school, needed anything, or were happy. They were just there to grow up as best they could.

As a result of these conditions, Elizabeth became pregnant.

Liz

Liz was a bright, attractive 15 year old whose family was forced to move to a new neighborhood. Before moving there, Liz was innocent with regard to sexual matters. She became friendly with a 16 year old, Jane, who lived next door. Subsequently, Liz became a popular member of Jane's high school crowd. Liz sensed that Jane's crowd was a bit fast but so enjoyed the popularity she had gained that she was loath to risk it by appearing puritanical. Through Jane and her friends, Liz met Jim.

As a result of these conditions, Liz became pregnant.

Betty

Betty was a bright, attractive 15 year old whose parents were affectionate but rather traditional in outlook. They felt, on both educational and moral grounds, that Betty's development would be best served by attending a parochial school. By and large, Betty enjoyed going to parochial school. However, there was one Sister who con-

[1] *Washington Post*, Nov. 9, 1961; brought to my attention by Harvey Sachs. Liz and Betty are my inventions.

stantly dwelled on the importance of chastity, and who displayed her views in an inquisitorial manner. Betty rather resented the accusations of the Sister, but being of basically sound personality managed to take them in stride. She frequently dated boys, but aside from an occasional kiss kept her virginity intact.

One evening, Betty and her new steady boy friend were sitting in his car just talking. Her boy friend, Dick, decided at 10:30 to take his nightly allotment of one deep kiss. At precisely that moment, Officer Larkin, who was the Sister's brother, threw open the car door. He proceeded to derogate Betty and Dick, calling Betty a slut and threatening Dick with a statutory rape charge. His tantrum spènt, Officer Larkin's manner turned fatherly and in the end he smiled and said, "You look like good kids so I'm gonna give you a break this time. But don't let me catch you up here again." Betty and Dick, who had remained speechless throughout, did not say a word for another 3 minutes. At 10:43, they simultaneously uttered the words, "what the hell!"

As a result of these conditions, Betty became pregnant.

A fable is a tale that conveys the wisdom implicit in the common sense in a disingenuous manner. This small collection of fables summarizes in spoofing fashion what we currently know about the process of becoming deviant. Thus, their appreciation may be regarded as a preface to comprehending that process.

Now that is quite a bald statement, and thus requires immediate qualification. *I do* not *mean that the three fables summarize the* details *of the many theories endeavoring to account for becoming deviant. No three or 300 fables could do that; each stresses different circumstances or combines them in different ways. However, the three fables adequately summarize the basic ideas or master conceptions that provide the strategy of explanation for the many theories which otherwise differ in countless ways. The fable of Elizabeth displays the idea of* affinity; *the fable of Liz that of* affiliation; *and the fable of Betty the idea of* signification. *Though each fable spoofs or mocks the master conception it expresses, I now want to treat each idea seriously.*

5

Affinity

The idea of affinity has been the key element in the staple explanation of becoming deviant. It has been the ascendant conception at least since the rise of positivism; so much so that it is echoed and sometimes mocked in the common sense. Most research and most theoretical accounts of the process of becoming illicitly pregnant, delinquent, criminal, mentally ill or just plainly immoral have been informed, perhaps partly misinformed, by the idea of affinity, whether the circumstantial details involved physical constitution, race, intelligence, family life, poverty, social class, educational failure, rapid social change, immigration, adolescent turmoil or anything else that struck the fancy of a scientific age. For instance, in a limited but important sense, many modern sociologists still closely follow Lombroso and the other early founders of positive criminology. Lombroso said bodily constitution and to his close or careful readers muttered something about social conditions; nowadays, we say social conditions and to our close and careful readers mutter something about organic conditions. With regard, however, to the logic and strategy of explanation, the idea of affinity has been persistent, consistent and dominant. What is this idea, and how suited is it to the study of subjects becoming deviant?

Affinity is a simple and fairly useful conception. Persons, either individually or in aggregates, develop predispositions to certain phenomena, say, delinquency, as a result of their *circumstances.* Accordingly, the key issue of affinity is: *which* circumstances? Why more delinquency here than there? The prime datum in this approach is the differential rate according to one or another circumstance. It is that differential rate which requires explanation.[1]

The logic of theory and the design of research has been to locate regularities of circumstance—constitutional, personal, social, economic, or cultural—by which those who are *more* delinquent may be distinguished or differentiated from those who are less so, and then to apprehend those differences by providing a cogent and, in principle, testable theory. Whichever the allegedly operative circumstances, whichever differential rates are to be explained, whichever theory is used to apprehend those differences, the same mode of reasoning underlies the idea of affinity: Certain antecedent conditions predispose persons or groups to certain predictable outcomes. The predictable outcome to which they are predisposed by their circumstance is the higher rate of deviation. With more complete knowledge, and more refined analysis, the level of prediction would become more certain; we would possess a cause, a necessary and sufficient set of conditions.[2]

By what process do cirmumstances move members of a group to certain predictable outcomes, such as a higher rate of delinquency? The idea of affinity speaks to that key question, and most often it has spoken in terms taken from another level of being. The easiest way of summarizing those terms is to suggest that the unspoken process by which circumstances move persons is gravity. Under the proper circumstances, persons gravitate to the appropriate deviant form.

Affinity has had many meanings, and technical usages have emerged in anthropology, biology, and chemistry. The meaning of affinity in the study of how persons become deviant has been closest to that used in chemistry. There, affinity refers to the attractive force exerted in different degrees

[1] The most influential and well-developed arguments for the differential rate as the prime datum appear in Emile Durkheim, *Suicide* (New York: The Free Press of Glencoe, Inc., 1951); and Robert MacIver, *Social Causation* (Boston: Ginn and Company, 1942).

[2] I have no wish to go into the general validity of such an accredited view. Many regard its continued accreditation as a sign of proof, a confirmation of its substance. Others regard the whole idea as rather quaint. I leave the discussion of the general or abstract validity of this accredited view to those who enjoy debating such matters: philosophers of science. Constrained by the topic of the volume, the subject of deviation, only one observation is really necessary or warranted: whatever its general merits, such a view really has little to do with the *subject.* The subject faces many issues in the process of his becoming deviant. Rarely, if ever, is the difference in rate between a category in which he may be placed and one in which he would be misplaced a relevant issue *for him;* certainly it is no prime datum. That does not make the issue of differential rate inappropriate or bereft of use; but it *does* make it irrelevant to the human subject becoming deviant.

between atoms, causing them to enter into and remain in combination. By analogy, this guiding idea suggests that persons of appropriate predisposition will be *drawn* to the phenomenon and to the social circles already sponsoring it; if necessary they will invent the phenomenon anew.

Thus, the underlying conception of those who utilize the idea of affinity is *attractive force*. This idea seems well-suited to the study of objects. It would seem self-evident, however, that to be applicable and useful in the study of *man,* the idea of affinity must be revised in a manner that *affirms subjective capacities even while recognizing their diminution.* It is amazing, and testifies to the habit of uncritical transfer between natural science and the study of man, that so few have really bothered with such a revision. Most have mindlessly accepted the transfer. Some have completely rejected the idea; but the real task, that of a humane revision recognizing the subjective capacities of man, has hardly begun.[3] It seems apparent that when man becomes object, his behavior may be illuminated by the idea of affinity. Reducing man to object is not the task of sociology, however; that diminution, if it takes place, is the work of ordinary members of society. *Their* work diminishes the subject and prepares him for gravitation; *ours* does not—unless he is foolish enough to believe learned tracts and live by them.[4]

A revision of the idea must begin with an understanding of the unusual ways in which a *subject* relates to the circumstances that allegedly move and shape him. An object, being merely *reactive,* is literally determined by circumstance. Life, being *adaptive,* responds to the circumstances making up the milieu.[5]

The existence of subjects is not quite exhausted by the arduous natural processes of reactivity and adaptation. Capable of creating and assigning meaning, able to contemplate his surroundings and even his own condition, given to anticipation, planning and projecting man—the subject—stands in a different and more complex relation to circumstance. This distinctively human capacity in no way denies that human existence frequently displays itself in ways characteristic of lower levels. Frequently man is wholly adaptive, *as if* he were just organic being. And sometimes, though very rarely, he is wholly reactive, *as if* a mere object. But mere reactivity or adaptation should not be confused with the distinctively human condition. They are

[3] See C. W. Mills, *The Sociological Imagination* (New York: Oxford University Press, 1959), especially Chapters 8 and 9.
[4] Floyd Matson has suggested that the learned treatises of social scientists have had the consequence of diminishing and objectifying man. If anyone believed these writings, in the rather relevant sense of living by them, I would agree with him. Otherwise the positivist viewpoint he criticizes may be regarded as misleading but inconsequential. See Floyd Matson, *The Broken Image* (New York: George Braziller, Inc., 1964).
[5] For an excellent discussion of the responsive character of plant and animal life, see René Dubos, *The Mirage of Health* (New York: Harper & Row, Publishers, 1959).

better seen as an alienation or exhaustion of that condition.[6] A subject actively addresses or encounters his circumstance; accordingly, his distinctive capacity is to reshape, strive toward creating, and actually *transcend* circumstance. Such a distinctly human project is not always feasible, but the capacity always exists, and must be explicitly appreciated to refashion the idea of affinity.

To gravitate toward that to which we are predisposed by circumstance, to become the kind of thing that may be comprehended by the idea of affinity, the subjective capacity must be pacified.[7] Otherwise, the predisposition, or any other product or element of circumstance may be encountered and overcome. A human affinity does not exist as a force separate from the persons that harbor it. Instead, it may be regarded as a natural biographical tendency borne of personal and social circumstance that suggests but hardly compels a direction of movement. Until released, the affinity remains latent. For affinity to become manifest, the subject's capacity to withstand and transcend circumstance—to develop projects—must be pacified or diminished. The subject must become more like an object. That transformation occurs in the world and may be termed *natural reduction.*[8] Once reduced, the subject is temporarily reconstituted. For a time he may become the kind of person who will choose not to choose. Periodically, thus, the subjective capacity is forgotten or foregone. Being objectified, the subject behaves *as if* he were object.

Objectification, the process culminating in natural reduction, is an ordinary feature of social life. Though its occurrence and intensity is magnified by specially suited features and specially equipped agents in certain inhuman settings—there is no more precise term for them—some measure of objectification, and thus natural reduction, appears in any milieu. In certain oppressive settings, being is systematically processed, typed, summarized in files, derogated, degraded, and dehumanized. But in any human milieu, being is occasionally put down, turned off or overlooked. In either

[6] I suppose this is the proper place to admit that the view commended in this book is quite similar to that expounded in Sartre's writings. Though little is gained in heralding the debt, suppressing it would be pointless. The really important point is not whether a conception of man may be derived from Sartre or any other philosopher, rather, whether a view of man draws authority from the common sense of operative participants in social life. Thus, the relevant authority for the assertion, "Man is seen to be above all capable of 'going beyond' his given situation through his 'project'," would be the common sense and not merely Wilfrid Desan, *The Marxism of Jean-Paul Sartre* (New York: Doubleday and Company, Inc., 1965), p. 59.

[7] Even illiterate peasants, it should be said, require pacification. Otherwise, they too may sometimes transcend circumstances. The subjective capacity is no monopoly of modern or civilized man. Indeed, it sometimes seems that the real expertise of modern man is the development of *forceful* instruments of pacification.

[8] These are rightly conceived by Merleau-Ponty as "catastrophic," by which he means a reduction from one order of being to another. See Maurice Merleau-Ponty, *The Structure of Behavior* (Boston: Beacon Press, Inc., 1963), p. 150.

case, though in different measure, the subjective capacity may be temporarily pacified. Once pacified, the behavior of persons, like that of objects, may be illuminated by a conception of affinity. Because social settings so regularly include features and agents who perform objectifying operations and naturally reduce being, an unrevised idea of affinity has survived in sociology. Thus, studies informed by a primitive conception of affinity may yield findings which, in a rather sloppy way, may be regarded as accurate. The discrepancy between sociological portrayal and the true phenomenon has been obscured by the objectifying activities that occur in the natural social world. Performed by ordinary persons and special agents, the reduction of subjects to objects is part of the social circumstance, or "breeding ground" for deviant behavior. This is especially true of the featured milieu in sociology's favorite affinity.

The Favored Affinity

Revised to suit the study of subjects, affinity is a useful though commonplace idea. Certain circumstances may be regarded as promoting a latent tendency, an attraction, to deviant phenomena that may be activated when the subject is naturally reduced. Many circumstances have been stressed, but despite variation considerable continuity and agreement has existed among sociologists. In various guises and for variable reasons, a similar circumstance was favored by sociologists in their search for a milieu in which deviation flourishes. Despite the frequent challenges, despite a debatable statistical basis, their choice survived. Most sociologists using the idea of affinity have continued to stress the relation between poverty and pathology. Affinity, already a well-developed conception when the correctional approach flourished, maintained the specific correlation posited in that view after its general decline.

The Chicago school maintained the general relation despite its fundamentally different style of formulation and despite its apparent antagonism to earlier students of "the social problem" who explicitly pointed to the coincidence of poverty and pathology. The Chicagoans went beyond earlier students by specifying the aspects of poverty that led to pathology, but earlier writers had also recognized the existence of a stable and respectable poverty. The terms of analysis shifted from undeserving to disorganized, but the putative habitat for deviation remained stable. In the twentieth century, as well as in the nineteenth, the strongholds of disreputable poverty harbored the circumstances, whether constitutional, personal or social, that spawned a population drawn to vice, pathology or deviation.[9] By stressing

[9] See my "Poverty and Disrepute," in eds. Robert Merton and Robert Nisbet, *Contemporary Social Problems* (New York: Harcourt, Brace and World, Inc., 1966), Chapter 12.

disorganization, the Chicagoans provided a device by which the tendency to disrepute, implicit in traditional conceptions of poverty, could be activated. Social disorganization amounted to the liquidation of ordinary controls; among the poor especially, lacking the vested interest in conformity common among the well-to-do, the breakdown of communal organization released deviant impulses. Vice and crime, and the circles sponsoring them, ecologically settled by the time of the Chicago school, magnetically attracted the unrestrained. And eventually new forms of deviant organization emerged to substitute for inoperative conventional forms. Statistically, surmised the Chicagoans, deviant behavior would appear with considerably greater frequency in areas suffering a breakdown of organization. And, apparently it did. The many ecological studies executed by the Chicagoans strongly confirmed their general hypothesis.[10]

But even if one grants, and it is granting quite a bit, that poverty, because it is frustrating, oppressive, and miserable, creates a strong tendency to deviation when organization breaks down, there are still difficulties with the affinity favored by the Chicagoans and subsequent sociologists. First, they relied on official estimates for the volume and distribution of deviant behavior. That dependence poses perhaps insoluble problems of evidence. These will be discussed later, but certainly not resolved. Second, and more pertinent here, is their neglect of any device by which subjects, poor or well-off, controlled or not, were transformed into objects and thus, themselves, became the kind of phenomena capable of gravitation.

Most people raised in poverty are not especially deviant, and those who are remain conventional in countless ways.[11] Disorganization provided a release, but another device was needed. To be free of control is the consequence of disorganization, but such freedom smacks of choice, not determination. One may take the official statistics on rates of deviation in the most disorganized slums quite seriously and conclude that most people choose convention rather than deviation. (It is, after all, the official statistics that are used to make a case for a deviant affinity.) If the slum fosters deviation, we observe that the temptation is frequently withstood or overcome. To be molded by circumstance, to gravitate to the prototypical tendency of slum life, the subject must be naturally reduced. And to understand that process we must distinguish resident agencies of objectification.[12]

---

[10] The classic studies are Robert Faris and Warren Dunham, *Mental Disorders in Urban Areas* (Chicago: University of Chicago Press, 1939), and Clifford Shaw, Henry McKay, *et al., Delinquency Areas* (Chicago: University of Chicago Press, 1929), and their *Juvenile Delinquency and Urban Areas* (Chicago: University of Chicago Press, 1942).

[11] See my *Delinquency and Drift* (New York: John Wiley & Sons, Inc., 1964), p. 37.

[12] See my discussion in "Poverty and Disrepute," of the situation of disreputable poverty and the process of pauperization. Both the situation and the process are amply supplied with elements and agencies that work arduously, though perhaps unwittingly, to naturally reduce the population subjected. Matza, *op. cit.*

The favorite affinity of sociologists—between poverty and pathology—was continued in the functionalist view. There it informed Merton's formulation, despite his preference, like the Chicagoans', for a more tangential statement. His central thesis about the social basis of aberrant behavior is developed in his essay, "Social Structure and Anomie." In somewhat modified form, Merton's formulation remained influential and provided a main part of the impetus for theories of delinquency later propounded by Albert Cohen, Lloyd Ohlin and Richard Cloward.[13] Avoiding the language of the more traditional statements of the favored sociological affinity, Merton contended:

> *The distribution of statuses through competition must be so organized that positive incentive for adherence to status obligations are provided for every position within the distributive order. Otherwise, as will soon become plain, aberrant behavior ensues. It is my central hypothesis that that aberrant behavior may be viewed sociologically as a symptom of dissociation between culturally prescribed aspirations and socially structured avenues for realizing these aspirations.*[14]

As it happens, the section of society subjected to this form of dissociation is the lower class. Bombarded, in Merton's new rendition of an old affinity, by the propaganda of success and prevented by class barriers from realizing that inculcated aim, the poor are more apt to stray from conventional avenues of achievement. The higher susceptibility of persons thus teased should be reflected in higher rates of registered deviation. And so it is, according to Merton. But to maintain that worldly confirmation of a hypothetical affinity, Merton had to uphold the reliability of the registration system. Too sophisticated to give the appearance of taking official statistics seriously, he conveyed a critical attitude. But that attitude, as will be seen, was to have a very peculiar use. Approvingly, Merton cited the pioneering study by Wallerstein and Wyle[15] of the frequency of undetected but admitted criminal offenses by persons deemed "law-abiding." Among the earlier attacks on the reliability of official statistics, this study became a cornerstone for theories stressing the part played by control and registration agencies in the selection of persons becoming deviant.[16] But for Merton it had no

---

[13] Albert Cohen, *Delinquent Boys* (New York: The Free Press of Glencoe, Inc., 1955). Richard Cloward and Lloyd Ohlin, *Delinquency and Opportunity* (New York: The Free Press of Glencoe, Inc., 1960).

[14] Merton, *op. cit.*, p. 134.

[15] J. S. Wallerstein and C. J. Wyle, "Our Law-Abiding Law-Breakers," *Probation,* XXXV (March–April, 1947), 107–112.

[16] Along with the work of Wallerstein and Wyle, Porterfield's studies of crimes admitted to by college students, Sutherland's studies in white-collar offenses, Clinard's work on black-market violations and, later, Clausen and Yarrow's research on paths to mental hospitals were to provide a tentative empirical foundation for a new logic

such implication. The study was cited and the results accepted, though they could have been challenged. Apparently following Wallerstein and Wyle, Marton granted that "unlawful behavior, far from being an abnormal social or psychological manifestation, is in truth a very common phenomenon."[17] It may seem as if Merton took account of Wallerstein and Wyle's study and grappled with the dubious reliability of official estimates regarding the distribution of deviation, but this is not so. His citation of Wallerstein and Wyle's study was meant to disarm rather than appreciate its implications for sociology's favorite affinity. Instead of challenging the findings, or dismissing them sardonically (as he did in the case of the older interpretations of the political boss), Merton used yet another technique: he cited the study approvingly and then ignored it. Not knowing quite what to do with their explicit challenge to the statistical basis, he simply reiterated his contention regarding the affinity between a dissociation of ends and means and the appearance of aberrant forms. After giving due consideration to these disturbing findings, he concluded:

> But whatever the differential rates of deviant behavior in the several social strata, and we know from many sources that the official crime statistics uniformly showing high rates in the lower strata are far from complete or reliable, it appears from our analysis that the greatest pressures toward deviation are exerted upon the lower strata.[18]

Thus, the challenge to official statistics is ignored. The inherent defects of those estimates appear as a clause in a sentence whose destiny is to overlook them. The moment of agony and indecision over, the favored affinity of sociology survives unscathed. There *must* be more crime and delinquency in the lower orders because "the status of unskilled labor and the consequent low income cannot readily compete in terms of *established standards of worth* with the promises of power and high income from organized vice, rackets and crime."[19] In the world the point remains moot, but in Merton's analysis the affinity between poverty and deviation remains clear and hardly qualified.

---

of explanation stressing not affinity, but signification. Early theoretical foundations for this approach appear in the work of Frank Tannenbaum. See *Crime and Community* (New York: Columbia University Press, 1938); Austin Porterfield, "Delinquency and its Outcome in Court and College," *American Journal of Sociology*, XLIX (November 1943), 199–208; Edwin H. Sutherland, *White Collar Crime* (New York: Holt, Rinehart and Winston, Inc., 1949); Marshall B. Clinard, *The Black Market* (New York: Holt, Rinehart and Winston, Inc., 1952); and John A. Clausen and Marian R. Yarrow, "Paths to the Mental Hospital," *Journal of Social Issues*, XI (1955), 25–32.

[17] Merton, *op. cit.*, p. 144.
[18] *Ibid.*, p. 144.
[19] *Ibid.*, p. 145.

The distribution of deviation—the rates by sector of society—is the worldly foundation for an asserted affinity. The favored affinity between poverty and pathology need not be dismissed simply because Merton and many others never bothered to defend the official estimates against the attacks launched by Wallerstein and Wyle, Porterfield, Sutherland, and other early critics. Nor need it be dismissed simply because of the obvious and inherent deficiencies of registration systems. Official estimates *may* reflect the actual distribution of deviation while necessarily underestimating the volume. That possibility was stressed by Albert Cohen. In *Delinquent Boys,* he defended the statistical basis for an affinity between delinquency and the lower class before considering the process by which it develops.[20] In cogent manner, Cohen explicitly confronted Porterfield, Wallerstein, and Wyle and countered their challenge. He conceded their discovery of considerable unacknowledged delinquency among the law-abiding. But what, he asked, of hidden delinquency in areas traditionally conceived as its strongholds?[21] Though the issue remains unresolved, Cohen's reasoned arguments that official statistics more or less reflect the true distribution is slightly more convincing than the thesis claiming little relation between officially registered deviation and the true distribution.[22]

The selection of the lower class rests, according to Merton, on the contention that dissociation between culturally prescribed goals and institutional avenues of realization is widest and most prevalent in that segment of society. If we focus on the paramount cultural goal in Merton's analysis, and thus in American society, we may discern additional similarity between his views and those of his Chicago predecessors. The goal of primary importance is *success.* However, it is overwhelmingly important only within a specific cultural context. When that context is specified, and fortunately Merton himself specified it, his continuity with the Chicagoans becomes even more pronounced. Success and wealth become preeminent because alternative goals lose momentum in modern urban society.

> It would of course be fanciful to assert that accumulated wealth stands alone as a symbol of success just as it would be . . . to deny that Americans assign it a high place in their scale of values. In some large measure, money has been consecrated as a value in itself, over and above its expenditure for articles of consumption or its use for the enhancement of power. . . . As Simmel emphasized, money is highly abstract and impersonal. However acquired, fraudulently or institutionally, it can be used

[20] Albert Cohen, *op. cit.*

[21] *Ibid.,* p. 41. Also see Fred Murphy, Mary Shirley, and Helen Witmer, "The Incidence of Hidden Delinquency," *American Journal of Orthopsychiatry* (October 1946), pp. 686–696.

[22] For a sophisticated discussion of the relation between the official and true *volume* of delinquency, see Thorsten Sellin and Marvin Wolfgang, *The Measurement of Delinquency* (New York: John Wiley and Sons, Inc., 1964).

to purchase the same goods and services. The anonymity of urban society, in conjunction with the peculiarities of money permits wealth, the sources of which may be unknown to the community . . . or, if known, to become purified in the course of time to serve as a symbol of high status.[23]

Thus, *urban anonymity* is the context within which the abstract capacity of money emerges; whereas a context of familiarity robs money of an unqualified and untrammeled value. Consequently, the trend toward deviation existing among the poor depends partly on a feature of metropolitan life stressed by the Chicago school, as well as by Simmel. As indicated earlier, *the* pathetic feature of metropolitan existence, anonymity was treated extensively and carefully by the Chicagoans. For Merton, it was an abstract condition, deserving little more than statement, which allowed money and success to emerge, in his analysis, as preeminent. If the care displayed by the Chicagoans in specifying the location of this pathetic feature had also been imitated and elaborated, Merton and his followers might have arrived at a more refined guess regarding *the particular sections of poverty* that nourished deviation. And the guess would have been precisely that of the Chicago school—disorganized poverty. An equally felicitous result might have followed, for related reasons, if Merton (and especially his followers, Lloyd Ohlin and Richard Cloward) had paid closer attention to detailed studies of working-class mobility that flourished during the same general period. For a thesis so dependent on class barriers which cruelly taunt as well as restrict persons lured by success, it is incredible that so little attention was devoted to a careful consideration of the character and extent of working-class advancement into the middle classes. A distinction between mobile and immobile contingents—between proletariat and *lumpenproletariat,* organized and unorganized—or even the hoary and tendentious contrast between deserving and undeserving—any of these would have helped specify the limited section of the lower class vulnerable to the dissociative condition so stressed by Merton.[24]

[23] Merton, *op. cit.,* p. 136.
[24] If nothing else, such a specification would do more justice to the official facts. However dubious their validity, official estimates of the distribution of deviant behavior usually indicate that only its most submerged section, and *not* the working-class in general, misbehaves with disproportionate frequency. This holds for delinquency, mental illness, divorce, and illegitimacy among other things. See Frederick Redlich and August Hollingshead, *Social Class and Mental Illness* (New York: John Wiley & Sons, Inc., 1958); William Kvaraceous, *The Community and the Delinquent* (Yonkers-on-Hudson, N.Y.: World Book Co., 1954); William J. Goode, "Family Disorganization" in Chapter 10 of eds. Robert Merton and Robert Nisbet, *Contemporary Social Problems* (New York: Harcourt Brace & World Inc., 2nd ed., 1966); S. M. Miller and Frank Riessman, "The Working-Class Subculture; a New View," *Social Problems,* IX (Summer 1961), 26; and S. M. Miller and E. Mishler, "Social Class, Mental Illness, American Psychiatry: An Expository Review," *Milbank Memorial Fund Quarterly,* XXXVII (April 1959), 174–199.

Affinity remains the staple strategy of sociology in comprehending the process of becoming deviant. But just as the favored coincidence of poverty and pathology was questioned and challenged within that tradition, so too the very idea of affinity has lost its uncontested preeminence. The gains in man-hours of effort dedicated to its distinctive mode of reasoning and research were perhaps matched by a loss in originality and vitality. Being staple, it has become pedestrian; being established, it has lent itself to ever more exacting procedures and elaboration. Affinity has been expressed in highly abstract or formal propositions on the one hand and methodology on the other. Concreteness, and thus naturalism, had little place in such surroundings; it found new lodging in the ideas of *affiliation* and *signification*. There, in *the context* of affiliation and signification the human meaning of *affinity* can, paradoxically, be discovered. Out of context, there is little more to be said about the idea of affinity; it is too abstract an idea. To make affinity meaningful, it must be returned to its natural human context. That is one task of the subsequent chapters.

6

Affiliation

The Chicago school maintained the affinity between poverty and pathology originating in the correctional view; however, it suggested another idea as a basis for that coincidence. Not clearly differentiated at first from the idea of affinity, *affiliation* emerged as a distinctive strategy of explanation in the work of Edwin Sutherland. The Chicagoans, and much more explicitly, Sutherland, intended affiliation to contest affinity as the key conception in apprehending the process of becoming deviant. Building on the ecological stress of the Chicagoans, and their recognition of different forms of social organization, Sutherland explicitly repudiated the logic and utility of affinity and began to substitute a new idea. Though initially it too harbored some of the same defects as the transplanted conception of affinity, affiliation was more easily revised to suit the study of human subjects. And the more the idea of affiliation was developed, the more illuminated the meaning of affinity became.

Affiliation refers to the adoption or receiving of a son into a family, and, by gradual extension, to the uniting or attaching in a close connection those who were previously unattached. In its most mature development, in its most human form, affiliation describes the process by which the subject is *converted* to conduct novel for him but already established for others. By providing new meanings for conduct previously regarded as outlandish or inappropriate, affiliation provides the context and process by which the neophyte *may* be "turned on" or "out." One distinction between a mature and a primitive conception of affiliation depends on whether the term "may" is intended literally and seriously or is a mere expression of a failure in deterministic nerve. So imprecise is the use of language in some networks of discourse that only italics can convey an intention to be taken literally. The reader may do whatever he wishes with the term "may" unitalicized. But if he is informed, he will read it as an equivocal "must." Between an italicized "may" and an equivocal "must," there is a world of difference. It is that difference we must explore to understand the process by which the idea of affiliation became humanized and thereby suited to the study of subjects.

Before humanization of the idea, the potency of affiliation rested on *contagion;* afterwards, on *conversion.* Profoundly lodged in the very method of epidemiology, consistently echoed in the lingering doctrine of pathology, contagion or infection literally shaped the primitive version of affiliation. Derived from another world—that of merely organic life—and justified by the prevailing generalization of the ideas as well as the method of science, the logic of contagion was applied to subjective being. So, tacitly, it came to be thought that human subjects, if properly placed and sufficiently exposed, must "catch" a deviation. And if things did not come out quite right, the "must" could always be made an equivocal "may." Typically, the equivocation corresponded to the recognition that, in addition, the subject had to be appropriately vulnerable to the infection. As in medical science, the subject needed to possess an affinity to what was being passed around in his milieu before succumbing to it. Thus, in the primitive version, affiliation was more or less forced to conspire with affinity in order for the subject to be vanquished. The two conspire in the mature version, too, but the subject is vanquished much less easily.

Did sociologists ever really believe that persons "caught" deviation? Not really; they simply acted and wrote as if they did. As long as deviation was conceived as pathology, as long as the language of research used the terms of epidemiology, as long as man's environment was likened to that of the ecological milieu of trees and foxes, what better inference regarding the *method of affiliation* could be imagined? Given the intellectual context in which the idea first flourished, contagion almost *had* to be the method by which the affiliation process did its work. It made sense; but, truly, the only sense it made was surrealistic. Contagion made *logical* sense; it fit beautifully with other aspects of the formal edifice. The loyalty of contagion was to *abstracted* pathology, *abstracted* epidemiology, *abstracted* ecology. And so, being an inference borne of abstractions, being fundamentally and patently disloyal to the subjective world, the idea of contagion became profoundly implicit. It became the unmentionable pinnacle of the primitive version of affiliation. To utter it except as heuristic analogy (the typical evasion of social science) would have been disastrous. The idea of contagion

itself might have been exposed. And that would have endangered everything else, for, as in surrealist architecture, it was the pinnacle that held up
the entire edifice.

Contagion was not simply unmentionable. More important, it was in-
defensible. Except as an easily refuted analogy or as a lingering popular
superstition, it could not survive the slightest scrutiny.[1] The result was that
no one seriously bothered to defend it. Dimly aware that its only sense was
surrealistic, the primitive architects were reluctant, perhaps, to subject the
transplanted idea of contagion to the stern test of the world. Once open,
once subjected to a test regarding its *realistic sense,* the idea would crumble.
The common sense which rules human reality would have doubled up in
laughter at the very idea of catching a deviation.[2] Because it was indefensi-
ble, because it so patently violated the common sense of reality, contagion—
the primitive method of affiliation—was surrendered. It was a sacrifice to
the world, a humble concession to our sense of reality. The rest of the
edifice was maintained. But that was an enormous error, a fatal compromise,
and that is why I have followed this perhaps frivolous digression.

The edifice being surrealist, being a model in which each abstract
component was loyal to the others rather than to the world, the loss of the
concept of contagion was fateful: the entire primitive architecture with
which the process of becoming deviant was conceived gradually fell into
disrepute. Pathology was spoofed out of existence. Ecology and epidemiology still exist in sociology, but as a source of ideas and commanding imagery, they have become almost mute. They tell us things but intellectually
have nothing to say; they harbor knowledge but not wisdom. Finally, they

[1] For a discussion of contagion of madness as a popular fear, see Michel
Foucault, *Madness and Civilization* (New York: Pantheon Books, Inc., 1965),
Chapter 7. Additionally, the idea achieved a certain currency in the conservative
view of "mobs," "riots," and other rebellious collective uprisings. Following LeBon,
this view has persisted despite being ably demolished by Rudé. See Gustav LeBon,
The Crowd (London: E. Benn, 1909) and George Rudé, *The Crowd in History*
(New York: John Wiley & Sons, Inc., 1964).

[2] That the common sense responded in largely the same manner to Pasteur
when he announced the germ theory of disease does not detract from my thesis.
Putting aside the persistent and increasingly modern medical view that the incredu-
lous response to Pasteur was partly warranted, the expertise of the common sense
may be usefully restricted to subjective reality. When extended to lower levels of
existence, it has a characteristic tendency to conceive things with a certain anthropo-
morphism. So upside-down is the perspective of the positivist tendency in sociology,
that one scientific contemporary grimly, condescendingly accuses spokesmen for the
common sense of being too anthropomorphic with regard to human matters. No
better example of the convoluted character of positivism and its dire need for what
would amount to intensive existential therapy could be imagined. See William Catton,
From Animistic to Naturalistic Sociology (New York: McGraw-Hill Book Company,
1966), pp. 20, 34. So confused and so bewildering is this sophistry that when accused
of conceiving human matters anthropomorphically, human subjects frequently are at
a loss for words in responding. The needed retort is patent: Nothing, it should be
said, would be more suitable in conceiving *anthropos.*

have come close to being simply methods, divested of the physical and organic imagery, theories and ideas with which they were originally associated. Now, but not originally and still not completely, they are just ingenious ways of collecting useful social data—data about which we are to theorize in human ways.[3]

Thus, I contend that the shift from contagion to conversion as the method of affiliation was a fateful turn.[4] Once made, the subsequent path of naturalism was clear, its agenda for speculation and research was implicit in that very choice. To understand that, we must appreciate what an idea of affiliation utilizing a method of conversion *chooses against*. Obviously, it chooses against contagion, but that is only a small part of its commitment. Equally obvious, there is nothing preordained about the path implied by choosing the method of conversion. Only a few—those who remained faithful to their commitment—followed it; the others reverted to older habits. Man, being able to make commitments, may renege on them also. If there is nothing preordained in the course of naturalism, if in that project commitments are made and reneged on, cannot the same be said about the equally human process of becoming deviant? As I will try to show, such a conclusion slowly emerges. In becoming deviant, there is no prospective unfolding of social process resulting from affinity and affiliation. Once the method of conversion is chosen and we appreciate what is chosen *against,* we will understand why a faithful naturalism had to repudiate a preordained or predictable social process.

Conversion and the Preordained

The function of a method of affiliation that utilizes conversion is, hopefully, to rid the study of man once and for all of the idea of being preordained. Instead, though only gradually, appears the less potent but thoroughly human idea of being ordained: a process in which a willing subject, an affiliative other, and a signifying other ordinarily share or collaborate.

Being preordained is the final part of the intellectual legacy transplanted to the study of man. It is the deepest manifestation of that legacy, joining in magnificent fashion the habits of mind deriving from the supra-

[3] For a different view, see Otis D. Duncan, "Social Organization and the Ecosystem," in Robert Faris (ed.), *Handbook of Modern Sociology* (Chicago: Rand McNally & Co., 1964), Chapter 2, pp. 37–82.

[4] For a recent attempt to conceive the elements of conversion in the process of taking on deviant world-views, see John Lofland and Rodney Stark, "Becoming a World-Saver: a Theory of Conversion to a Deviant Perspective," *American Sociological Review*, XXX, No. 6 (December 1965), 862–875.

human and the subhuman. Having bothered to create *God,* and slyly hiding his hand, man paid a price for so profound an alienation. His being was preordained by the supernatural. That old conception began to break down when it was enunciated in its full logical absurdity. Until Calvin and his followers, the idea had been qualified and otherwise mystified. Thereafter, descendants of the sponsors of so fanciful an idea turned to the subhuman and found there a new source of inspiration. The fantasy of preordination—nightmare for the subject, but a Faustian daydream for the analyst—was henceforth maintained in the very bones of what has come to be called science. The idea of preordination was rendered secular. It became prediction. The scientist, an ordinary human, delved deep into the world of the subhuman, especially the physical world of the mere object, and he discovered the idea of prediction. Armed with the discovery, he transplanted it to the human realm. Amazed by the lack of cheer and congratulation at this stunning transplantation, he grew weary of the subject, first constructing a hundred theories discounting his objections and then forgetting about them altogether. If ordinary men did not like his theories, so much the worse for them; he could always find a more receptive audience among others of similar delusion or ambition. And more effective, he could begin schools and reward or otherwise train an audience to believe as he did. In that way, the primitive disciplines emerged.

But there were always heretics, always persons among whom the training never took. And there was tolerance of them since the architects were not aware that they were constructing a secular orthodoxy built around the idea of subhuman preordination—prediction. So the idea of conversion was not banned; from the architectural viewpoint, it was simply another means of achieving the Faustian dream. No narrow orthodoxy this: Everyone was encouraged to weave his own systems, to join in the quest, as long as he didn't take his subjects too seriously and as long as he had the common decency to utter occasional obeisance to the idea of secular preordination. (The two stipulations come to much the same thing.) The primitive architects should have known better than to be so tolerant of an idea like conversion. It was a religious idea, and like any religious idea that refrains from or retrieves the alienation—that maintains for humanity things originating in man—the idea of conversion could subvert the secular orthodoxy. Stripped of the supernatural connotation of "calling," as in all decency it was obliged to be to apply to sinful behavior, conversion was the cornerstone for a thoroughly human account of the process of becoming deviant—an account that scrupulously excluded subhuman processes.

The choice against being preordained emerged slowly and partly unwittingly. Explicit in their repudiation of the potency of antecedent circumstance, those originally favoring affiliation seemed hardly aware that conversion, being a fully human process, was incapable of sustaining preordained being. The being who is converted is a subject. He engages his milieu and the others in it, grapples with them, considers their beliefs, tries their style, anticipates or imagines the place he will have among them, and worries about whether choosing them will preclude others. Once engaged, he continues as subject, either building his commitment (a process that itself is not so very easy) or creating a distance between himself and the social role he occupies, in which case we might say he is reconsidering his choice.[5] In either case, though more expressly in the latter instance, being affiliated or engaged is hardly being without *doubt* or *regret*. Doubt and regret are implicit in human engagement and they indicate in dramatic fashion the *continuation* of consideration, assessment, imagination, and worry *after* conversion. The subject is never mindless and especially not after he has gone through the immense trouble of converting himself. Conversion is the most human of processes because it involves a transcending of at least part of one's circumstance. The subject who experiences conversion, like the sociologist utilizing the notion, has made a choice. In both cases, they have in some measure *chosen* to be human and are thereby transformed. For better or worse, they must begin to live with that choice and to refashion their lives in terms of it.

The sociologist's choice to be human necessitated grappling with an enormous task: a rendering of the process of becoming deviant in restricted human terms. The choice was against any utilization of processes originating in other worlds, and if that meant the surrender of a Faustian fantasy of discovering the bases of being preordained or the factors of prediction, then so it was. There were other compensations—most of them implicit in the sociologist's taking his subject seriously.

The choice against being preordained was not attained in Sutherland's formulation of the affiliation process. But he prepared the way for that choice.[6] Clearly rejecting the preordination of affinity—the tyranny of antecedent circumstances—though late in life conspiring with its trifles, addressing himself in the only way possible to a doctrine of contagion that was too incredible to be explicit, by reiterating beyond all apparent necessity, Sutherland developed the idea of affiliation. Taken alone, his rendition, *differential association,* seemingly depends only on the method of learning, simpler than conversion, and slightly less human since there is little choice and no competition over the loyalties of man. But taken together with *differential social organization,* as Sutherland clearly intended, his method of

---

[5] Howard Becker, "Notes on the Concept of Commitment," *American Journal of Sociology,* LXVI (July 1960), 32–40. Erving Goffman, in *Encounters* (Indianapolis: The Bobbs-Merrill Co., Inc., 1961), pp. 85–152.

[6] The best summary of the development of Sutherland's thinking on the twin conceptions of differential association and differential social organization may be found in the *Sutherland Papers,* edited by Albert Cohen, Alfred Lindesmith and Karl Schuessler (Bloomington: Indiana University Press, 1956).

affiliation harbors an idea of conversion.[7] Differential social organization pointed to the conflict or competition among different cultural worlds. Sutherland was, if anything, hypersensitive to the possibilities of pluralism, as he was greatly influenced by the ethnography of the Chicago school, part of that tradition in his stress on the "behavior system"—a radical way of maintaining the integrity of peculiar worlds by describing their *own* workings. Unless one always was deviant, in which case little illumination is required, *becoming deviant* depends on being converted.

Though sensitive to pluralism, as manifested in the central place accorded the conception of differential social organization, Sutherland was not always appreciative of the movement of ideas and persons between deviant and conventional realms. Partly obsessed by the idea of ecology, Sutherland nearly made his subject a captive of the milieu. Like a tree or a fox, the subject was a creature of affiliational circumstance, except that what Sutherland's milieu provided was *meaning* and *definition of the situation*. Sutherland's subject was a creature, but he was half a man. Had Sutherland appreciated the interpenetration of cultural worlds—the symbolic availability of various ways of life everywhere—and more important, had he appreciated that men, but not trees and foxes, intentionally move in search of meaning as well as nourishment (and that sometimes such a move is only to the next street, as was brilliantly shown by Zorbaugh); if, in other words, he had rejected the doctrine of radical cultural separation along with an ecological theory of migration well-suited for insects but not man, his creature would have been wholly human. But he did not, and in the same measure his conception never makes the full transition from simple learning to full-fledged conversion. Accordingly, the concept of being preordained—this time by an overpowering affiliational network—managed to survive despite being set mainly in the remarkably uncongenial idea of conversion. Betrayed by an intellectual heritage, the Chicago School, that had abstracted radical cultural separation from isolated primitives and unintentional and meaningless movement from the trees and foxes, Sutherland and his followers were trapped in a profound mixing of metaphors, an unwitting mixing of worlds. Affiliation provided meaning and definition of the situation—that was its human method—but the subject sometimes remained like the tree or the fox without the capacity for choice and sometimes like the insular primitive without alternatives from which to choose; he could not create meaning, shift it, or shift himself away from it. That remained idealistic foolishness—whatever the subject may have thought about it.

But Sutherland had gone far enough. He had brought the subject to

---

[7] Sutherland, *ibid.,* pp. 20–21. Also Edwin Sutherland and Donald Cressey, *Principles of Criminology* (Philadelphia: J. B. Lippincott Co., 6th ed., 1960), pp. 82–85. Also, Thorsten Sellin, *Culture, Conflict and Crime* (New York: Social Science Research Council, 1938).

the brink of humanity by providing a setting for his conversion consisting of definitions of the situation, beliefs, reasons, justifications, techniques, or, in summary, *meaning*. Though it was possible to conceive these as "forces" or "factors," their ordinary human character was in full display. Behind the blown-up physicalist rhetoric were little people talking, perhaps cajoling or intimidating, no larger or more mighty than you, me, or for that matter, the subject himself. And though sociologists could huff and puff to bloat these "forces" larger than life—almost as if their professional pride depended on it—the older convictions would never achieve their previous strength. The day of reckoning for the Faustian daydream was not far off.[8] All that remained was a strengthened and thus human recasting of the subject *as he existed within the affiliative context*. That accomplished, being could no longer be preordained, only ordained; unless, of course, a new preordination was fabricated.

The missing element—a human recasting of the subject—lay in wait. That conception had never been entirely vanquished. Implicit in the common sense of social life, developed in the philosophical psychology of George Herbert Mead, nurtured in American sociology in the writings of Herbert Blumer, cultivated and elaborated in European existence philosophy, and popularized in the café existentialism of two continents, the diffidence of so human a conception was soon overcome. That it was diffident is readily understandable: until the surrealist architecture of primitive sociology decayed, there was no place for a human conception of the subject in the empirical accounting of social process. The human conception existed as sociological perspective or philosophical theory or youthful commitment, but largely it kept its distance, maintained a principled aloofness from substantive social description and analysis. Efforts to engage social phenomena were made under the banner of "symbolic interactionism," but they were largely unsuccessful, and probably had to be. Symbolic interaction—the human recasting of the subject—could hardly be applied in an intellectual context in which all the other elements had already conspired to dehumanize.[9] Fundamentally committed to the active *creation of meaning* and thus human being, it was incompatible with an architecture whose foundation was preordained being.

Until affiliation utilizing the human method of conversion appeared

---

[8] The huffing and puffing took various forms. Most commonly it was called "role theory." For an excellent critique and a humanized recasting of that theory, his protestations notwithstanding, see Erving Goffman, *Encounters* (Indianapolis: The Bobbs-Merrill Co., Inc., 1961).

[9] See Herbert Blumer, "Sociological Analysis and the 'Variable'," *American Sociological Review*, XXI, No. 6 (December 1956), 683–690. Among the best attempts to reconcile the symbolic interactionist perspective with more conventional sociology were Donald Cressey, *Other People's Money* (New York: The Free Press of Glencoe, Inc., 1953); and Alfred Lindesmith, *Opiate Addiction* (Granville, Ohio: Principia Press, 1947).

and subverted the surrealist architecture, the human recasting of the subject—symbolic interaction—was well-advised to remain disengaged from social phenomenon. At their best, the symbolic interactionists just theorized about the nature of man. Consequently, they appeared to the world of sociologists—especially in the writings of Herbert Blumer—as if they were just huffing and puffing. But that appearance was deceiving. They were not huffing and puffing but attempting to breathe a special kind of life—human nature—into a dormant subject.[10]

The task of joining the idea of conversion to a subject rendered in human terms fell to Howard Becker. And in keeping with the spirit of the method and theory of naturalism, he joined the two ingenuously, without fanfare or polemic. It was done so unnoticeably and so matter-of-factly that his contribution was welcomed in the sociological literature as if it were simply a bit of excellent research. The tolerant orthodoxy had long since learned that the best way of managing heresy was to blind itself to it. And since they had been well-trained, the orthodox were skilled at such an incapacity. Its heresy unseen, "Becoming a Marihuana User" itself became part of the edifice supporting the pinnacle of preordination. And its author, too modest to point out the enormity of the heresy, seemingly went along with the prevalent misinterpretation. Indeed, between the first publication of the essay in 1953 and its revised form ten years later in *Outsiders* there was a slight shift of tone in the introduction that went slightly toward a recanting, but easily averted that fate. Considering the motivated obtuseness of the orthodox, and Becker's modesty, an important task remains: the heresy of humanism must be made explicit. At the level of subjective existence (and thus in the process of becoming deviant) there can be no being preordained; there can be only the ordaining of the self and others, which is altogether another matter.

Becoming a Marihuana User

In "Becoming a Marihuana User" the sociological conception of man became thoroughly human. In describing that event, we will see why the heresy remained obscure. To see the heresy of humanism, one must read

[10] See the following works by Herbert Blumer: "Sociological Analysis and the 'Variable'," *American Sociological Review*, XXI, No. 6 (December 1956), 683–690; "What Is Wrong with Social Theory," *American Sociological Review*, XIX, No. 1 (February 1954), 3–10; *Critique of Research in the Social Sciences: An Appraisal of Thomas and Znaniecki's The Polish Peasant* (New York: Social Science Research Council, 1939); "Society as Symbolic Interaction" in Arnold Rose (ed.), *Human Behavior and Social Processes* (New York: Houghton Mifflin Company, 1962), pp. 179–192; "Sociological Implications of the Thought of George Herbert Mead," *American Journal of Sociology*, LXXI, No. 5 (March 1966), 535–548.

Becker's essay in a peculiar, almost obsolete fashion: one must take it literally and seriously. (In certain learned literatures, this amounts almost to tearing an author out of his disciplinary context.)

Like any good naturalist description, Becker's is one that may be regarded as having a use in the world. Taken from the natural world, made conceptual, it may be restored to the world as "insight" or guide to action.[11] Accordingly, it may be regarded as a "recipe," a faithful summary of how to do what people have somewhat unwittingly been doing all along.[12] Being faithful to the world, indeed paying homage to it, the recipe elevates or makes explicit two basic features of the natural social process of human subjects: *consciousness* and *intention*. Profoundly implicit in the world because they are so basic, taken-for-granted because they are so elementary or obvious a part of human existence as it is commonly sensed, they are alienated to the suprahuman perhaps because they so tire the human spirit; they are thus viewed thereafter as the sin of humanist pride. Within itself, the recipe pays homage to consciousness by telling us how to do what we have been doing *less consciously* all along; at its margin—at its *invitational* edge—it pays homage to intentionality. Here is how it can be done, says the recipe, *if perchance you should want to.* Because Becker's essay affirms both features of the recipe, it could well have been titled "How to Smoke Pot." And because the recipe affirms consciousness and intention in the world, it may be regarded as the archetype of humanist naturalism.

A basic feature of the recipe must be reiterated and fully appreciated. It does not *invent* consciousness and intention; it *affirms* what appears in the world through conceptual elevation, or making explicit. What it found in the world is not unwitting or unintentional; it is merely a consciousness and intentionality that did not bother announcing itself or making itself explicit because it was too engrossed *doing* the thing. It did not describe itself bringing something into being. But, nonetheless, in doing the thing that is summarized in the recipe, persons in the world *used* consciousness and *assumed* intention. Being human, they could do no other. And being naturalist, Becker's rendition remains faithful to these intricate processes as they appear in the world. He, like those that do the thing, only more explicitly, utilized consciousness *in the conversion process,* and assumed intention *at the invitational edge*. Let us follow Becker, as he follows the ordinary subject in the process of becoming a marihuana user. Like both, we begin at the edge, and only later enter the process. As in the phenomenal summary and the world it reflects, the process will be rendered *easy* and *open;* it becomes apparent that *anyone* can become a marihuana user and that *no one* has to.

[11] Barney Glaser and Anselm Strauss, *The Discovery of Grounded Theory* (Chicago: Aldine Publishing Co., 1967).

[12] Harold Garfinkel, "Conditions of Successful Degradation Ceremonies," *American Journal of Sociology,* LXI (March 1956), 420–424; and Harold Garfinkel, "Some Sociological Concepts and Methods for Psychiatrists," *Psychiatric Research Reports,* VI (October 1955), 181–195.

Becker announces his intention to utilize the idea of intention almost immediately. But he does it so disarmingly, so matter-of-factly, that unless read seriously and literally it is overlooked. It is misinterpreted as simply another heuristic device. Accustomed to "as if" formulations, the trained sociologist might think that the only strange aspect of Becker's device was its anthropomorphic quality. Becker begins his analysis with a *willing* subject—one who wants to try marihuana. With a slight assist from Becker, who means something quite unusual when he parenthetically adds that he will tell us how the subject became willing in the next essay, the reader perhaps went along with the heuristic game, not realizing that no "as if" was intended.Why should he not pretend for a moment that the subject was capable of being willing? He had pretended almost everything else.

At the invitational edge, at the point of choosing whether to enter the process, before the recipe can work, Becker's subject is to be willing. What could be intended by so strange a beginning? Becker never explicitly tells us. Thus, a conception of being willing must be provided.

Being Willing

One notion of what Becker means by being willing must be dismissed. In that interpretation, being willing is simply a popularized or vulgarized version of being predisposed toward a certain kind of behavior. It takes affinity and, in bad faith, renders it will.[13] Such a rendering would smack of bad faith because it attempts a devious grafting of will on to a conception of being predisposed—or being preordained. That this was *not* Becker's intention is clear. His most general purpose in this essay was to cast doubt on "theories which ascribe behavior to antecedent predispositions."[14] Instead, he aimed to suggest "the utility of explaining behavior in terms of the emergence of motives and dispositions in the course of experience."[15] In the event that there was still confusion or in case the reader failed to notice that instead of predispositions there are now "dispositions" built "in the course of experience," Becker affirmed his antagonism to being preordained by displaying his allegiance to the philosophy of George H. Mead—the viewpoint that maintained the human conception of the subject. Paraphrasing the Meadian perspective, Becker said:

The presence of a given kind of behavior is the result of a sequence of social experiences during which the person acquires a conception of the

---

[13] Bad faith here has a curious meaning: being untrue to the subanthropomorphism implicit in a primitive conception of affinity.

[14] Howard Becker, "Becoming a Marihuana User," *American Journal of Sociology*, LIX (November 1953), 235.

[15] *Ibid.*

*meaning of the behavior, and perceptions and judgments of objects and
situations all of which make the activity possible and desirable.*[16]

Thus, Becker cannot be accused of merely smuggling predispositions into a
conception of being willing. Nonetheless, predispositions or affinity enter
the process of becoming willing. They do so in the world, and suggest the
way in which a conception of affinity may become more thoroughly humanized. In the natural world of the subject, *the consequence* of affinity is being
willing to do a thing, no more and no less. So conceived, the ordinary consequence of affinity becomes apparent.[17] Affinity permits self-ordination.
Under proper circumstances, the self as it encounters the invitational edge
of novelty experiences an option. Thus the ordinary affinity yields permission instead of compulsion. Its consequence is liberty, or, if one prefers,
license. The response is open to the invitation implicit at the fringe of
affiliation. Thus, the ordinary consequence of having been exposed to the
"causes" of deviant phenomena is not in reality *doing* the thing. Instead, it
is picturing or seeing oneself, *literally,* as the kind of person who might possibly do the thing. *The self ordains itself* but initially only as open. While
such ordination is apt to occur at the concrete point of invitation, it may also
occur at a distance in fantasy. Needless to say, given different circumstances
the subject may prejudge the behavior: he may see himself as closed to it.
Accordingly, different circumstances and the affinities implicit in them
result in a variable *sense* of option or closure.

But as any young woman engaging in her first infidelity knows, being
willing is not quite the same as being able. The pondering of self and the
reconsideration of one's project is a continuous experience; it never ceases.
Even commitment—a decisive alliance between the self and its projects
against other lines of action—is reneged on. Thus, the willing young woman
embarked on but hardly committed to a deviant course may decide *in
process* that she is not able. And by that decision she may learn that she was
not willing after all. She *becomes* unwilling. This is not mere self-delusion
or self-serving reconstitution. It is just as, indeed more, real as the sense of
closure to novelty that is never tested in experience. Though she may reconsider the matter again even at the very next invitation, during the period
of remission, she may sense her fidelity with a certainty unknown among the
untested. Her fidelity has been refreshed. Among those for whom the matter
seems closed, fidelity itself remains an article of faith. They may never know
whether they are the kinds of persons destined to remain faithful and dimly
they know it. Not surprisingly, therefore, they are for strict enforcement.
They do not trust their affinities, and for good reason. The common sense
knows, whatever sociology thinks, that the yield of affinity is slight; it is

---

16 *Ibid.*
17 There is a special, or extraordinary consequence to be discussed below.

limited to intentions—good or bad. Thus, the seemingly closed subject—in this case the one holding good intention—must face and live with the possibility of suddenly discovering that she is able though not willing. Unaided, the sense of closure would be no more predictive of not doing something than an option of doing it. But a sense of closure, being an agency of conventional morality, is enormously aided by the intentional elaboration of mechanisms of avoidance and suppression. Both mechanisms are well-manned and heavily invested-in. The purpose of each is to keep the invitational edge of deviant phenomena out of sight and reach. With temptation reduced through intentional and elaborate human institution, the prediction of closure appears weightier than that of option. And so it is, but only because we have structured it that way. Without the conspiracy of social structure, the yield of ordinary affinity is slight, whether it be a sense of option or closure.

How can we know whether the ordinary yield of affinity is in reality so slight? How can we tell whether the consequence of social and personal circumstance is only being willing or being unwilling—senses which in either case are considered, reconsidered, revised, or revisited by the self in *its* project of continuous creation? How can we be sure, to follow the suggestion of positivism, that tentative or undefinitive option and closure are not the very illusions pointed to in the so-called fallacy of humanism?

The human sense of option and closure, being willing or unwilling, may be known and appreciated by contrasting it with literal captivity. This may be done through designating the special features of certain circumstances and their extraordinary predictive yield. In human terms, the general feature of captivity is that it exerts a *tyranny* over the affairs of the subject. In the hold of effective tyranny, the subject is reduced to object and acts accordingly. The only limitations on prediction inhere in the recalcitrance of the reduced subject—he may somehow decide to risk all and assert humanity—and in the resources and sentiments of the tyrant—he may somehow decide that the game is not worth the candle or that he does not like regulating things. More instructive than the tyranny exerted by man over other men is the tyranny of the organism. It is more instructive because most of us in the world today do not know the concrete meaning of full-blown political tyranny. Thus its illumination of the option yielded by ordinary circumstance would be dim. It would fail as a contrast because most extant political tyrannies are replete with option. The tyranny of the organism is more instructive precisely because in some instances it is more compelling. It may serve as the archetype for the natural reduction and thus present a most fitting contrast to the equally natural situation in which the subject exists at his ordinary condition—the level of human being. Being reduced is no less natural than being human, just less common.

Organismic tyranny yields the captivity of specified neurosis. That is the extraordinary relation between circumstance and being which was glimpsed brilliantly by Freud and overgeneralized, especially by his followers but in some measure by Freud himself. Instead of conceiving psychoanalysis as a determinism—something one can do if one prefers—it is more instructive to deem it a changing body of theory and practice that *treats actual determinisms* as they appear in the world of the subject. So unusual and pathetic are literal determinisms in the world of the subject, so unaccustomed are we to actual captivity that, rightly, we ponder the need for therapy and understandably, though perhaps wrongly, we conceive the condition as illness. A more modest conception of dis-ease would have been more to the point since the feeling experienced by the captive subject is disquieting and strange. Unaccustomed to so mighty a grip, confused by the periodic waning of intention, frightened by the inhuman sense that he is not conscious of a reason for his behavior, the subject *himself* experiences the condition with dis-ease. It is not so much the behavior itself that necessarily strikes him as strange; more precisely, it is the lack of a sensed relation between himself and the thing being done. For good reason, the subject *expects intention* and *exists in consciousness.* That is his nature, and that all social organization and normative life is built on those assumptions is no denial of man's natural condition; it is the most compelling confirmation.

But there is a bit of a problem: The subjective capacities develop *within an organism,* and thus arises the possibility of a tyranny exerted by a lower order of being. Freud referred to the effects of such a tyranny as "overdetermination," a curious, most revealing, and remarkably well-chosen term—so revealing that it is usually misconstrued. (Could we not say that the misconstruction was motivated?) The meaning of overdetermination should be apparent: literally *being determined.* One's behavior can not be more than determined; but the idea of being determined can be weakened through sloppy or metaphoric usage, and Freud himself followed in that tradition. But he had the brilliant sense to realize that if by fiat all women are deemed beautiful then the one who is really beautiful is best called "over-beautiful."[18] Freud's contribution was hardly limited to a spilling of the beans implicit in a conception of overdetermination. And as is implied in the phrase "spilling the beans," he had no intention of contributing to the assault on the idea of being preordained. He worked arduously at maintaining the edifice of determinism and is usually granted an honored place within it. He did after all assert the principle of psychic determinism, and he clearly had faith in it. But that, it must be said, is not the real point of Freud's contribution.

Psychic determinism in Freud's work is fiat, overdetermination a co-

18 For a delightful discussion of the process by which the literal meaning of words is dissipated, see Peter Fryer, *Mrs. Grundy: Studies in English Prudery* (London: D. Dobson, 1963).

gent and magnificent theory. The latter, and not the former, specified the forms taken by the captivity of the subject and, more important, located a prime source of tyranny. Various neuroses (provided that term, too, is not dissipated) amount to existence in captivity. When behaving within the terms of the neurosis, the subject is captive. He is overdetermined, or literally determined. The source of so curious a human state—so strange we rightly conceive it an affliction—is the lingering hegemony of the organism over the subject. Thus, the captive existence of a subject may be located or grounded. It develops within a context: Neurosis emanates from failures to come to terms with and thus *to transcend* our organic being. The deepest meaning of instinct is not animal lust or aggression; it is *aim,* determination, or preordination.

This stress on an emergent subject *within* an organism struggling to transcend it is central to the Freudian scheme. Such a stress is the reason why weaning, toilet training, oedipal drives, and the rest are the *least* expendable components in the Freudian system. They must be taken quite seriously because they are precisely the occasions during which the incipient subject strives, with more or less help, to transcend his organism. Is it actually so absurd, for instance, to regard the regulation of defecating and urinating as a profound experience in which a potential subject must struggle with organic being? For Freud and his orthodox followers the *embodied subject* remains the central figure. More important, this imagery provides the dialectical context that in the event of organismic victory yields a lingering tyranny manifested in a captive existence. Revisionist psychoanalysis and social psychiatry, having disembodied the subject, lose the source of the overdetermination by minimizing the organismic or "instinctual" context in which it emerged. Left without a grounded theory of overdetermination, they followed the more abstract tendency also implicit in Freud: the principle of psychic determination. And to make up for the lost ground, they added some abstract cultural determinism.

By confusing overdetermination with psychic determinism, revisionist psychoanalysis, Freud and his orthodox followers went somewhat astray. They confused being captive with being willing or unwilling. Overdetermination comprised a lucid account of captivity in terms of the fusion of organic and subjective existence and the variably pathetic consequences of so vain or human a project. But the captivity of the subject was *localized;* the tyranny of the organism could never be complete until death. With that exception, its continuing hegemony even in the neuroses was partial, manifesting itself as localized eruption, and sensed by the subject with dis-ease or, as Freud suggested, as *enchantment.*

Psychic determinism is quite different. Rather than a grounded theory including a source and specific manifestations, it was a principle capable of abstract formulation and indiscriminate application. The manifestation or "eruption" could be diffuse. One's entire being could be affected. A theory of overdetermination grounded being preordained in the earthy reality of a subject struggling with his organism and yielded the localized captivity of neurosis. The principle of psychic determinism took an altogether different path: It found being preordained in the sky or in the Faustian fantasies that brought it to earth, and it yielded an abstract—one might say diffuse—captivity. It yielded a captivity with quotation marks around it, which is to say its result was *affinity*, not captivity. Like all ungrounded determinisms, its yield was significant but slight: a subject who upon engaging novelty would sense himself as being willing—or unwilling. Psychic determinism had a place along with its brethren emanating from other disciplines: it pertained to an *ordinary* rather than extraordinary relation between self and circumstance. Thus its yield, like those antecedent circumstances typically stressed in sociology, was of limited potency and diffuse applicability. It affected all behavior, but not very much.

We may appreciate the meaning of being willing or unwilling by contrasting both with the literal and localized captivity of existence; and, as suggested, a prime instance of such a curious human state may be found in an embodied theory of overdetermination.[19] Being willing or unwilling is the ordinary form of affinity, the ordinary yield of antecedent circumstance. Unless a natural reduction lurks in the biography of the subject, exposing him to the compelling potency of the organism, unless a natural reduction is implicit in the agencies that define his current situation, making him the kind of creature subject to gravitation, the hold of circumstance, antecedent or contemporary, is limited. This limited hold is *not* a result of our incomplete knowledge of the determinants of human behavior. It is in the nature of the case—man—that happens to be before us.

To recognize and appreciate the meaning of being willing is by no means to assert the existence of a free will. Indeed, it is the very opposite. The logic of one's past, the human agencies in one's situation are certainly real. They are the grounding for the conduct of will. Free will, as the phrase itself implies, takes will out of context, converting it inexorably into an abstraction of as little use as any other. Will is the conscious foreshadowing of specific intention capable of being acted on or not. It is a sense of option that must be rendered in context. But to put will in its place is not to imprison it. Will need not be untrammeled, abstracted or "free," nor need behavior be determined, preordained or predictable. Thus viewed, being willing is the human leap that allows an open process to continue. Will

[19] The preceeding discussion is influenced by the writings of Dennis Wrong, "The Oversocialized Conception of Man in Modern Sociology," *American Sociological Review*, XXVI (April 1961), 183–193; Philip Rieff, *Freud: The Mind of the Moralist* (New York: The Viking Press, 1959); Ernest Becker, *Revolution in Psychiatry* (New York: The Free Press of Glencoe, Inc., 1964); Michel Foucault, *Madness and Civilization, op. cit.*

exists in the world; its absence in sociological theory gives readers the unmistakable impression that the author striving for a causal account is doing some leaping of his own. As usual, the lesson of naturalism is clear: Sociologists would do better to describe the ways in which their subjects proceed through an open process by being willing than to substitute procedures derived from a subhuman world. The first is a dynamism suited to our topic of inquiry—man; the second is an insult—and like all insults, its function is to obscure our own deficiencies.

Being Turned On

By being willing, the subject may begin a process that neither holds him within its grip nor unfolds without him. Without the subject, the process has no meaning since it must be mediated through him and take its form from him. To enter the process, the invitational edge of the deviant phenomenon must somehow be hurdled. To do that a leap is required—an act of will; the phenomenon is engaged, but not abstractly. The subject is actually doing the thing—an immersion in concrete activity which is essential. The remainder of the process of becoming deviant can hardly happen if the subject continues to gaze at a phenomenon kept at a distance. And having done the thing is certainly not the end of the open process of becoming deviant. Hurdling the invitational edge merely makes the person someone who has tried something once, and we all know many people like that. Whether the subject proceeds, whether the open process continues, whether he becomes deviant depends on a great deal more. Having come along this far, the next issue for the subject, and thus for the sociologist, is whether the phenomenon and those affiliated with it succeed or fail in "turning him on" or converting him. All that has been accomplished thus far is that a subject has become actually open to conversion. However small, it is an accomplishment, for he is open concretely; he is open to a consideration of the phenomenon *from inside it*. There is nothing even approximating a guarantee of his conversion. But the terms of consideration have been shifted with the change of perspective. No longer outside the phenomenon, the subject proceeds to a new level of consideration. He has succumbed to the slight yield of affinity, and is now simultaneously subject in the process of affiliation and subjected to it.

Just as in a subsequent part of the process the subject may discover *concretely* that the deviation is actually wrong, so too he first discovers that the deviation is an experience with its own features and problems. Outside the phenomenon, the knowledge that agents of society will really act as if it were wrong to deviate remains abstract and in that measure irrelevant; more profoundly, and more immediately pertinent, knowledge that there is really something to be done remains similarly abstract and thus similarly irrelevant. Outside the phenomenon, the only issue before us, and thus the only one worth considering, is that of affinity. And even *that* issue need not be very concrete since—as member of society *or* as sociologist—our affinity may be to remain closed to it. Accordingly, the issue of affinity is highly abstract when limited to a consideration of those still outside the phenomenon. It speculates about those who are themselves only speculating; it measures those who are themselves only taking their own measure.

Inside the phenomenon, new issues arise, but the old issue of affinity does not cease to exist. Contrarily, it is only in the course of experience— first affiliation and later, signification—that the *meaning* of affinity, and thus its yield, is built. The yield of ordinary affinity outside the context of experience is mainly whether the subject can imagine himself experiencing the specific deviation. As suggested, such a yield may be regarded as slight. But inside the phenomenon, actually doing the thing and possibly being with others who also do it, the subject becomes so situated as to sense the meaning of affinity: *He* builds its meaning. In the context or situation of affiliation, affinity takes on new and multiplied meaning. One way of summarizing that amplification is to say that the meaning of affinity becomes concrete or relevant. The subject may now reconsider, *in light of the disclosed meaning built in the course of experience,* whether his initial understanding of his own affinities—as he pictured them—was sound.

That reconsideration is the project that links affinity to affiliation. The subject discovers himself in process. There is no other way. Not being preordained, the subject is fated to continuous reconsideration. But the terms in which he reconsiders his affinities are not the same as those that guided his initial consideration of himself as one who might deviate and thus, under proper circumstances, one who might well leap the invitational edge. Now *in the situation,* engaged in the phenomenon, the terms on which he is to reconsider his affinity are provided by the affiliative circumstance itself. New issues arise, intrinsic to the context of affiliation. And it is those issues that henceforth will loom largest in his overarching project—the relation between himself and the alternate possibilities open to him. Thus, it would be accurate to suggest that the subject is bound by its terms and its issues— until he makes another move. He need not leap or even run to escape the clutches of the affiliative context—its terms and issues are not so constraining. After due reconsideration, he may simply stroll away from it, though perhaps with regret, indecision or second thoughts. Or, he may remain and be "turned on" or converted, though again perhaps with regret, indecision or second thoughts.

Whatever the outcome of reconsideration, the subject has entered the affiliative context sponsoring a deviant phenomenon. His intention displayed, not as explicitly as in the decision to use a recipe but just a tentatively, he engages the experience. Henceforth, the question of affinity can be rendered in a manner that makes common as well as sociological sense: How *well-suited* or *attuned* are phenomenon and subject to each other? The description of that process of reconsideration is the main task of Becker's two essays on marihuana use. The key element in the subjective process of reconsideration is precisely that which is elevated and honored in the recipe: human consciousness. In becoming deviant, nothing happens behind the subject's back or despite him. Indeed, to be converted he must be fully open to the experience. Partly closed to it, the subject can be inside the phenomenon yet not see and evaluate it on its own terms. The continued reliance on the old terms diminishes the chance of conversion, though it does not preclude it.

Conversion is mediated through a reconsideration of the self and its affinities. In the context of experience, consciousness may shift itself so as to incorporate new terms of reference, new issues of relevance. Only the context of experience can provide the terms and issues that are the very tissue with which meaning is built and disposition discovered. Though peers or other educators are part of the experience, it is a mistake to reduce the affiliative circumstance to a process in which the initiate capitulates, or does not, to the pressure of others already converted. The others are considered —but with the phenomenon they represent, practice and sponsor.

Doing something for the first time may be regarded as an exploratory leap, providing, perhaps unknown to the subject, the occasion for a reconsideration of his action in terms of what he already knows about himself and a re-evaluation of himself in terms of what he now knows about the activity. At each point of participation, the novice may learn concrete details unanticipated in fancy. He may sense himself as well-suited to the smoking of marihuana, and even to its illicit procurement, but awkwardly *unsuited* to the purchase of its publicly and legally dispensed accoutrements. The would-be philanderer may love his women, but hate the brief moments of necessary interaction with clerks or other minor functionaries more worldly and matter-of-fact toward such pursuits than any single activist could possibly be. In the fabric of activity, the subject may witness its seamy side; but that is quite different from a correctional conjuring of a surface seaminess. Marihuana is not likely to make the user wild or aggressive, but it may make him quite fat. The possible reality of the latter may be as important to ongoing reconsideration, and thus to the process of becoming, as the quickly-discovered unreality of the former.

Viewed in this way, Becker's essays may be considered a specification of the terms and issues provided by an affiliative circumstance—marihuana use, and thus the occasion through which being may be converted. To become deviant, the subject's willingness must survive reconsideration. Let us consider, using Becker as guide, the building of meaning and the continuous ordaining of self as the subject proceeds through the open process of becoming a marihuana user, for it is only the affiliative circumstance that the subject, and thus the sociologist, can discover the human meaning of affinity.

Even in the seemingly simple matter of *learning the technique*—the first issue faced by the subject in Becker's summary of the affiliative process —the meaning of affinity emerges, and reconsideration is set in motion. Unless he has read Becker's essay, all the American subject knows is that marihuana is to be smoked—providing, of course, he is not introduced to the substance in the chic and thus unwittingly Francophile circles in which it is put in pastry and eaten.[20] That exception aside, American marihuana use—before anything else—is an act of smoking. The student of abstracted affinities seeking correlations outside the context of experience who neglects that "antecedent condition" does so at his own peril. This does not mean that the subject must already be a smoker to learn the technique; but if he is not, the task is that much more complicated and arduous. For as Becker implied, the technique required of the subject if he is to get "high" is not simply one of smoking; it is an esoteric elaboration of the only competence really special to smoking—*inhaling*. An informant in Becker's study described the special method of inhaling:

> *Take in a lot of air, you know, and . . . I don't know how to describe it, you don't smoke it like a cigarette, you draw in a lot of air and get it deep down in your system and then keep it there. Keep it there as long as you can.*[21]

The implication seems clear enough: before becoming a marihuana user, the subject must become a special kind of inhaler. That he may be deterred, or discouraged by that necessity is true, but it is of no great importance. More important is the reason why a skill so easily learned would make any difference in whether the subject proceeded to become a marihuana user. If he is simply learning a technique, its moment is small: He can just practice. But the subject is not simply considering the experience. He is considering himself in relation to it.[22] He is reconsidering his project. Viewed in that way, the crucial meaning that is built in the course of the experience is not the meaning of marihuana; it is the meaning of affinity in its most concrete and

[20] For a summary of Baudelaire's description of the influence of hasheesh see Robert De Ropp, *Drugs and the Mind* (New York: Grove Press, Inc., 1961), pp. 68–74 (originally published in 1957 by St. Martin's Press).

[21] Howard Becker, *Outsiders* (New York: The Free Press of Glencoe, Inc., 1963), p. 47.

[22] This, and the remainder of the chapter, draws heavily from the general orientation of George H. Mead and Herbert Blumer; to a somewhat lesser extent, it is influenced by Sartre's perspective.

relevant sense. The *subject* engaged in a *project* is presented with a method by which the two may be related, and their fit actually considered. That is the human meaning of affinity, and its method quite naturally is relation—not gravitation. Relation, the method, is the mental representation of being engaged, the activity.

Existing in the project—for the time being that is where he *is*—the subject has the remarkable capacity to conceive himself in terms of the essence of that or any experience: *relation*. Not only does he have the capacity to resolve intuitively the first ontological question, he utilizes it constantly. If the subject did not intuit the idea of relation from his existential situation, and if he did not then utilize it in a manner to be described, he could not proceed. Everything human would just stop. For the subject, though apparently not for the philosopher, the resolution of the ontological question is child's play: Existence not only precedes essence; it suggests its very character, relation. More difficult, though still done by children, is utilizing human intuition to continue being human in the world—in other words utilizing the intuition in order *to proceed*. How to proceed; not how to proceed in any specific direction, but how to proceed in any direction at all? For man, this is a matter of life or death, though only of course in the subjective or higher sense of those terms. How to proceed, or how to continue being human in the world is the second ontological question, and the more profound.

The resolution is simple: *The subject conceives himself*. Happily, he is provided with all it takes: human consciousness. First, he pictures himself doing the thing, *as* he is doing it. In Meadian terms, and at this early point in process he objectifies himself *as an inhaler*. Second, he builds on to the meaning of affinity, which is itself being enriched in experience, the intuition of relation derived from existing in a project. The yield of this combination is *correlation:* the relation of *himself as an inhaler* to *himself in other projects,* past, present or future, that he sees or depicts—the ones of which he is *reminded*.

The resolution of the first ontological question—the intuition of relation—and the utilization of the simpler capacity of consciousness have a limited yield: only the subject's picture of himself as inhaler. To proceed, to do something with that picture, he must correlate it with others—all of those in fact of which the subject is reminded.[23] That is a very complex operation; indeed, it is one that could be performed only by members of a species that could conceive a computer. Since, fortunately, we are concerned with precisely that species, it is fair to assume that the operation is performed. Independent evidence of a sort may be suggested, though certainly it will not

---

[23] At any point, of course, given a properly constituted subject, the unconscious may enter, grip the entire process and preordain the outcome.

convince those who regard the entire discussion as "too anthropomorphic." Human being in the world does not stop; the subject continues to proceed using no power other than his own.

The subject is now at the verge of movement. The correlation between himself as inhaler and projects he is reminded of suggests a direction. The suggestion need be no more than faint. The subject, if not the sociologist, knows that he can always reconsider or "change his mind." Thus, he does not demand a firm instruction to stop or go. Since the whole process may only take a few seconds, there is only time to be reminded of several projects.[24] Thus, the subject proceeds on the basis of sloppy correlation. He does what he can in the limited time allowed him. In most instances, after all, he doesn't have all day—or night—to "make up his mind."

Accordingly, he *makes up his mind,* literally. After correlating the picture of himself as inhaler with a picture of himself in reminiscent projects, say, that of appearing graceful and competent in company, of learning to inhale cigarettes, of avoiding arrest, of being instructed, or perhaps even of avoiding cancer and other irritations of the lung, the subject makes up his mind one way or the other. He might as well, since almost anything he does will have that appearance in the world. He can hardly ask for "time out." It just isn't done, except by beautiful women, who can get away with almost anything, and athletes, who are really—not metaphorically—just playing games.

His mind made up, for the time being at least, the subject puts an appearance of it in the world. What his mind made up is projected into the world. This is the final and deepest level of "conceiving himself." Being pregnant with meaning, he gives birth and contributes to the flow of experience: He creates an act. Being is continued in the world. In other words, and less pompously, he takes another drag, or perhaps passes the joint on, nodding no; but also, he may fake it, or he may excuse himself and leave for another part of the world, nearby or far-away; he may even "create a scene," which obviously ought to be regarded as a projection into the world of a mind made up.

The point is that the subject has mediated the whole experience. There was no process of becoming without him. He "made it up" and the positivist

---

[24] Here a basic rule of social organization operates to hurry the subject along. That rule does not repudiate the process being described. Instead, it recognizes, confirms and affirms the ease with which the subject may perform the stunts being described. The rule is that experience must flow. Exceptions are made in games like chess, poker or flirtation, but even there patience is easily strained. More serious decisions may be put in abeyance, but that does not constitute a stop in the flow of experience. The subject appears to be doing other things while making up his mind. Pauses in the flow of experience display themselves in embarrassment and confusion. When the pauses become unduly long, or are unmitigated by reason, we have part of the stuff of which the social categories of mental illness and retardation are constructed.

took the wrong meaning of that evocative phrase. Positivists took it to mean the figment or fallacy of humanism, when it actually means composed or constructed.

To suggest that the subject maintained authority throughout this tiny part of the process is not to say he did anything he wanted or that he performed with free will. The latter phrases either say nothing or utter things outside the context of experience. All I mean by *maintaining authority* is that throughout the process of decision, the subject was the author of each key element. *He* made an object of himself. *He* intuited the idea of relation. *He* built the meaning of affinity. *He* correlated his present project with those *he* was reminded of. *He* gave birth to, or created an act. The subject made up the process, but out of material provided by the context of affiliation.

Thus far, the affiliative circumstance has been regarded as relatively permissive or benign. All it requested, and not too insistently, is that the subject "make up his mind." In that sense it is an easy circumstance, and thus one which fully illuminates the open process of decision. One need not romanticize the circumstance of general affiliation, of deviant affiliation, or of marihuana use specifically, to appreciate the value of an illumination produced by an unusually permissive part of the world. And even so permissive a world as that of marihuana use is not so enlightened as to exert no pressure toward conversion. One need not conjure the line, "Sorry, fella, you're in this too far to get out alive now," a statement and thus perhaps a reality to be found mainly in the worlds of police, moviemakers and other agents of correction, to appreciate the intimidation of the dare that is implicit in every deviant context, and the part played by simple expectation in every circumstance of affiliation.

Additionally, since the sponsors of the particular enterprise do not necessarily exist only in its light, they may be esteemed or attractive on other grounds. Thus, however permissive of second thoughts or changes of mind, the affiliative circumstance possesses a number of *general assets* over and above the terms and issues provided by the specific phenomenon. The additional consideration of these general assets surely affects the process, for the esteem of personnel, the intimidation of the dare, the appeal and the sociability of expectation are resources implicit in the affiliative circle, and are often quite useful in conversion. *But they do not foreclose the authority of the subject.* The process remains open, but it becomes more complicated and, as between the decision to stay on or get off, perhaps a bit more even. During reconsideration, the subject must consider the general terms and issues of affiliation as well as those specific to the phenomenon before him. Thus, beginning with an unusually permissive conception of the affiliative context illuminates the subject in the process of deciding. He must decide in every circumstance, however overbearing. To have begun in the grip of overt pressure would have obscured the fact that the subject takes *group pressure*

into account. Too often, it is said, he then produces the appearance of succumbing to it.

In returning to the unusually permissive part of the world—marihuana
use—one last point regarding the general assets of the affiliative circumstance should be made—lest the reader mistakenly believe that I have left
the subject with an empty authority, one that he rarely if ever exercises. He
does sometimes have empty authority, a subjectivity oppressed by context
or circumstance. Aside from the fact, however, that such matters are normally the province of students of political or family life, it must be said that
the potency of the general assets of the affiliative circumstance are as capable of being romanticized as the permissive character of marihuana use.
This is especially true with regard to *peers,* who, as it happens, are the concretely embodied assets of the affiliative circumstances presently at issue. It
takes a great deal of huffing and puffing to render peers more mighty or
larger than the subject himself, though, plainly, no more than sociologists
are capable of. And it takes almost as much oversight to celebrate the
clear fact that peers outnumber the subject, while overlooking the frequency
with which the subject removes himself and thus replaces them. Cut down to
size, peers, the embodiment of the general assets of the affiliative circumstance, must be considered. And in that life-like form, they *are* considered
by the subject. Thus, it is a mistake to confuse the relevance of affiliative
circumstance with a celebration of group potency. The actual potency of
peers is a matter to be considered by the subject, and, as such, part of the
general reconsideration of doing the thing.

The relevance of affiliative circumstance is that *it provides matters to
be considered by the subject.* The medium for such provision is the experience itself. But for the experience to matter, the subject must be able to
continue considering it. It is this necessity that brings us to the second phase
in Becker's rendition of the process of becoming a marihuana user. In some
ways it is the simplest aspect, in others the most complicated. Whether simple
or complicated, it is the crucial phase of *recognition:* when the subject must
learn to perceive the effects of marihuana.

Why, to use Becker's terms, need the subject "learn to perceive the
effects" of marihuana? Why are they not self-evident? One way of viewing the
matter is implicit in Becker's method of answering these questions. In one
sense, he answered: The subject cannot reach the next phase unless he learns
to perceive or recognize the effects. But Becker hardly considered the more
relevant sense of "why": why are the effects *not* self-evident? By not considering that question, Becker meant to suggest, I suppose, that effects of
novelty are rarely self-evident, that to locate and sense them requires assistance from others. That is quite a suggestion, and harbors considerable
truth. However, it is also quite an exaggeration of the human incapacity to
sense oneself. By not specifying the concrete and thus limited context of the

incapacity to recognize effects without assistance, Becker diminished somewhat the central part consciousness plays in the entire process. By the same
token, without meaning to, he lent credence to the deservedly discredited
theory that the whole experience may be regarded as an example of the
"placebo phenomenon," one in which the effects derive wholly from suggestion.

There is another way to conceive the necessary recognizing of effects
that maintains the central role of consciousness, and, more important, leaves
part of the reason for the necessity to the *substance itself*. After all, marihuana itself is part of the phenomenon being discussed, and it would be a
curious phenomenology that rendered it useless in its very use. Such would
be a phenomenology of appearances at the expense of essence, which is to
say a phenomenology without the very tension that informs and sustains it.
This is not to suggest that Becker was guilty of such an error, merely that his
appreciation of its essential effects seemingly began one phase too late. He
omitted marihuana's effect on consciousness, and to make up for the oversight, perhaps, he, the analyst, diminished the role of consciousness slightly.
For that tiny diminution the substance itself will do.

More informative, I think, than the view that the subject must learn to
perceive the effects of marihuana is the suggestion that he must be *awakened*
to them. Grasping the distinction between the two is essential: it allows us
to understand the key role of consciousness; it helps specify the concrete
circumstance in which the subject needs assistance in perceiving the effects
of something on himself, when, in other words, effects are not self-evident; it
helps avert the placebo conception of marihuana use; and finally, it clarifies
a basis for appreciating or "learning to enjoy the effects," the final phase
described by Becker.

Wide-awake, our subject needs no instruction in perceiving the effects
of most things happening to him—even when virgin territory is being
broken. Ordinarily, he is better equipped than anyone around to make such
judgments. Perhaps, as marriage counselors proclaim, someone should tell
persons what a sexual experience *is,* but ordinarily no one bothers despite
the plain fact that its nature is somewhat problematic. Indeed we assume
the applicability of the legendary words of Louis Armstrong: "like, if you
don't know, no one can tell you"; similarly, with most internal experiences,
even with alcohol, we do not typically go about explaining to people what it is
they're going to experience the first time they indulge. What is so different
about marihuana?

Why in this experience must the subject be assisted in perceiving effects? Why in this case is the ordinary assumption, "if he doesn't know, no
one can tell him" dropped? Why, in other words, do we no longer assume
that the subject presides over the things happening to him? The answer, I
think, is simple, but of necessity controversial since it may be easily misinter-

preted: *Momentarily,* the subject ceases to preside; *momentarily,* he is half-asleep. In that limited sense, a first effect of marihuana is a diminished consciousness. In the lay meaning of the term, the subject is "drugged," though only slightly; and thus under proper affiliative circumstance only temporarily.

Half-asleep, the subject cannot perceive the effects *on himself* of the substance he is using. But quite easily, he can be awakened to them. That awakening consists of being told more or less accurately the effects he is to perceive. It is sheer nonsense to believe he could be told anything. He is not *that* drugged, unless of course he has taken an overdose, in which case he will usually fall fully asleep. The medium for the awakening is talk: simply being told what in all likelihood he would be perceiving if he did not momentarily exist in a state of diminished consciousness, if he had not momentarily fallen half-asleep. Moreover, the consequence of that reawakening is inexorably to reinstate the mind, to restore the subject to the condition in which he presides over things happening to the self and the small society before him.

But being reinstated *after* being half-asleep, the mind neither quickly returns to the condition of ordinary consciousness nor does it simply slumber back into diminished consciousness. It does both and yet something else. The mind returns to ordinary consciousness when the effect of marihuana has worn off; it slumbers back into diminished consciousness periodically during the experience; and it exists in *altered* context in the time between the occasional diminutions. "Being high" is perhaps the best way of rendering that altered context of mind, and thus those who do the thing use precisely that phrase. Everything that will be *appreciated* or not, in Becker's third phase, is, as he himself suggested, a symptom of "being high." The latter is the essence that lies behind the manifold and quite variable appearances. Thus, before going on to the phase of appreciation, we must understand what happens in the condition of altered consciousness known as "being high." What happens is in principle enormous, but in degree it is slight, in duration, short-lived.[25] Because "being high" is essential, and because comprehending it requires a rudimentary grounding in a theory of consciousness, a seemingly wide detour is mandatory.

What could it mean to "be high"? To what reality does ordinary language point in that expression? There are really only two serious possibilities, and we will see that choosing between them is largely unnecessary. Indeed, we will be driven to the conclusion that properly viewed the two possibilities are different sides of the single reality pointed to in the expression "being high."[26]

[25] The enormity of what happens in principle is more fully realized in the LSD experience. For descriptions of that experience, see David Solomon (ed.), *LSD: The Consciousness-Expanding Drug* (New York: G. P. Putnam's Sons, 1964).

[26] This discussion is limited to being high on marihuana. Being high on alcohol, though neighborly, is in some ways another thing altogether.

The first possibility exploits the idea of *essence:* Whatever it is that is becoming high is being altered *in itself.* The second possibility exploits the idea of *relation:* Whatever it is that is becoming high is being altered in context, in the place or standing occupied in a configuration; more simply, its alteration is *in something else.* Clearly we need never choose between the two. And, in a way, the principle is well-established: In the whole universe, and certainly in the human world that, after all, produced the man who promulgated the *only* universally applicable idea, one never happens without the other; alteration of essence *is the other side of* alteration in the place occupied in a time-space configuration. The two are equivalent because they are the two basic human perspectives on the very same thing and on everything. That the so-called relativists in "social science" butchered the idea of relativity in the process of transferring it should, by this time, not surprise us. They did so by denying essence, thereby leaving the brilliant and human intuition *uniting* essence and relation or process in a sadly one-sided state. Reduced to a *non sequitur,* it came out in a form now familiar: "everything is relative." Relativity reverted to sophistry. In that form, it is taught to sophomores, and has great appeal to them.

Thus, whatever it is that alters does so in the double sense; "it" seems higher than itself prior to the shift, and "it" stands "higher" in relation to something else than before. What is "it"—this matter that can be sensed or experienced in higher and lower states? For the moment, let us refer to "it" as mind. And what is the something else; that which mind stands in relation to? What better answer than Mead's? Mind stands always in relation to its context: the *matter* from which it is continually formed and over which it continually presides—self and society. Thus conceived, "being high" is an alteration of consciousness, the essence, or energy, of mind; and, on the other side, "being high" is a shift in the standing of mind relative to self and society in the light of consciousness. Whichever side of the equation we prefer, it should be clear that the net result is a changed configuration. Furthermore, it should be plain as day that *in principle* something enormous has occurred; something so strange that, if misunderstood, if glimpsed quickly from outside the phenomenon, it would not be tolerated for a moment by right-minded spokesmen of society. The very fabric of social order, they would shout, is endangered by so satanic a substance. "It puts you out of your mind," they would sputter. And never realizing how amusingly close to the truth they had come in their utter falsification of the phenomenon, they would ban it. There is always a reason for proscription. Those who would prohibit always glimpse something about that which will be banned; but being, by definition, *outside* the phenomenon, their vision is bent. Thus, as is their bent anyway, they act on the basis of bloated principles instead of reality.

In principle, the altered configuration of mind, self and society is so enormous as to be dizzying—in consequence as well as in our capacity to conceive such a possibility. But in reality, the enormity is illusory. In reality, the altered place of mind relative to self and society experienced by the subject as "being high" capitalizes on the most ordinary of human processes —a shift of mood. Moreover, the very way we conceive the altered configuration, "being high," capitalizes on a perfectly ordinary linguistic trick— what might be called sleight-of-word. And, finally, the consequences of the changed configuration, the "symptoms" of "being high" may be unified and summarized by capitalizing on the full and serious meaning of the most ordinary condition of modern life: banality.

To comprehend the meaning of "being high" on marihuana, in reality, each of these assertions must be elaborated. Eventually, we must return to the point in the actual experience at which the subject was put to rest. Half-asleep and then awakened, he must be followed through the experience of "being high"; otherwise, the description of what happened, thus far given *in principle,* will never come down to earth. But the problem is that we are not yet ready for a landing. Without a conception of various states of being —only one of which is "being high"—there is no ground to land on. Thus, the reader must be patient. The subject cannot be brought down to earth without first exploring a rudimentary theory of conscious mood. Any other approach would be misleading.

Being Awakened

The experience of being awakened from drowsiness, half-sleep or even sleep is not uncommon. Being awakened in a certain way is less common, though not unique to the marihuana experience. The *mood* or state of mind with which the subject reenters the flow of experience depends partly on the quality and duration of respite; slightly more pertinent here, though being refreshed is clearly a matter of moment to the mind, is the precise configuration of mind, self and society at the time of reawakening and shortly thereafter. That configuration *in the subject* is one key meaning of mood. With mood, whatever its configuration, he reenlists in the flow of experience, sensing the world *temporarily* in an uncustomary manner to which, since he has grown to know himself, he is pretty well accustomed. In due time—it takes some longer than others—his operative mood, the one the subject associates with himself in everyday life, is restored. That mood is *for him* the ordinary configuration of mind, self and society. What is the meaning of this restoration, so common that among the ablest of men it occurs daily? More pertinent, how does it clarify the mood of marihuana?

The meaning and reason for this restoration of the operative mood, experienced by everyone save those who allege to be fully-awake the moment of reentry, is that awakening occurs *unevenly.* What we are generally restored to is *consciousness*. What occurs unevenly are the matters from which it is formed and reformed, created and recreated, born and reborn; the matters with which, naturally, it is stored and restored. Consciousness, the essence or energy of human existence, provided with matters for consideration, self, and society, conceives itself as mind. Thereafter, since it *too* has been conceived—pictured once brought into being—the mind, as well as self and society, can be made the object of consciousness. True, consciousness can be accused of playing with itself when attentive to mind rather than self or society, but those things happen. Being conscious of mind is being attentive to what consciousness made of itself, what it *became*, provided with the matters of self and society. Accordingly, mind, consciousness growing up, becomes additional matter, joining self and society as objects of consciousness and thus as additional sustenance for growing up even more. A clever thing, this consciousness; it knows how to conceive. It brings things into being by just picturing them, and uses everything around it from which to draw pictures—including itself growing up. In consequence, mind grows up even more.

A key issue in an awakening is the sequence with which consciousness alights on its objects—mind, self and society. Being awakened can only mean one thing: Dormant the moment before, each, in its turn, now exists *alighted by consciousness*. The illuminated existence of each may be dim, partial or full with little necessity and even less likelihood that each restoration to operative level will be complete before the next begins. At the moment of awakening, consciousness alights unevenly on the matters it exists in and makes objects of: mind, self and society. Refreshed, consciousness is *available* to begin its daily tribulation. Gradually, the diminished consciousness of sleep will be undone. The key question is the sequence in which consciousness alights and restores its objects. Among those available for alighting, what does it alight? More basically, what does that question mean? Until the meaning of the uneven spread of consciousness to its objects is grasped, we can hardly comprehend what happens to the marihuana-user awakened from half-sleep, a subject I want eventually to reach.

The problem is that the consciousness of mind, self and society are *integrated*. Whether wide-awake or just awakened, there is no consciousness of mind oblivious to self and society, no consciousness of self oblivious to mind and society, no consciousness of society oblivious to mind and self; except, it is sometimes said, under the influence of LSD, or much more plausibly, under rigorous discipline of mysticism, or, much more involuntarily, under the grip of certain extreme forms of "mental illness," or, much more theatrically, under the hold of hypnotic trance. These extraordinary exceptions aside, the integration of consciousness of mind, self and society remains in the ordinary shifts of configuration. Once composed or put together—a process described by Mead—the ensemble or "system" ordinarily holds together. That system—the subject—shifts frequently in configuration, or, as he senses, in conscious mood. But the shift occurs as a whole; the impossibility of segregated consequence is the very meaning of integration, or "system." Thus, however unevenly distributed at the moment of any particular configuration, the illumination of consciousness is spread among its objects; but the spreads differ. One way of understanding this process is to focus on three ordinary, but instructive states, each pointing to a different configuration of integrated ascent. All three are different from the operative mood—the "even keel"—familiar to each of us. That it *is* so familiar to each of us is in large measure due to the commonplace departures. We know even keel because, often enough, we are not there; instead, we exist in one or another configuration of integrated ascent, each commonly sensed. The three exemplary departures from even keel may be termed *being self-conscious, being engrossed* and *being reflective*. Each specifies a shift of consciousness and thus a different configuration of integrated ascent.

Three Moods of Consciousness

Consciousness of mind, self, and society remains and composes each ordinary departure from even keel. Put another way, the objects of consciousness in descent, as well as the one ascending, are contained in all. The shift is only in configuration of the objects—in where each stands in relation to the other in the light of consciousness. Viewed in this way, which object ascends and which descends is not the primary matter. What matters first is where each object stands in relation to the other.

So integrated are shifts of consciousness that as sure a guide to human experience as ordinary language appears somewhat misleading. Actually, however, ordinary language is not misleading; instead, it simply takes for granted what is commonly sensed and, thus, can effect a certain economy. By elaborating the ordinary meaning of key phrases, one can make explicit that which is taken for granted. The loss in economy is matched by the gain in sensible meaning.

In the lay usage, "being self-conscious" does not at all mean being oblivious to mind and society, nor does it imply the conscious use of self to persuade others so celebrated by educators, social workers, Marxists and businessmen. The ordinary meaning of "being self-conscious" takes for granted the maintained consciousness of mind and of society in descent; it is that ordinary meaning that clarifies the mood under discussion. The professional meanings are calls to virtue of a sort and are best referred to as self-service. *That* self-consciousness is not a mood, only a manipulation. Whatever virtue and the disciplined organizations serving it and themselves pretend, ordinary language *knows* that "being self-conscious" is neither the triumph of the self nor even something to hanker after. It is not the self in command; rather, it is the quite ordinary sense of momentarily being ill-at-ease or awkward. *That* being self-conscious, not the self-serving usage, points to a shifting mood that maintains the integrity of consciousness and its playthings, or objects. Self-service is ordinarily done at even keel, though a few people get engrossed in it; even fewer, sad to say, are self-conscious about it.

Being self-conscious is the mind taking notice of the self existing in a peculiar society. Caught in that predicament, consciousness alights on the self. An essential part of being self-conscious is mind being conscious of an immediate and concrete society—one that is right before the subject—that he momentarily exists in. The natural context for being self-conscious is consciousness of a small society that appears untowardly focussed on or, in the terms of Sarte and Merleau-Ponty, "fixed" on the subject. Thus two model situations occur, both presenting the appearance to conscious mind of untoward focus: being stared at, quite a deviation in primitive societies, and still a minor though easily mitigated transgression in the not-so-primitive; and being seriously misplaced, or out of place, quite a mistake in the countryside, and not so good an idea even in metropolis. In those situations, the configuration may shift away from even keel: consciousness alights on the self, but the objects from which it is drained, mind and society, are right there in the mood.

The difference between being stared at and being out of place is very small. A moment's reflection tells us that, being out of place, we stand out and thus stand in danger of being stared at. Hence, in the situation of being misplaced by age, sex, race or anything else that matters, the rapid shift from even keel to being self-conscious first passes through a tiny moment of reflection, the integrated ascent of mind. Either immediately or after a tiny moment's reflection, therefore, mind notices the self being discovered or exposed in a concrete society that was or seemed untowardly focussed or fixed on the subject. In this departure from even keel, the self draws consciousness from its other matters. Being becomes self-conscious.[27] But in so doing, the integration of mind, self and society—the composition of consciousness—is not unduly disturbed; rather, it is *moved as a whole* to a

[27] In two special cases—which can be reduced to one, if one prefers—a bit of a problem occurs. The main question, though, is whether it is a problem for the conception being discussed or the special cases. Celebrities and beautiful women live in a fishbowl—that is their nature in the world. They *ordinarily* stand out and thus are *ordinarily*—actually or reflectively—being stared at. The question, thus, is whether they grow accustomed to their predicament, whether that state of being gradually becomes even keel for them. If so, their operative configuration differs essentially from those of most others. If not, they exist chronically in a sense of being awkward. My guess would be that eventually they grow accustomed, and then exist at an essentially different even keel. The pity, perhaps, is that shortly thereafter the world is no longer so outwardly focussed. Thus, though admittedly self-serving, my suspicion is that the problem lies not in the conception presented, but rather in the lives of celebrities and beautiful women.

somewhat different configuration, and thus a differently sensed and experienced state of being.[28]

Just as consciousness may be drawn to the self, so too, and in the same wholistic manner, it may be drawn to society. To reiterate, I do not mean society, the abstraction. By society, I intend the concrete and immediate society the subject momentarily exists in; I mean his *project*—what he is doing in the world at a moment in time. Subjectively and existentially, the project *is* society. Conscious of society-in-the-project, the mind has already drawn into it the relevant rules, procedures, techniques and sentiments. Except in the mind—if the word may be used loosely—of abstracted sociology, the rules, procedures, techniques and sentiments do not exist elsewhere. They exist in projects, some of which may be written or otherwise displayed. Just as conscious self and mind exist in the project, society exists in it; the project is a concrete repository, conceivable by everyone, for a tiny portion of what abstract society, conceivable only in the most grandiose moments of reflection, has collectively and historically come to. Thus it is that society can be an object of consciousness. In the project, concrete, limited, and immediate, society can be conceived; it is managable. Accordingly, everyone can be and is conscious of society-in-the-project. Whether it be skiing, conversation, selling, baseball, flirtation, plumbing, burgling, writing, political activity, digging, painting, or making love, a consciousness of each society-in-the-project exists in the subject. But at the same time, given integrity, consciousness of the mind and self remains. In the project, consciousness may be drawn to any of the objects. The subject may act at even keel, self-consciously, reflectively, or, if the subject is fortunate, he may just *do* the thing. He may exist temporarily in what according to the most reliable authority—man, himself—is the best of all states of being, the most sought after, the most elusive. Being engaged, the subject is *engrossed* in his project. *Entranced* by the thing he is doing, the subject *loses,* or at least forgets, *himself.* In so doing, the subject is more than ever completely "selfish." In this mood of integrated ascent, in the drawing of consciousness to society, man becomes fully human: He "makes it." That is why Mead—not Freud— poses the more profound relation between man and society. Conceived in society's image, mind and self are at ease when consciousness dwells in the matter used to create them. But the ease and the joy of such experience has nothing to do with conforming or adjusting to society. Almost the opposite: Being entranced is "making *it.*" And to what does "it" refer? The answer seems relatively clear: "it" is society-in-the-project. To "make it" is to create, even if just a very little bit, a revised society-in-the-project. Being engaged, man contributes bits of consciousness to the world; he makes so-

---

[28] A differently conceived discussion of these matters may be found in Erving Goffman, "Embarrassment and Social Organization," *The American Journal of Sociology,* LXII, No. 3 (November 1956), 264–271.

ciety, not abstractly, but in his project. After his penetrating presence, after his *concentration,* that project—whatever its specific character—will never be quite the same. Being engaged in it, being so engrossed as to contribute or add consciousness to it, the subject has helped fashion or make what the project is to become. More simply and directly, he has left his imprint on the project, and thus on the society in it. Altogether, thus, we may observe that *man has made society,* meaning something relatively concrete; he *made it* by concentration, by contributing or adding bits of consciousness to the world when entranced by the thing he was doing. But not being especially generous by nature, and, at any rate, not having much else to rely on, man capitalizes on the collective consciousness spent on man-made society: society-in-the-project is utilized in the incessant project of forming new selves in tiny human organisms, provided with consciousness, as they appear in the world.[29]

As if that were not enough utilization of society-in-the-project, man does one more thing. Using consciousness, he may *reflect* on society and on the self composed from society. Provided with such matters, and reflecting on them, consciousness matures into mind. Thus, consciousness develops yet a third object for alighting: itself grown up, or *mind.* Consciousness focussed on or playing with itself grown up is the final configuration of integrated ascent to be considered; and, as will be apparent, it returns us to the subject in the mood of marihuana. Not so good as being engrossed, it is, one would imagine, at least better than being self-conscious. The pity is that many intelligent people confuse it with being engrossed. And they buttress a confusion that is quite understandable when half-asleep by being that way all the time, or by never really being engrossed; or they play with words saying they are engrossed in the substance and its effects. They do all those things because, being intelligent, they fancy being engrossed.

Of the three, perhaps, being reflective is the mood most difficult to conceive. Partly, this is because of the inherent difficulty in conceiving something that already has doubled up on itself. In reflection, consciousness alights on itself grown into mind; and to seriously consider and then reflect on that possibility is inexorably to begin construction of a mirrored maze. Moreover, mind stores consciousness of past self and society, and even—in service to the self—collaborates in suppressing, or making *less memorable,* disquieting material. Composed from the conscious existence of self in society, mind contains the past history of the objects that figure in any current configuration. This would be no problem if the integrated ascent of mind merely pointed to reverie, but such self-serving playing out of memory is really the least integrated form of being reflective. Done alone, and without self-consciousness, reverie can itself become a rather curious project and

[29] For a discussion of being engrossed in activity, see Erving Goffman, *Interaction Ritual* (Chicago: Aldine Publishing Co., 1967), Chapter 6.

thus something in which the subject can be apparently engrossed. But at best that is a semantic duplicity—at worst, madness. Ordinarily it is simply reverie, about which nothing more need be said.

The more pertinent, and the more integrated ascent of mind occurs in company or other projects beyond simple reverie. These are more difficult to conceive, for the configuration we move to is one in which consciousness is drawn to a mind that stores consciousness of past projects *in the face of yet another* present project. My concern is not with reflectively pausing from the world, as good a definition as any of ordinary reverie, but rather with being reflective *while* doing a thing—while in the world. In that state of being, the things we do take on a strange, though not wholly unfamiliar character, all the more so if the integrated ascent of mind is lightened by a still drowsy and thus a *dim* consciousness. We have now just about returned to "being high," the mood of marihuana. With a ground in sight, we go back to our subject.

The Mood of Marihuana

Half-asleep, the subject is well situated for a shift in mood. Wide-awake, too, his mood may shift, but not quite as easily. Drowsy, the subject's consciousness is more available for relocation and subsequent movement of configuration. Though consciousness may go in the direction of any of its objects in that condition, it is most likely to go *where it is told*. Two features inherent in the common use of marihuana concretely and literally *tell* consciousness to go to mind and thus to be reflective. These features are established in the first few learning experiences. Thereafter, they are instituted in the subject, and thus he can do it himself.[30] The fact of the matter

---

[30] A pharmacological interpretation would probably hold that any shift in the configuration of consciousness is chemically based and reflected in the nervous system. One could hardly disagree. The only issue is whether the neural shift preceeds or follows what consciousness is told to do. Irrespective of which formulation is preferred, it should be apparent that neither relies on the idea of placebo. Even if the phenomenological interpretation is chosen—as opposed to the pharmacological— marihuana is surely not without substance and thus not without consequence. Marihuana makes the subject drowsy; it opens him, more than usual, to a shift in mood; and whether as the result of marihuana, or because of the time-honored tale associated with its use, a shift in mood occurs. Of two things there can be little question: that the shift in mood has a neurological counterpart; and that time-honored tales contain a great deal of substance. Thus, there can be—and should be—a unity of phenomenological and pharmacological interpretation. The time-honored tale merely tells what is somewhat likely to happen anyway, but it enormously increases the likelihood of it happening. Although the experimental test is quite easy to imagine—the fabrication of false tales—it would be nearly impossible to implement. As will become apparent, given what is told, there can *be* no false tale. Anything he is told will lead the subject to the mood of being reflective—even the utterance that he will become engrossed or self-conscious. To be put on notice is a signal for reflection, no matter what you are told to notice.

is that, even before going half-asleep, consciousness has begun shifting in the direction of mind. The subject has been put *on notice*. He has been *told* that something is going to happen. Why else would he be there in the project trying the thing? Consciousness is already at work noticing the self and society through mind. Mere noticing is already a movement in the direction of plain reflection, but thus far, the shift is quite ordinary in two senses. It may be partial: sufficiently close to even keel as to still include the easy possibility of becoming engrossed, self conscious, or return to even keel. Or it may be properly discounted: the kind of reflection that everyone is accustomed to. Nonetheless, the first tale has been told, and the subject has responded accordingly; he is on notice. That done, he is ready to become high.

Once drowsy, the subject is awakened. That is all there is to the second tale. He may wake or alert himself or he may be awakened by others. In either case, he is *told*, by the logic of the situation if not by others, to continue noticing. Since he is not fully asleep, he may even have noticed himself becoming drowsy. Awakening begins to occur in the half-sleep. He is awake to his own drowsiness, and subsequently he will notice, or be told to notice, other symptoms. But *essentially* he is now ready to be awakened to a shift in mood from which everything else he experiences will be derived. *Continuing to be drowsy, and continuing to be reflective,* his consciousness alights on mind in the face of a continued consciousness of self and society. Since the subject is drowsy, his consciousness of all three objects is somewhat dimmed. Since the subject is reflective, consciousness is unevenly drawn to mind. That peculiar combination is the meaning of "being high" on marihuana. The meaning of the phrase "capitalizes" on and then hides a linguistic trick: sleight-of-word. As usual, ordinary language, affecting economy, obscures the context of meaning and the tricks by which it is achieved. Also as usual, however, phrases take on more sensible meaning when the context taken for granted in ordinary language is made explicit. In the interest of clarity, the sleight-of-word must be displayed. Otherwise, people might develop quite a romantic conception of the mood and uses of marihuana—especially students and other intellectuals. As usual, the left bank of naturalism, romance, is almost as misleading as its right opposition, correction.

Being high is an unusual form of being reflective, and the phrase is an expression of that sense. Taken for granted, and thereafter left implicit, or unsaid, is the context of being high; therein lies much of the meaning and the sleight-of-word. In this state of being, the mind is high: consciousness is drawn to it. But the context is low, a diminution of overall consciousness. The configuration has shifted in two senses. The integrated ascent of mind develops within the context of a general diminishing of consciousness. Consciousness of the other objects, self and society, *descends* more quickly than that of mind mainly because the subject has been told to be on notice. Alerted to stay awake, his mind loses consciousness at a considerably slower rate than self and society, the other objects. The sleight-of-word is apparent: Consciousness of mind is "high," even though it is lower *absolutely* than the moment before. In integrated descent, mind ascends since *relatively speaking*—therein lies the sleight-of-word—its descent is slower than that of the other objects in the configuration of consciousness. In this dim reflectivity, reference to a mind being *lightened* would be more informative and accurate than any conjuring of the always remote possibility of mind becoming enlightened. There is an integrated ascent of mind, but in the context of an integrated descent of consciousness. Drowsy throughout, unless "turned off," the subject may capitalize on a linguistic trick and thus accurately refer to his condition as "being high." And as long as he refrains from seriously concentrating his newly found acuity, the subject will delight in how conscious his mind has become of itself and the objects surrounding it. Being high, the subject may now exert his dim reflectivity.

The consequence, it should follow, as it would of any mood, is a *sensibility.* Surface romance and superficial romanticism aside, the sensibility that follows being high is to *banality.* Though banality itself is a most ordinary condition of modern life, a sensibility to it is not. In that very special and limited sense, the mood of marihuana may be regarded as extraordinary. Something extra is added to the *ordinary,* the definition of banality. What is added is sensibility, an appreciation based on a glimpse of how a thing is composed. Thus, the sensibility to banality is the appreciation of the ordinary based on a glimpse of its composition: a precocious and unformulated insight of how the ordinary is put together. For many people, though by no means all, as Becker indicated, such an experience can be pleasurable. The term pleasurable, however, is too general, a bit too broad for the referent. More precise is the term "fun," especially since glimpsing the composition of the ordinary can often be extremely funny.

Once the meaning of banality is clarified, *once a sensibility to it is developed,* we have already moved to Becker's final phase of becoming a marihuana user. The final phase he calls "appreciation," or "learning to enjoy the effects." Everything to be appreciated—all the objects in the "symptoms"—are well covered by the term banal. And appreciation itself —the subject in the "symptoms"—is the very meaning of sensibility. To understand how this curious aesthetic develops, the relation between the dim reflectivity of being high and the sensibility to banality must be further examined, and the composition of ordinary banality (redundancy is, for once, justifiable) must be more seriously assessed, as frivolous as it may seem.

Being high is the mood of dim reflectivity. Consciousness of mind, self and society in descent, that of mind descends more slowly, and thus, relatively speaking, it is ascendant, or "high." The closest the subject comes to expressing the double and complicated shift of configuration is sometimes to say he feels "light-headed"—not so very far from the truth, all things considered. That truth, rendered as well as can be reasonably expected by the subject, is *internally* consequential. The sensibility to banality to be displayed in the world follows from, develops from, the internal consequence of the doubly altered configuration of consciousness of mind, self and society.

What is the internal consequence of being "light-headed"—the doubly altered configuration of consciousness? At this point, if not already, the reader's willing suspension of disbelief will be strained beyond its probable breaking-point. My only defense, it should become apparent, is that he will be asked to do no more than the subject must do if he is to become sensible to banality. The only difference is that the reader must momentarily suspend disbelief while the subject suspends belief. If either refuses, the composition of the ordinary and a sensibility to it will remain incomprehensible. In other words, both reader and subject must allow relativity to have its say.

A link between "being high," or more specifically being "light-minded," and a sensibility to the ordinary must be provided. To suggest the character of that link is to ask the reader to believe that the mind not only can be conscious of itself—not an especially unreasonable request, but also that, *dimly,* the mind can be conscious of the current configuration in which it exists, however curiously altered, however deviously come to. Consciousness-in-mind *pictures* the whole mood—the current configuration and how it came to be—*conceives* it and *projects* it into the world as *sensibility*. The internal consequence of being high, the link, casts *its* shadow on the world. The way in which that internal state is dimly conceived will be enough to create the suspension of belief necessary for an emergent sensibility to banality. Conceived in relativity, the configuration is conceived *as* relativity. How in the world can the mind be dimly conscious of the configuration in which it exists and the tricky or devious manner by which it got there? In the same way, perhaps, that it knew enough to provide ordinary language with the expression "being high" when mind, absolutely, was low; and in the same way mind inspires an ordinary language to take relativity for granted in the sleight-of-word. But there is a simpler way of resolving this apparent puzzle: the whole mood—the configuration of consciousness and how it became or got there—*is* the perception. It is the way we view the world. Since the ascent of mind of this configuration exists only in relativity, it has little choice but to peer out at or perceive the world *as* relativity. In dim reflectivity, thus, relativity will be projected in the world as a special sensibility. Conceived by *relatively speaking*—the only way the mind could devise to picture what was happening to the configuration in which it exists—relativity commences to have its say.[31]

All that remains now is a coincidence to connect dim reflectivity with a sensibility to banality: what relativity says, how it peers on the world, must be suited to, must *match* the composition of banality in the world. Obviously, the coincidence—the perfect match—is hardly coincidental. The method by which banality is put together is precisely the method that is suspended by the human perception of relativity. Relativity suspends *belief,* and belief is the method by which the ordinary is composed.

For something to become ordinary it must be taken for granted. That taking for granted is all I mean by belief.[32] Things become ordinary, or banal, by being alienated from their history, meaning, or form—in short, from their context. Ordinary, they are seen purely as surface. An ordinary chair is just a chair; it possesses no character, it wasn't made by anyone, was never designed, was never anyone's project, does not affect nearby objects, does not bear any relation to the thing next to it. To take the chair for granted, to believe in it, is to render it empty of human meaning. In the somewhat stilted terms of phenomenology, the chair is *bracketed;* henceforth it will not be an object for reflection. It will be believed in or trusted on its face. Unless antiquated, another thing altogether, the chair becomes *unappreciable.* What lies behind the appearance, its human meaning—an obvious definition of essence—is suppressed or lost from view. A good thing, too; otherwise, we'd never get on with the business of the everyday world. We'd be forever hung up on all the meaning around us. We should incessantly say in the wondrous manner of the child—or marihuana user— "Golly gee! Look at that chair!" Or, more generically, of everything we should say, *"fancy that!"* We would fancy everything and almost never get engrossed in the world's business.

What does relativity say that suspends belief? One thing can be certain: it does not say everything is appearance. That is sophistry, and it leads to the sophomoric view that nothing has essential meaning, the very *opposite* of what relativity, in a seemingly losing battle, struggled to convey. Relativity tells us that everything exists in a context, and that the context is equivalent to the meaning or essence of the appearance. In saying that, of course, relativity merely reflects the bias of its own origin. The way it was conceived—the doubly shifting configuration—is not only its perception, or

---

[31] This may all sound like word-magic. Such a charge would be true, but misdirected. There is a magic in words, utilized by the subject through much of his life. How the magic works seems reasonably self-evident: Once a thing is conceived in a word, something transcending both has emerged and has a life of its own. That something is a conception; with it man composes his world and, like any good magician, hides his hand.

[32] To imbue belief with more profound meaning somewhat misses the point, and leads inexorably—as happened historically—to giving marihuana its bad name— the devil's substance.

window on the world; it is its *commentary,* or sensibility. But when one is half-asleep, all of these remain dim. Thus rarely, if ever, is the sensibility fully evident or recognized by the subject. There is a glimmer, a dim and precocious intuition of the composition of banality, an appreciation of *part* of the taken-for-granted or suspended meaning of the ordinary. But even if partly, belief is suspended by the perception of relativity. That done, context or meaning will be on display to be perceived by the subject.

Lest the reader romantically misinterpret my remarks, a number of reminders are in order, all implicitly taken for granted by those who use marihuana without abusing it: the perception of relativity, based as it is in dim reflectivity, is human and needs no chemical inspiration; the sensibility to banality is fickle and thus often unconsummated with respect to any particular object; the meaning that lies behind the ordinary glimpsed by the perception of relativity is what we have known all along but taken for granted. The three reminders taken together should indicate its nature to users and prohibitors alike: *Marihuana should not be taken seriously.* Whoever takes it seriously mistakes and thus abuses its nature: fun. As usual, correction and romance conspire, taking opposite roads that lead in the same direction—away from the nature of things. How could they do otherwise? Neither believes that things have a human nature. That correction leads to prohibition, and romance to celebration is hardly surprising. The respective abuses are in their nature.

Becker's rendition avoids both correction and romance. The experience of being high is neither wild nor profound. Instead, it is experienced by some as "pleasurable," or as suggested more specifically, as "fun." The fun of marihuana use is the sensibility to banality made possible by the perception of relativity, suspension of belief, and the consequent display of meaning—all directed to whatever happens to be around the mind of the subject. Belief suspended, an aesthetic of the ordinary may appear. The unappreciable may be appreciated. Thus, any object may attract the fancy of the subject; at even keel, they all have suspended meaning. The "symptoms" of being high, therefore, are in principle infinite, the only limitation being the environment of mind. Meaning restored, and glimpsed, the ordinary becomes extraordinary. Music may be heard as wholly musical, possessing tempo, melody and other elements of *its* composition; water may be experienced as wholly thirst-quenching; fire as wholly burning, shimmering and glowing; pictures as representations projected in the world by someone who saw things that way; expectations, say, to engage continually in conversation as just that—expectation; long silence as acceptable, inoffensive and meaningful; food as appetizing and tasty; time as wholly a matter of ebb and flow, punctuated not by clock but the movement or *tempo* of experience; sex as sensual, or even sexual; jokes—if well composed—as wholly funny; if not, as terribly flat; conversation as an oscillation of relevance and irrelevance;

and so on, indefinitely. Irrespective of the object of dim attention, a similar apprehension appears: the child's "golly, gee!" Part of the meaning of ordinary things is uncovered, recovered or discovered. But still covered or obscured in the mood of dim reflectivity is the most wondrous aspect of a sensibility to banality—the conscious realization that the subject knew the meaning of the ordinary all along.[33] Therein lies the illusory character of marihuana use. Since he is *dimly* conscious, the secret way in which the world composes the ordinary eludes the subject. By taking for granted that the sensibility derives *from marihuana*—by instituting belief *in it*—the user loses the possibility of retrieving the more profound alienation: the human meaning that is regularly suppressed in the taking for granted or belief by which the ordinary is composed. Thus viewed, the illusory character of marihuana use may be summarized without implying a conception of placebo: The display of meaning was always there implicit in the ordinary, right before our eyes but suppressed through belief, or suspended meaning; through the use of marihuana and its consequence of "being high," the display of meaning becomes apparent since belief is suspended; by connecting the display of meaning with the substance, marihuana, the process by which it is achieved itself becomes taken for granted, reified or "bracketed"; its human meaning is lost. Restored to even keel, the method of composing the ordinary—belief—is as evasive and effective as ever, and thus our sensibility to banality remains obtuse—unless, of course, the subject becomes conscious of the human nature of the whole process. In the literal and thus profound sense, the whole thing is a trick; the mind working its magic over the matter it is formed from. Marihuana makes the subject drowsy; *he* takes it from there.[34]

But there is another side to a sensibility to banality that, simultaneously, testifies to the precarious and delicate psychosomatic foundations of "being high" and points to part of the reason that many persons dislike the experience and find it anything but fun. Being high can be quite easily interfered with or disturbed. Many objects of reflection, including the self, are freshly or meaningfully experienced under the perception of relativity, since belief in them is suspended. Perceiving most objects in that novel manner almost certainly implies pleasure or fun. But there is one object that poses a special problem and thus, potentially, a main exception: other people. Viewed wholly—viewed in the terms of "Golly, gee!"—some people can sometimes be an enormous "drag." Though it need not, a sensibility to that reality—the most ordinary of the world's banalities—may "turn off" the

---

[33] Certain advanced elements of the "hippy," or drug community have allegedly achieved that level of consciousness. When they do, drugs are no longer necessary.

[34] To reiterate, this does not at all imply that no neurological traces could be found, reflecting the curious shift of consciousness. The error, I think, is in viewing the traces as independent, or prior to what is happening to consciousness.

user. The less accomplished the user, the less used he is to the method of marihuana and its mood, the more likely he is to be "turned off." If *very* unused to it, he may be "turned off" permanently, deciding quite understandably that the experience is *not* fun. If only slightly accomplished, he may be "turned off" for that evening. Still drowsy, he will be restored to something very much like even keel, despite the substance. But even keel may be sensed as unpleasant *because* of the substance. If somewhat more accomplished, the user may see that though some people are wholly a drag, their ability to drag depends wholly on *his* continued presence. That understood, the subject may wisely use two options always open to the drowsy —especially when they have seen that expectations are just that, only expectations: he may leave for another part of the world, nearby or far off, or he may fall fast asleep, exerting a most fitting way of coping with someone perceived as wholly a drag. And if the subject is even more accomplished, if he is well-used to the method of marihuana and its mood, he may understand that it is almost as easy to "turn off" a drag as to be "turned off" by one. Dimly reflective, he may observe to himself: "Fancy that! Here is someone who is wholly a drag." After considering *that* banality for awhile, he may move to some other object. The accomplished user will have "turned off" the "drag," providing, of course, he is not followed by him. But, being a "drag," he may well do that. Thus, the necessity for a mental note about persons whose presence intrudes and disturbs the delicate and precarious mood of being high. The mental note instituted as a consequential feature, marihuana users tend to be quite selective in the company they keep or invite. That selectivity is not just for reasons of security—though it certainly speaks to that issue too. For internal reasons of maintaining the delicate mood of "being high," as well as the external reasons of maintaining security, the company of marihuana users tends strongly to become cultish. Why do it, it may be asked, if it's going to be a drag?

Banality appreciated and its inherent weakness—a drag—checked, the subject has become a marihuana user, but, still, only in a tentative and limited way. There are more terms and issues to be met in the process of becoming a marihuana user, only one of which is the rather obvious but crucial matter of getting the substance. (It is, after all, poor manners to be a guest continually.) But the additional terms and issues, dealt with by Becker in the companion essay, "Marihuana Use and Social Control," all derive from a predicament of marihuana use that is somewhat different from those connected with affiliation: in America, the substance is "deviant." It is proscribed, banned or signified; it is under "social control." That reality—the state and its apparatus—poses another set of terms and issues that will also shape the open process through which the subject proceeds; it provides another set of matters for him to consider continually. *But they will not be separate matters.* Just as the meaning of affinity was built—not forgotten—

in the process of affiliation, its meaning will be built further in the process of signification. Affiliation, too, will develop new meaning.[35]

Before proceeding to the part of signification in becoming deviant, a brief word of explanation is required in bringing to a close the chapter on affiliation. Briefly, was the choice of marihuana use to exemplify the process of affiliation and its human method of conversion a good one? Is not marihuana use too "druggy" an example to represent the general part played by affiliation in becoming deviant? Does my example illuminate or obscure the general process of affiliation and its part in whole process of becoming deviant?

My answer, as evasive as it may appear is yes and no; yes, because any special deviation will have features unique to it; no, because the "general part played by affiliation" is an abstraction, which must be composed or constructed from a multitude of specific deviations. Every affiliation with specific deviation, every conversion to its terms, issues and viewpoint will bear the mark of that deviation. But the truth of specificity simply enforces the truth of generality, since it is its other side. The *general* truth of affiliation and its human method of conversion is that the *subject mediates the process of becoming.* The *specific* truth of affiliation and its human method of conversion is that the subject mediates the process of becoming *in the terms and issues provided by the concrete matters before him.* Thus, we may conclude that becoming a marihuana user is like nothing else and everything else.

[35] If the model presented by Neil Smelser is appropriately termed value-added, I suppose the one suggested here might be called "value-multiplied." Aside from the dubious arithmetic difference, not especially relevant in any case, there is a difference between the two approaches. Though hardly necessary in its development, the approach of value-added has not taken the subject and the matters of concrete concern to him as the prime social datum. In that sense, the approach developed by Smelser is quite "objective" and, not surprisingly, "scientific." For discussion of the value-added approach, see Neil Smelser, *Theory of Collective Behavior* (New York: The Free Press of Glencoe, Inc., 1963). For an attempt to apply the same model to deviant behavior, see Marvin Scott, "Value-added Theory of Delinquency," paper read at the Annual Meeting of the American Sociological Association, Chicago, 1965.

7

Signification

That anyone—sociologists especially—could write as if the authoritative fact of ban was of minor importance in the process of becoming deviant is hardly believable. To ignore the impact of ban is tantamount to suggesting that Leviathan can be irrelevant in the lives of the ordinary men who fall within its oppressive ambit. One could suggest that, of course; and, tacitly, most sociologists have—but not without first becoming more or less one-eyed.

The scholar's or scientists's way of becoming partially blind is, inadvertently perhaps, to structure fields of inquiry in such a way as to obscure obvious connections or to take the connections for granted and leave the matter at that. The great task of disconnection—it was arduous and time-consuming—fell to the positive school of criminology. Among their most notable accomplishments, the criminological positivists succeeded in what would seem the impossible. They separated the study of crime from the workings and theory of the state.[1] That done, and the lesson extended to deviation generally, the agenda for research and scholarship for the next half-century was relatively clear, especially with regard to what would *not* be studied. Scientists of various persuasion thereafter wandered aimfully, leaving just a few possibilities uncovered, considering how deviation was

[1] For a brief discussion of the positive school, see my *Delinquency and Drift* (New York: John Wiley & Sons, Inc., 1964), Chapter 1.

produced. Throughout, a main producer remained obscure, off-stage due to the fortunate manner in which fields of inquiry were divided. The role of the sovereign, and by extension, instituted authority was hardly considered in the study of deviant behavior. That lofty subject, unrelated to so seamy a matter as deviation, was to be studied in *political* science. There, as in the curriculum in government or political sociology, Leviathan had little bearing on ordinary criminals. And in criminology, the process of becoming an ordinary criminal was unrelated to the workings of the state. It was, it must be granted, a pretty neat division.

Even later, when the neglected producers of deviation began being brought to account in the premature contributions of Tannenbaum and in the work of Lemert, Goffman, Becker, Erikson and others, the effort seemingly struggled against the ordinary context of inquiry. Their contributions were to be absorbed into a tradition of inquiry whose first premise was a separation of crime and state; thus, the absorbtion was not without a certain measure of distortion and misfit. Left unassaulted, the historic misconception of the positive school—the separation of crime and state—could remain the cornerstone of a sociological study of deviation that heeded the possibility that the correctional system's effects sometimes boomeranged. But as long as the misconception maintained, such a possibility could be regarded as easily rectified instead of as a profound irony lodged in the very nature of the intimate relation between crime and the state. Thus, while still basically out of context, law, police discretion, total institutions, and "labeling" could be taken into account by the sociologists reading and often applauding the work of the neoChicagoans.

Until the relation between organized authority and crime became a topic of conjecture and research, a crucial part of the process of becoming deviant was omitted. Outside the context of its central part in the very conception of crime and deviation, its key role in the selection of those destined to continue becoming deviant, and its ancient but amazingly resilient commitment to the method of penalization, the state's relation to deviation was easily conceived as *correction*—with due allowance made for deficiency of knowledge, inefficiency, corruption, or mistake. In context, as one might expect, its role has been a bit more devious and even in principle not so beneficent. So potent an apparatus as Leviathan should display its effects in manifold ways and even on those not yet patently in its grip. One need not be in prison to be affected by Leviathan; nor must Leviathan be a police-state to cast a shadow over its subjects.

This connection between the organized, though diversified authority of state and becoming deviant is the broadest meaning of signification I want to consider. Persons unrelated to organized authority may signify too, but not so potently, or meaningfully. Besides, non-authoritative members of society who choose to collaborate in the control of deviant behavior can be discounted or otherwise put in place—at least in principle. Strictly speaking, it's none of their business—and all the more so as the signification of deviation becomes a specialized and protected function of the modern state. The main substance of that state function is the authorized ordaining of activities and persons as deviant, thus making them suitable objects of surveillance and control.[2] However awesome the state apparatus and however active its agents may be in affecting deviation, the same general principle developed in the discussion of affiliation will maintain here: The subject mediates the process of becoming. Confronted with a more mighty authority, however—Leviathan and not that of mere peers—the subject's authority over the process may be dwarfed. That diminution is part of the process—when it works well. Thus it will not do to anticipate the conclusion of the entire process and prematurely place the subject in chains. It makes considerably more sense to begin where the subject was left at the end of the last chapter—presiding over the process by which he affiliated with a deviant activity. However, his affiliation with marihuana use as described there was more or less *innocent*. Before considering anything else, I must elaborate, for in truth the marihuana user is already guilty, though only in a certain sense. To make that correction, we turn to the first element of signification —ban—and its meaning. Afterwards, we may consider *apprehension*—its more patently consequential aspect.[3]

[2] In considering the part played by signification in the process of becoming deviant, there is little necessity to denounce the state or accuse it of unwarranted oppression. All that is required is an appreciation of uncontested aspects of its rudimentary nature and consequences—elements of state conceded by conservative and liberal political theorists alike. Furthermore, no slight is intended in using the term Leviathan; after all, Hobbes was commending, not condemning, the contrivance that would achieve a unity of meaning and thus order in society. Finally, connecting the state with the oppressive business of signification in no way implies that that is its only work. The state organizes welfare, makes wars and does many things in between. The important matter here is that we not be unduly misled or otherwise confused because state agents and spokesmen sometimes call internal control and other elements of signification "welfare." Recently, our capacity to see through that deception has been inadvertently augmented by what is otherwise an ugly and brutal affair: other spokesmen for the same state have taken to conceiving war, too, in the honeyed terms of the welfare and correction of far-off peoples who have allegedly wandered from the righteous path. To complete the mystification, perhaps, yet other spokesmen of the very same state have begun to conceive of their modest welfare program in terms of a "war." Instead of rendering us fully dizzy, it may be hoped that so curious a concatenation of misused terms will prove instructive and help restore a closer correspondence of words and things.

[3] A final aspect of signification, penalization in the form of imprisonment or institutionalization will not be considered in this discussion. It is omitted for two reasons: it has already received adequate treatment in the numerous studies of institutional life and, more pertinent, my main concern is with the establishment of an identity deviant enough to be deemed unsuited for ordinary civil life. Imprisonment for crime and hospitalization for mental illness are clear signals that from the viewpoint of authority deviation has become established. Penalization confirms the belief that the main part of the process of becoming deviant has been concluded.

Ban: Being Bedeviled

Whatever the deficiencies of using marihuana to exemplify the affiliation process, it should be clear that few deviations provide a sterner test of the significance of ban. Despite its increasingly acknowledged benign character and a concomitant increase in dissent as to the propriety of prohibition, despite a solidary and thus supportive pattern of use including even a romantic apologia, the fact of authoritative ban casts an unmistakable shadow on the moral status of marihuana use. If ban makes even marihuana use shady, that it has the same effect on other less controversial deviations may be more or less assumed. Consequently, the task of elaborating the consequences of the first element of signification, ban, is greatly simplified: marihuana can be used to stand for or exemplify general deviation.

That ban imbues an activity with guilt is hardly surprising or unintentional. The moral transformation of activity is the purpose of ban; the simplest way of summarizing the legislative and purportedly public intention is to predict that with time the activity will exist in guilt. This need not mean that the guilt of banned activity inevitably rubs off on the subjects or that they do not eventually get over their initial trepidation and unease; but it does indicate a number of manifest tendencies and thus matters to be considered by the attentive subject. That the guilt of banned activity may be managed or perhaps even neutralized testifies to the eventual capacities of the subject and not to the inconsequentiality of the sovereign's intention.[4] The consequences of ban may be manifold and mixed but their serious consideration requires that we begin with the phenomenon as it morally exists— guilty. Only when that is granted may the social responses of participating subjects be traced.[5]

[4] The definition of signification suggested by Berger and Luckmann is especially appropriate in this regard though perhaps it is wanting in other respects. Signification, they said, "is the human production of signs." And a sign "may be distinguished from other objectivations by its implicit intention to serve as an index of subjective meanings." A ban is a potent and explicit example of just such an intention. See Peter Berger and Thomas Luckmann, *The Social Construction of Reality* (New York: Doubleday and Company, Inc., 1966), p. 34. For an excellent literary treatment of the unease associated with the initial stages of becoming a pimp, see Colin McInnes, *Mr. Love and Justice* (London: MacGibbon and Kee, 1960).

[5] Occasionally, the impact of ban may be thoroughly negated; usually it is contended or coped with. Such a negation is infrequent because wholly to negate the impact of ban at issue—making the activity guilty—requires a sustained growth of collective consciousness of the oppressive relations between the state and its subjects culminating in a sense of local autonomy or cultural separatism. Thus, an attitude of virtual innocence in the face of public ban is best viewed as culturally revolutionary and though such things happen, as in the case, say, of isolated centers of

The consequence of ban on those who refrain from participating in deviant activity—the right-minded—may be dismissed quickly, and one aspect of the endless squabble regarding the effectiveness of deterrence thereby avoided. A self-evident consequence of so moral an act as ban is to restrict and discourage access to the designated phenomenon at its invitational edge. An inculcated attitude of avoidance is intended by the sovereign and it would be the height of folly to imagine that a ban did no work toward that end. As an example, one need only speculate on the relative incidence of cigarette smoking—announced as dangerous and potentially deadly but not banned—and that of marihuana use—denounced in much less direct terms but banned—to grasp the appreciable achievement of the intended attitude of avoidance. To keep the right-minded away from guilty phenomena is a main purpose of banning and it should be clear that the argument against the deterrent capacity of ban speaks to a different issue when framed properly, and hardly discounts the relative ease with which the righteous are kept that way. Opposition to the devil, too, may thus be given its due.[6]

Fortunately, the really relevant issue in the controversy regarding the effectiveness of deterrence is the one currently before us: the consequence of ban on those sufficiently wrong-minded to have tried the activity anyway. Properly put, obviously, the issue is *not* whether or not they will be deterred. That question answers itself—in the world if not elsewhere. Ban did not deter the wrong-minded; they did the activity anyway. But that incontestable failure hardly exhausts the consequences of ban. Leviathan may have its say even when disobeyed. In making the activity guilty, Leviathan bedevils the subject as he proceeds and thus is partly compensated for its gross failure to deter. Gradually, the mistake of innocent affiliation is rectified. Under an authority more weighty than his own, the subject will come to act as if innocent affiliation with guilty activity is untenable—even if he does not see it in

---

bohemian experimentation with drugs, it is best not to generalize from what is almost surely an esoteric exception. The usual fate of participants in banned activity is much more prosaic: their consciousness never expands or otherwise develops. A discussion of levels of consciousness in rebellious activity and their relevance is a main contribution of E. J. Hobsbaum in *Primitive Rebels* (New York: W. W. Norton & Company, Inc., 1959).

[6] The proportion of a particular population that will scrupulously heed a ban is variable and obviously difficult to estimate. But that does not mean that the righteous are negligible in number. One *minimal* estimate, perhaps instructive, may be derived from a study of compliance with traffic signals in which full stopping motivated by considerations of safety arising from the peril of cross-traffic was discounted. After all, we might not wish to count among the righteous those who perhaps merely wanted to avoid breaking their necks. The study, based on direct observation of drivers, concluded that about 15–20 per cent of the driving population are clearly righteous with regard to stopping fully: they stop because the sign says so. See Johannes Feest, "Compliance with Legal Regulations: Observation of Stop Sign Behavior," *Law and Society Review*, II, No. 3 (May 1968), 447–461.

precisely that way and despite the fact that he and his collaborators may claim to see little guilt in the activity.

Ban bedevils the subject in a very concrete way. Working arduously, it virtually guarantees that further disaffiliation with convention will be a concomitant of affiliation with deviation; put slightly differently, that the scope or range of disaffiliation will surpass or go beyond the amount implicit in the deviation itself. The logic of ban creates the strong possibility that the subject will become even more deviant in order to deviate. In its effect on the wrong-minded, ban compounds disaffiliation and thus contributes to the process of becoming deviant—unless, of course, the subject reconsiders the entire matter and returns to a righteous path.

Ban hardly makes commitment to a deviant path inevitable; it only assures the compounding of deviation as long as the path is maintained.[7] Such a consequence is neither surprising nor unintended. A main purpose of ban is to unify meaning and thus to minimize the possibility that, morally, the subject can have it both ways. Either he will be deterred or bedeviled. And by bedeviled, I mean nothing mysterious—merely, being made a devil as a result of being put in a position wherein more deviation and disaffiliation than was originally contemplated appears in the life of the subject. Bedevilment must be counted a product of ban on the wrong-minded; surely, it does not result from an internal proclivity of deviation to reproduce.

The compounding of deviation and the subject's further disaffiliation from convention are among the topics of Becker's second essay, "Marihuana Use and Social Control."[8] Everything considered in that essay flows from the existence of ban. Though apprehension and penalization, the less likely elements of signification are also operative, they are hardly necessary. Ban is sufficient, though, of course, ban itself plainly includes the other possibilities as subjective anticipation. That is a key meaning of ban, as is well known to the subject. Attentive to the methods of Leviathan even before their concrete appearance, the wrong-minded subject acts in terms of them. He takes into account the meaning of ban and, for that reason, proceeds to become somewhat more deviant.

The three issues faced by the subject as posed in Becker's summary of the impact of social control on marihuana use are supply, secrecy and morality. Each flows from the fact of ban; each, when resolved *within a context of continued use,* deprives the activity of the innocence of abstract affiliation. By maximizing his safety, by consciously accommodating to the reality

---

[7] The view that signification through one or another of its elements commits the subject to deviation is common and represents yet another attempt to graft the idea of preordination onto a human process.

[8] Howard Becker, *Outsiders* (New York: The Free Press of Glencoe, Inc., 1963), Chapter 4.

of guilty activity, the subject may begin to build the fuller meaning of being deviant. As a guest at an informal gathering at which marihuana happened to be used, the subject would be in no position to become familiar with the meaning of that state. Besides, being so occupied with considering his affinity with marihuana, he would be too busy perhaps to consider the more general moral question of being deviant.

Outside the informal gathering, though sometimes during it, the subject begins to encounter the issues flowing from the fact of social control, or ban. Presented in a variety of ways, the issues can hardly be avoided, since their context and source is the frequently insinuated existence of the state. So immersed is the subject in the context of state that no sequence in the appearance of issues can be posited. Issues simply appear and a resolution must be devised by the subject as he continues his still ordinary life within a society regulated by a state that has chosen to ban something he is doing. In devising a resolution, the mistaken belief in the possibility of innocent affiliation is rectified. Thus, the state's project of correction begins long before the subject is apprehended and irrespective of whether he ever is. A first order of business for Leviathan in its corrective project is to deter the possibility of innocent affiliation with guilty activity. Otherwise, the subject would be unprepared for meaningful apprehension. To prepare the subject for what might happen to him and to put him in a properly guilty frame of mind, he should be bedeviled. His sense of wrong-doing should not be limited to the occasional commission of a single deviation. Its meaning should spread a bit, permeate brief periods, at least, of his conventional existence.

Being bedeviled is an inner experience though its outward manifestations enhance the deviant subject's adaptation to social control. These adaptive maneuvers are stressed by Becker in his discussion of secrecy. Once the neophyte has gone beyond occasional indulgence and become a regular user, he must concern himself with appearances in public when under the influence of marihuana. No more than a brief excerpt from Becker's summary is necessary. He explained:

> If a person uses marihuana regularly and routinely it is almost inevitable . . . that he one day find himself high while in the company of nonusers from whom he wishes to keep his marihuana use secret. Given the variety of the symptoms the drug may produce, it is natural for the user to fear that he might reveal through his behavior that he is high, that he might be unable to control the symptoms and thus give away his secret. Such phenomena as difficulty in focusing one's attention and in carrying on normal conversation create a fear that everyone will know exactly why one is behaving this way, that the behavior will be interpreted automatically as a sign of drug use.[9]

[9] *Ibid.*, pp. 69–70.

How such fears may be managed may be worth elaborating, but first the user should be considered at a much earlier point in the process. Still a neophyte or at most an occasional user, the issue of secrecy nonetheless appears to the subject though in a somewhat different manner. That secrecy matters so early in the process of becoming affiliated, that the subject internally experiences the risk of discovery, and that he does so outside the context of use or overt danger is cogent evidence of the profound impact of ban.

Transparency

Before any necessity of keeping or managing his secret when high, the subject faces the problem of keeping or managing it when *not* high. Aware in most instances that he need not keep it from everyone, a question still remains: *from whom must it be kept?* Beneath that question, though perhaps suggested by it, lies one that is more basic: *can the secret be kept at all?* That childish question raises the primeval issue of human transparency, an issue that for good reason is rarely resolved to the complete or final satisfaction of the subject. Under the spell of ban, the deviant subject almost surely senses himself as transparent, if only for a time. But though ban is implicated it would be improper to give it full credit. Ban merely provides the facilitating context. It is the subject who causes his own sense of transparency.

Taken for granted, the sense of transparency may be suppressed or overlooked despite the fact that it is the best evidence of ban's enormous potency and despite its considerable consequence. Occurring within the subject, and for reasons of personal security commonly excluded from ordinary discourse, a feeling experienced by almost everyone is lost from public view. Moreover, the sense of transparency is eventually managed and overcome—though it may return when new deviations are essayed. Consequently, the subject may himself forget the experience and tacitly conspire in the public process by which a prime instrument of social control is lost from view. Even if recalled—something everyone does when reminded—the experience may be seen as too fleeting to be taken seriously; but it should be. Being bedeviled is no small matter even if eventually managed, and a first signal of being bedeviled is the common fear that we appear in the world looking that way.

Conscious of ban, and conscious that he has flaunted it, the subject becomes self-conscious. Little else need be assumed to raise the possibility of human transparency. Neither morbid personality nor mystical predilection seem necessary, though both help. The concerns underlying the fear of transparency are quite ordinary and are based on the common understanding that social communication occurs through inadvertent cues, gestures and expressions as well as plain talk, on the common sense that the subject may "give himself away."

Few things are more difficult to achieve than the certainty of possessing a poker-face. Before gaining the confidence of persistent self-possession, the fear that we can be seen through is nagging. And even when confidence is gained, keeping a poker-face is rarely an effortless activity. Internally, the violator of ban is in a situation analogous to that of a bluffer. Both are liars. High no longer, he reenters the world acting as if the hand he held a short time ago did not include marihuana. He acts that way even if no one asks him. For a brief period, perhaps only episodically, the subject is "on."[10] He assumes the face of one who shortly before did nothing out of the ordinary. In that way he makes an appearance in the world—a bluffer, he exists slightly bedeviled.

To work at being opaque is in its very nature conducive to being sensitive to the possibility of being transparent. The heightened sensitivity to the possibility of being transparent may be thought of as yet another mood of consciousness. Reinforced by tales spun for children—Pinnochio for instance—transparency is an internal replica of Leviathan's desired vision of the subject who violates its law: omniscience. So conceived, a sense of transparency depends on the mediation of consciousness, and not necessarily on the pangs of conscience. It is a mood in which consciousness alights rapidly back and forth between its objects—self and society. That shifting back and forth is all there need be to the sense of transparency. Consequently, the subject may experience the mood irrespective of how he resolves the moral issues before him. Even though he views himself as one who has done nothing especially wrong, there is still the problem of whether he can be *recognized* as the kind of person who has done that thing. When among the right-minded, the subject may sense his transparency. He may avoid that possibility by increasingly avoiding them, but such disaffiliation is an even more potent way of compounding deviation. In one way or another, Leviathan bedevils the undeterred subject; it will even get him to collaborate actively toward so righteous an end.

The possibility of hiding from righteous scrutiny—of being opaque— is subverted by the conscious existence of society in mind. This need not mean that the subject always, or even often, experiences himself as transparent. But such a sense may occur when something leads consciousness to oscillate so rapidly between self and society that the two are taken together. In this way the subject may experience a heightened awareness of the society within himself. Internally, the subject *is* transparent. Though no one else

10 See Sheldon L. Messinger, Harold Sampson and Robert Towne, "Life as Theater: Some Notes on One Dramaturgic Approach to Social Reality," *Sociometry*, XXV, No. 1 (March 1962), 98–110.

may suspect it, he projects that appearance into the world—or so he fears.[11] Fully aware of Leviathan's attitude toward marihuana use, the subject may keep in mind society's ban. And fully aware that he has used marihuana, though perhaps only once, that fact too exists in the self kept in mind by the subject. Not immediately or without good reason, but on an appropriate occasion soon after use, the two facts will be brought together, or commemorated. Unless he hides in his room, the subject is bound to encounter a situation that will occasion a commemoration.

Far from depending on an extrasensory capacity of persons to read each other's mind and thus mutually guess recent activities, the fear of transparency rests on the prosaic but nagging uncertainty regarding the limits of ordinary human sensibility.[12] The only mind-reading required of others and the only capacity imputed to them is a sensibility to the cues emitted by the deviant subject and the appearance projected by him. And at the basis of mind-reading or diminished versions of that sensibility is the subject's own tendency to "give himself away." In fearing transparency, the subject fears *himself* along with others. As Santayana suggested, woman's intuition rests on man's propensity to feed it.

In association with the right-minded, the deviant subject may consider whether he has given himself away when talk approaches things he has done or the authority he has acted against. On those occasions a coincidence prompts concern. Reflecting the internal connection of a fused consciousness of self with society is the outer proximity of human beings: the intricate and sensitive network of gestural cues, shifting eyes, tell-tale expression, nervous avoidance, assiduous interest, informational slips and everything else that composes the sensibility of suspicion. The subject has himself wondered about others; why would he not wonder whether they wonder about him? Thus, the coincidence: an inner and outer proximity of self with society work toward the same end—a mood of transparency.

The deviant subject's new perspective on ordinary conversation may be more or less guaranteed by his new position—known only to himself—in the participating circle. Consider an innocent and abstract discussion of the appropriate deviation among the right-minded who can hardly avoid the topic if at all exposed to the mass media. Our subject has engaged in such talk before using marihuana and is at least as likely to encounter it after-

---

[11] Folk beliefs, being part of vulgar or common knowledge, take subtle processes and render them in remarkably simplified form. A most common means is the substantiation of the spiritual and ethereal. Thus, the reality of a continued hold of the dead upon the living is given substance in ghosts and haunts; just so, the reality of human transparency is given substance, in vulgar tradition, by the belief, say, that the solitary sin of self-abuse will become public in the form of facial complexion or manual disfigurement. In both senses the phenomenon of human transparency is substantiated in the common sense.

[12] See Tamotsu Shibutani, *Society and Personality* (Englewood Cliffs, N.J.: Prentice-Hall, Inc., 1961), pp. 139–140.

wards. But *now,* the neophyte deviant stands in a different relation to the discussion and the chatty participants.[18] Relatively speaking, he has become something of an expert—if only he could reveal his activity. Whether the talk is about burglary, homosexuality, infidelity, armed robbery, prostitution or consorting with prostitutes, premarital pregnancy or marihuana use, the subject who has experienced each begins to sense how little the participants know about the matter under discussion. They take on the appearance of outsiders; in limited measure, the subject has been inside the phenomenon at issue. The temptation to flaunt his superior knowledge is easy enough to restrain; that tiny bit of enforced modesty is neither unusual nor hard to come by. The feature of interaction that seems most consequential is that the subject must continue being cagy; he must persist at managing himself throughout the conversation. He watches himself to be sure he behaves naturally or casually: at the precise level of involvement, with the exact wisdom and style he thinks his associates expect of him. He is engaged in a remarkable project of imitation—being himself as he thinks he is ordinarily. In his own eyes, he has become a center of attraction since he has done something that is being discussed as if no one had. Moreover, since a performance is being staged for those around him, the subject is "on" in another sense. The part he is playing, the performance he is staging is peculiar —one might say inverted. He tries to minimize the conceivable contribution he could make to the discussion, but to do so in a way that will not arouse suspicion—a rather convoluted aim given the ordinary nature of verbal discourse.

In so stilted a mood, the subject is likely to hear himself and others in a somewhat altered way. The conversation may take on an added and ulterior meaning. Thus the perfectly ordinary disclaimers—his own or another's—frequently verbalized and plainly intended as modest expressions of ignorance and uninvolvement may begin to sound suspiciously like the tale of the young maiden whose "friend" became inappropriately pregnant. The disclaimer stands out. It has become a relevant issue for one of the participants whereas the others perhaps continue treating it matter-of-factly, as of no account. More generally, the deviant subject becomes more fully attentive to the setting and its nuances. Fleeting glances may take on added meaning. The response of others to something the subject has said—or has not said—may be listened to more carefully than usual. On this occasion, others must be attended, their behavior scrutinized for signs of possible oversensibility.

Thus conceived, the sense of transparency need hardly depend on the literal belief that one has been seen through, though such things some-

[18] For an extended discussion of the management of information that is potentially discrediting, see Erving Goffman, *Stigma* (Englewood Cliffs, N.J.: Prentice-Hall, Inc., 1963), Chapter 2.

times happen; instead, it depends on the conscious attention spent on averting that possibility. The neophyte user of marihuana, or the newcomer to any other deviation, has devoted psychic effort to keeping his secret. As a result of that endeavor—especially if done well—the subject has built the meaning of duplicity, enriched the meaning of being devious, temporarily established the feasibility of being opaque; finally, he has created some distance between himself and right-minded associates. Acting with guile, he has misled them; he has worked the bluff. Even if only slightly, he has alienated himself from their company. Spurred by ban, the subject has behaved deceptively. In that process, he is led to discover certain features of the right-minded—their gullibility, their misunderstanding, and perhaps even an over-assiduous interest which may later be conceived as a sign of hypocrisy.

Being bedeviled is the key consequence of ban because it prepares the subject for meaningful apprehension, the more potent element in the signification process. Other consequences of ban either contribute to preparation in a similar way and thus require little additional discussion or are so dubious as to require scepticism instead of serious consideration. An example of the first is stressed and amply discussed by Edwin Schur and Howard Becker and is implicit in Sutherland: Ban "criminalizes" the subject's field slightly by forcing him to consort with persons providing an illegal service who are likely to be further along in a deviant career than mere users.[14] An example of the second is the claim that forbidden fruit is more spicy and that, by analogy, prohibition or ban may thus increase the level of deviation. Aside from the dubious validity of the statement itself—a grave shortcoming when dealing in metaphor or analogy—there are other difficulties. A stress on the attraction of forbidden fruit reckons without the subject's capacity to taste, and thus to evaluate and consider from within features easily and romantically imputed from outside an activity. Furthermore, many of the activities presumably illuminated by Eve's experience remain sufficiently spicy even if placed in the penumbra between permissible and prohibited forms. But most important, the indirect evidence available gives little support to so strong a thesis regarding the effects of ban. The massive increases in drug use in the United States did not occur immediately on the advent of prohibition, but apparently long after—about twenty years later in the slum and thirty years on the campus. The prohibition of alcohol had little consequence one way or the other on the total volume of indulgence. The main impact of prohibition was a rise in the consumption of more easily produced wines and spirits and a decline in the consumption of beer.[15] And, if age may be substituted for historical trends, the incidence of

---

[14] See Edwin Schur, *Crimes Without Victims* (Englewood Cliffs, N.J.: Prentice-Hall, Inc., 1965).
[15] See Andrew Sinclair, *Prohibition* (Boston: Little, Brown and Company, 1962), p. 255.

driving hardly declines at the age of permission—though, admittedly, it does not increase as much as might be hoped. Thus, it would seem premature, if not presumptuous, to place much weight on the state's capacity to elicit illicit behavior merely by prohibiting it.[16] Irony does not work so simply.

By itself, ban serves to make activity guilty—to rectify the mistaken belief in innocent affiliation. By making secrecy and security sensible, ban maneuvers the subject into a compounding of deviation. But the permeation of character implicit in such a development is slight, and not widespread. To become more fully deviant, the subject ought to experience more tangible and direct contact with the state. More generally, his deviation should become known or public—open to authorized disapproval. To consider that eventuality, we turn to the more familiar element in the signification process.

Apprehension: Being Selected

To become deviant is to embark on a course that justifies, invites or warrants intervention and correction. By definition, then, to deviate is to run the risk of apprehension. Not an empirical proposition, the relation between deviation and societal reaction is incontestable. The relation exists in the very meaning of deviation. If no reminder of the correct path is justified, no arrest warranted, a path has not been strayed from; one simply not so well-worn has been taken. Thus, deviation is actionable activity.[17] Inherent in the very conception of deviation is a double reality. Right in the deviation is a warrant to be told *not* to in whatever terms and tone righteous authority chooses to speak. That is the meaning of deviation—what distinguishes it from merely "being different."[18] As real as the behavior itself, the warrant to be corrected may not appear very real to the subject—not until it is made to materialize before his very eyes. But elsewhere—in organized institutions—the reality of warranted correction is already quite concrete. And there too, it never exists separate from the reality it seeks to

[16] For an opposite view, see Kai Erikson, *Wayward Puritans* (New York: John Wiley & Sons, Inc., 1966), pp. 114–136; also, Isidor Chein, Donald Gerard, Robert Lee, Eva Rosenfeld, Daniel Wilner, *Narcotics, Delinquency and Social Policy: The Road to H* (London: Tavistock, 1964), p. 6.

[17] I do not wish to equate deviation with crime, though sometimes it does seem as if most jurisdictions in the United States desire just such an equation. Many activities are actionable and thus deviant even though well outside the jurisdiction of criminal law. Torts and many varieties of mental illness are only the most obvious examples. Despite the existence of non-criminal deviations, my discussion will stay close to the criminal on the grounds that they best reveal the part played by signification in the process of becoming deviant.

[18] See Edwin Lemert, *Social Pathology: A Systematic Approach to Theory of Sociopathic Behavior* (New York: McGraw-Hill Book Company, 1951), Chapter 2.

control and correct. Without each other, the two elements of deviation—infraction and reaction—suffer a loss of meaning.

The relevance of signification for becoming deviant may be introduced by considering its various meanings. A first meaning of signification, to be *registered,* is roughly equivalent to being labeled, defined or classified. It refers to the event or process of assigning persons to categories, usually as a result of demonstrating that someone has actually done something "wrong." Secondly, signifying implies a "putting down" or derogation as in the term stigmatizing. This sense of signifying is part of the vernacular of slum Negroes, as indicated for instance in the many versions and widespread knowledge of "signifying monkey." In this meaning, signifying refers to baiting, teasing, humiliating or exposing another on the basis of presumed deficiencies or airs.[19] Signifying ranges wide in many sections of the Negro ghetto. The term may refer to a store-front preacher signifying a backsliding member of his congregation or it may equally refer to the barbed rhymes by which slum youth playfully derogate each other. This meaning is important since it clearly denotes what might otherwise be taken for granted or obscured: the registration of a subject as deviant is an act of derogation, even if warranted. Unwarranted, it is defamation of character, a pursuit itself deemed sufficiently harmful and dangerous as to be usually both criminal and civilly actionable. The view that the registration of persons as deviant is serious, consequential and derogatory receives full confirmation in law and common sense.

The final meaning is perhaps the deepest. To signify is to *stand for* in the sense of representing or exemplifying. An object that is signified, whether it be man or thing, is rendered more meaningful. To be signified a thief does not assure the continuation of such pursuits; but it *does* add to the meaning of a theft in the life of the perpetrator, and it does add to the meaning of that person in the eyes of others. To make someone or something stand for yet something else is an act of genuine creation requiring an investment of meaning. Thus, signifying makes its object more significant—as we might expect. The object enjoys—or suffers—enhanced meaning. To be signified a thief is to lose the blissful identity of one who among other things happens to have committed a theft. It is a movement, however gradual, toward being a thief and representing theft. The two movements are intimately related; without a population selected and cast as thieves, we might have to look everywhere to comprehend the prevalence of theft. The casting comes first. Its consequence is to provide a working account of the prevalent level of theft—and to thus safeguard most of us from suspicion

---

[19] For a discussion of signifying among slum Negroes, see Roger Abrahams, *Deep Down in the Jungle: Negro Narrative Folklore from the Streets of South Philadelphia* (Hatboro, Pa.: Folklore Associates, 1964), pp. 64, 267.

and interference. In that sense, those selected and then cast as thieves come to represent the enterprise of theft.

Being Cast

The *activity* of signification distinguishes it from the natural selection of traits exerted by a milieu over resident species. Darwin's principle of selection illuminated a process in nature that was blind, fortuitous or without purpose. In that limited sense, the natural selection in the organic realm is *passive*. Without motive, it maintains consequence. That is one of the reasons the principle is so intriguing and Darwin's apprehension of it so startling.

The human selection of persons to be cast in one part or another is not blind, fortuitous or without purpose. No less natural than selection in the organic realm, human selection develops along different lines. The irony of direction (evolution is a direction) produced by no intention whatsoever is replaced by one that is less bold. In Darwin's natural selection evolution occurs without Author. Human selection restores active authority to a central place, but an irony is maintained. Being merely human, he who casts another as deviant may intend something quite different or if conscious of his activity may view it as inconsequential, as *following* the formation of character rather than contributing to it. In the human realm, the irony of selection is that it is done with good intentions; not with no intentions whatsoever. Self-deception, bad faith, the limitations of perspective and short-sightedness replace the fully blind forces of nature. Motive restored, consequence becomes more devious.

To be cast a thief, a prostitute, or more generally, a deviant, is to further compound and hasten the process of becoming that very thing. But the compounding implicit in being called something, cast as that, or even treated as one who is that thing would not be so very meaningful if the subject—in this case, the object of signification—were not already rehearsed in being more deviant than, externally considered, he apparently is. Because of ban, and his collaboration with *its* logic, more of the subject's character may be devoted to deviation than he could have reckoned initially. He has to be devious in order to be deviant. Consequently, he becomes prepared for a more stunning spread. Though here too the subject must collaborate, he is now as well situated as could be imagined to begin conceiving himself in the terms of the signifier. That the signifier conceives him in that way is readily understandable once we appreciate that the conception is a workaday simplification. More difficult to understand is why the subject would be willing to concur in such a simplification. Let us briefly consider what the signifier does and why. Then we may turn to the more difficult matter of the subject's possible collaboration.

No relentless Javert, the agent of signification need only perform his limited duty in a professional (it used to be called officious) manner to provide *terms of identity*. Unless he is malicious—something that is possible but hardly entertaining when developing irony and hardly noteworthy when describing human behavior—the signifier when developing and refining these terms of identity does not mean them for the eyes or ears of the deviant subject and does not intend them as caricatures. He means them for himself and others involved in the duties of signification. He intends them as routine notations and observations by which his work may be expedited. As such, the signifier's terms of identity, like those developed in any bureaucracy, bear the signature of limited perspective and the stipulation of convenient simplification. Why blame me, the signifier might well ask, when the otherwise attentive deviant subject has remained unattentive to both signature and stipulation. The terms of identity are not intended as ontological statements regarding the essential condition of the signified subject. To say or note of someone that "he is a thief" or, even stronger, "he's just a plain drunk" certainly sounds exhaustive; but in context the statements refer to the limited aspect of being that is of direct relevance to a bureau assigned limited duties. The designation reflects the intentionally limited perspective *of the signifying agent*. Routine, and made for convenience rather than profound assessments of character, such simplifications are rather like the employment counselor's observation, "he's a public relations type." Thus, the terms of identity contain an ellipsis. Obscured from view, the modifications may remain inoperative. Consequently, the deviant subject may easily take the terms of identity out of their intended context. He may fail to realize that, though invited to his apprehension, arraignment, trial and other formal processes considering him, still he is in many ways an interloper in them. Like the patient on a ward, the young child among adults, or the stranger at his trial, he may become shop-talk in his very presence. In that way, he easily overhears the elliptical statement of his character.[20]

[20] The internal relevance of terms of identity, as well as many other services provided by bureaus signifying deviant activity is a central thesis of the emerging neoChicagoan view. As such it provides a basis for a criticism of modern social institutions. Edwin Lemert has pointed to this aspect of a stress on secondary deviation as a possible reason for its new and perhaps spurious popularity among so many students of sociology. This perspective starts, Lemert has suggested, "with a jaundiced eye on the collective efforts of societies to solve problems of deviance, particularly when this work of social control is propagandized as primarily in behalf of the deviants." Moreover, Lemert observes with considerable justification that because of this feature, "secondary deviance may be a convenient vehicle for civil libertarians or young men of sociology to voice angry critiques of social institutions."

Additionally, of course, the same statements may be uttered directly as accusation or denunciation. If malice and sadism did not exist, impatience and the flaring of temper would suffice, as even parents know, to provide the most sweeping derogations of character in terms that at the very least are easily equated or confused with those of identity. These displays occur, and are quite useful in augmenting terms of identity less directly provided.

Whatever the reasons for providing terms of identity, a more difficult question remains: why would the signified subject collaborate in widening the meaning of his deviant acts; why go along with a spread that confuses or equates the things he sometimes does with what he is? To attempt answering that question, we must first appreciate that often enough he does *not;* with that fact taken for granted, a few possibilities may be considered. The possibilities may be ranged according to the measure of subjective complicity, the extent to which the subject collaborates in absorbing the terms of deviant identity. At the extreme of non-complicity is the possibility of being excluded from occasions and circles providing competing and conventional terms of identity.. At the opposite extreme—that of subjective complicity —are two subtle matters; one having to do with the equivocal language of identity, the other with a built-up equivocation at the time of next commission. Between the two is the frequent tendency of the subject to concede that a display of authority is, after all, authoritative.

Exclusion

Without access to the occasions and circles in which various identities are realistically embedded, the chances of continuing to conceive oneself in their terms, or to do so anew grow small. Continued identification in the face of exclusion depends on fantasy, not an unimportant phenomenon but

---

Whatever its polemic uses or origin, there can be little doubt that the view that officials and professionals are mainly engaged in self-service is strong and entrenched among most sociologists sympathetic with the work of the neoChicagoans. For example, see Erving Goffman, "The Medical Model and Mental Hospitalization" in *Asylums* (New York: Doubleday & Company, Inc., 1961 [Anchor]); Thomas Szasz, *The Myth of Mental Illness* (New York: Harper & Row, Publishers, 1961); David Sudnow, "Normal Crimes," *Social Problems* (Winter 1965), pp. 255–276; David Matza, *Delinquency and Drift* (New York: John Wiley & Sons, Inc., 1964), Chapter 4; Jerome Skonick, *Justice Without Trial* (New York: John Wiley & Sons, Inc., 1966), Chapter 8. Aaron Cicourel and John Kitsuse, *Educational Decision-Makers* (Indianapolis: Bobbs-Merrill, 1963); Aaron Cicourel, *The Social Organization of Juvenile Justice* (New York: John Wiley & Sons, Inc., 1968). For the discussion of the polemical uses of the concept of secondary deviation and, more generally, an excellent reconsideration of the idea, see Edwin Lemert, "The Concept of Secondary Deviation," in *Human Deviance, Social Problems and Social Control* (Englewood Cliffs, N.J.: Prentice-Hall, Inc., 1967).

something which even in the most fertile imagination requires the eventual refueling of experience. Thus, the consequence of exclusion—minimizing the chances of competing terms of identity—is easily recognized and almost taken for granted. That exclusion occurs due to past deviations is hardly debatable. If one is sceptical regarding the methods of social research, he may suit himself and inquire into the specifications for entry into many colleges and universities, the U.S. military service, a great many jobs and marital—as well as trade—unions.[21] This does not deny the persistence, perhaps even the growth of an enlightened attitude that gives past sinners a chance to redeem themselves. Many organizations devote themselves to precisely that aim. Nonetheless, gross exclusion persists. And, as Goffman has striven to show, devotion to the care or cause of the stigmatized sophisticates exclusion but does not remove it.[22]

Thus, the gross exclusion suggested by Becker is augmented by the more bewildering and subtle forms recounted by Goffman. For a man to refuse a homosexual a job seems cruel and unduly vengeful, something limited to practicing Neanderthals. But to refuse him a place next to me in a shower—now, there is something that even a committed civil libertarian might fail to take issue with. Unfortunately, the apparently reasonable exclusion may be just as effective—though in a different way—as the unreasonable form in establishing the deviant terms of identity. Gross exclusion withers the possibility of ancillary identities. Reasonable exclusion speaks to a narrower and more pertinent issue.

The basis for gross exclusion, according to Becker, is in the tendency to regard the new, deviant status of the subject as controlling or overriding. It is treated by others as central or essential, not as peripheral. After apprehension, Becker suggested:

> One will be identified as a deviant first, before other identifications are made. The question is raised: "what kind of person would break such an important rule?" And the answer is given: "one who is different from the rest of us, who cannot or will not act as a moral human being and therefore might break other important rules." The deviant identification becomes the controlling one.[23]

Because of the fear that he "therefore might break other important rules," the exclusion pointed to by Becker goes far beyond what might be deemed reasonable. It covers almost all aspects of the deviant subject's life. Since other aspects are affected in a negative fashion, the possibility of maintaining

---

[21] For an especially well-designed study of exclusion see R. Schwartz and J. Skolnick, "Two Studies of Legal Stigma" in Howard Becker (ed.), *The Other Side* (New York: The Free Press of Glencoe, Inc., 1964), pp. 103–117.

[22] Erving Goffman, *Stigma*.

[23] Becker, *op. cit.*, pp. 33–34.

the primacy of ancillary identities—ones having little relation to the fact of deviation—is reduced. The possibility of figuratively saying, "I am a thief but also a pretty good husband" is sharply reduced by a notification that one's wife plans to divorce him; so too is the possibility of figuratively saying "I am homosexual but a very successful businessman" by being discharged from *that* responsibility. As the competition of ancillary status is reduced, the deviant identity may come to be controlling for the subject too. Becker concluded:

> *Treating a person as though he were generally rather than specifically deviant produces a self-fulfilling prophecy. It sets in motion several mechanisms which conspire to shape the person in the image people have of him. . . . One tends to be cut off, after being identified as a deviant, from participation in more conventional groupings. . . . In such cases, the individual finds himself deviant in these areas as well. The homosexual who is deprived of a "respectable" job by the discovery of his deviance may drift into unconventional marginal occupations where it does not make so much difference.*[24]

If Becker's implicit villain is a garden-variety bigot, Goffman's in *Stigma*— and in most of his writings—is the liberal professional, willing to accept the stigmatized on the condition that those bearing stigma accept themselves as they exist in his eyes. The acceptance is conditional on the tacit agreement that certain limited exclusion is in the best interests of all concerned. Henceforth, if all goes well, the limited exclusions take on the character of being reasonable. But for that very reason, they testify in a very pointed and one-sided way when considered in light of the issue of specific identity. This issue of specific identity is much narrower than that of primacy among competing identities. The more rudimentary issue of whether I am a thief or not replaces the question of whether my identity as thief or good husband is to predominate.

Consider a most reasonable of reasonable exclusions—that of a one-legged man excluded from a company of dancing two-legged women. Everyone has difficulty: the man feels put down, the women awkward and embarrassed; the entire enterprise of dancing suffers. Equally important, the enterprise of one-legged men accepting themselves as they are is interfered with. Nothing especially surprising follows from this exclusion. One-legged persons are reminded that they are one-legged. It is as simple as that. The trouble is that most other issues of specific identity are not quite that simple and that nevertheless the logic of reasonable exclusion prevails.

Consequently, known thieves may be provided jobs, allowed wives and children—but not bonded. Equally reasonable is the exclusion of known

[24] *Ibid.*, p. 34.

homosexuals from my shower, of known pederasts from the company of my children, of known cheats from the dignity of my professorial absence during exams. Reasonable exclusion has the general feature of testifying to the issue of specific identity. It points the subject to a conclusion steadily permanent in the case of one-legged men (though even there over-drawn), but unquestionably premature and untenable in most other cases. Both thief and not thief, as all thieves are, his identity *as* thief is *intensified* by reasonable exclusion. In gross exclusion, that identity is *extended* until it predominates over ancillary identities.

Thus exclusion, whether gross or reasonable, tends to focus the deviant subject's attention on the terms of identity initially provided by the agent of signification during apprehension. Though meaning different things, both forms of exclusion testify to the same conclusion: he *is* a thief. As in most forms of exclusion, the subject need hardly collaborate for the appropriate lesson to be drawn. All that really matters is that occasions and circles which sustain competing identities be inaccessible to him. Such a method of inculcating the terms of deviant identity does not require the subject's presence; other methods do.

The Display of Authority

Until apprehension, the deviant subject exists in an abstract relation with organized authority. The warrant to be stopped or arrested is there, alongside the activity of deviation. However real, organized authority lacks a certain substance. When it finally materializes—if it does—its appearance is likely to include some elements of surprise. Partly because he is usually taken without warning, and partly because a most notable feature of authority is quite superficial—right there on its face—the deviant subject is likely to experience the shock of concrete discovery. Of course, the shock of concrete discovery is familiar enough. Not especially connected with new knowledge, the shock derives from the sense or appearance of discovery associated with a shift from abstract to concrete understanding.[25] The increment of understanding is in intensity; little is added to extent. Consequently, the subject may grow reluctant to publicize what, after all, "everybody knows." Having been reminded a few times that he is rather retarded in mastering the self-evident, the subject learns to keep to himself the way in which he managed to grasp the knowledge about which he is most certain. And reminding others of their retardation, he contributes to the collective

---

[25] For an excellent literary treatment of the shock of discovery, see Anton Arrufat, "The Discovery," in J. M. Cohen (ed.), *Writers in the New Cuba* (Middlesex: Penguin Books, Inc., 1967).

process by which the difference between abstract and concrete understanding is suppressed and lost from view. To appreciate the impact of authority, that difference must be made explicit.

Until being signified, the deviant subject does not concretely understand the reality of organized authority; just as he did not understand the reality of deviation until affiliation. Understood abstractly, the most superficial features of authority appear of little or no account. Experienced and understood concretely, they are the most compelling features. They are what stand before the deviant subject when a figure of authority takes him by surprise. Shocked, he will rediscover what everyone claims to have known all along—that in several respects, authority is terribly authoritative.[26]

Being authoritative is the most superficial feature of authority. Dressed that way, rehearsed or trained in its tone of voice, inculcated in its posture and very demeanor, explicitly taught and henceforth conscious of its essential part in commanding respect, the agent of signification appears. Being authoritative is his display in a world that a moment before existed without so imposing and arresting a presence. That display may subsequently become familiar to the subject—and thus devoid of shock and consequence. It becomes devoid when the subject grows innured, accustomed, or even weary of it—but that is just another way of saying that authority has already made its imprint. Dressed properly and acting his part, the personification of authority, whether policeman, judge, or someone less notable, impresses; by being impressive, he helps a bit to cast the subject in his deviant part.

A main purpose of the entire display of authority is to convince the apprehended subject of the gravity of what he has done—to restore the *unity of meaning* that Hobbes correctly saw as basic to the kind of order imposed by Leviathan. In that unity of meaning, it is not enough that the subject concur in assessing his behavior as wrong; equally important is an attitude of gravity. The authoritative display aims at the creation of an attitude of gravity toward what he has done—within the deviant subject. Needless to say, perhaps, it is a bit difficult to add gravity without making more of something that has been done than it appeared the moment before. To attain a unity of meaning regarding the gravity of deviation, authority adds meaning to that previously envisaged by the subject. In shocked discovery, the subject now concretely understands that there are serious people who really go around building their lives around his activities—stopping him, correcting him, devoted to him. They keep records on the course of his life, even develop theories about how he got to be that way. So confident

[26] Though the reader may recognize this process as quite similar to the appreciation of banality experienced under the influence of marihuana, it should be evident that using marihuana is unnecessary. Being taken by surprise, and several other readily available human events do just as well in preparing the subject for concrete discovery. Thus, there is no intention of limiting the relevance of these matters to the marihuana user. They apply equally to other apprehended forms of deviation.

are they of their unity with the rest of society, so secure of their essential legitimacy, that they can summon or command his presence, move him against his will, set terms on which he may try to continue living in civil society, do, in short, almost anything of which only the mightiest of men are capable. What enormity has the deviant subject managed to uncover? Only the concrete reality of Leviathan, armed with an authority more potent than his own.

Pressed by such a display, the subject may begin to add meaning and gravity to his deviant activities. But he may do so in a way not especially intended by agents of the state. Their aim was to impress upon him the unity of society, their method to utilize the bare surface of authority. Faced with the appearance of authoritative being, the deviant subject may join society in seeing that what he had done could not be taken lightly, that instead it was a matter of considerable gravity. And dazzled by a display of the unity of meaning in society, he may conceive himself as included. But equally possible—therein lies the irony—he may get everything confused, take all that was presented him and proceed in a direction different from that intended. Impressed by the show of authority, persuaded of the gravity of his infraction, reminded of a unity of meaning, he may proceed inward. That is all he has to do to prepare himself to spread the deviant identity.

The way in which authority displays itself—authoritatively—provides matters to be considered by the subject. Once again in a position to reconsider the meaning of his behavior, still, the deviant subject is peculiarly placed. His own authority to bestow meaning has been temporarily reduced, dwarfed by an authority clearly more mighty. If not a child, he can be made to feel like one. Though possible to resist and discount the attitude of gravity conveyed by a display of authoritative being, it is difficult and unlikely. For a brief moment at least, the apprehended subject may join society in confirming the unity of meaning regarding the gravity of his behavior. What he did is in all likelihood quite important; why else the production?

But important to whom? To which unity of meaning will the subject now refer an attitude of gravity of which he has been made conscious? Though dwarfed, his authority has not been liquidated. On the one hand, thus, the subject maintains an option: The attitude of gravity may be referred to society *or* self. And on the other, authority itself may assist in expediting the wrong choice: Its agents may help in directing consciousness to the self. What you have done, they may say, is a matter of gravity both for yourself and society. And given the benefit of appropriate on-the-job training, they may even say that, mainly, it is a matter of gravity for yourself. In either case—with the explicit assistance of organized authority or without —the subject may refer the consciousness of gravity to the self. Even *without* the explicit instructions of authority, implicitly he has already been turned in that direction: He has been made to feel self-conscious. He has been apprehended.

To direct a consciousness of gravity toward the self is to add meaning to already consummated behavior and to embark on a path leading to widespread deviant identity. To maintain that path, however, the subject must build the meaning of identity. To the logician, the way in which the meaning is built may seem faulty, unfortunate and even incomprehensible; for the subject, too, it may prove unfortunate, but it is not so incomprehensible. He builds the meaning of identity with the materials provided him. If twice he equivocates the meaning of key terms related to issues of identity, he is really not at fault. In truth, many terms related to issues of identity *remain* quite equivocal—even for specialists in the field.

The Building of Identity

The first equivocation develops from the choice to refer the matter of gravity to the self instead of society. What he did has become important or grave and the object of that gravity is himself. He now faces a second choice: is the meaning of importance to be indication or consequence? Both are reasonable interpretations of the realization of importance. He may choose consequence and thereby retrace his steps, retrieve his error. To think that his theft was important in the sense of being consequential is tantamount to repudiating his initial choice. Such a thought restores consciousness to society and diverts it from self; consequently, it adds little to the growth of identity. To realize that theft is consequential—for him—is merely an indirect way of locating the importance in society. Since others are hurt by the fact of his theft, they will act against him when given the chance.

If, however, the apprehended subject maintains his initial choice and takes importance to mean indication he may continue to build the meaning of identity. Quite different from consequence, indication points the subject to a consideration of himself; to the question of the unity of meaning of the various things he does and the relation of those things to what he conceivably is. To consider the possibility that the theft was important in the sense of being indicative of him puts the subject well into actively collaborating in the growth of deviant identity by building its very meaning.

A main issue in the question of identity is the relation among the many things we do, and between all that doing and being. There is a simple way of summarizing that enormously complex question. In summary, the question of identity is one of indices, or indicators: Of all the things I have done or may conceivably do, which is the best index of what I am? Which most accurately reflects or represents my true being? If nothing is a good indicator, if none of his activities are indicative of him, the subject has settled the question of identity in a radical but defensible way: the unity of the phenomenon under consideration, the self, is renounced.[27] However defensible the radical resolution of renouncing unity, and thus the very possibility of something being indicative, it is not the position of the deviant subject under consideration. Quite conceivably it could be, but such a possibility will not be followed. Since my concern is with the subject who collaborates in the growth of his deviant identity, it is his path that I will follow. He has not chosen to resolve the question of identity by renouncing a unity within himself. On the contrary, it has just occurred to him that something he did was important—to him in the sense of being indicative of him. Implicitly, he is engaged in self-contemplation, a project limited to intellectuals only when conceived as explicit, permanent or salaried. And tentatively, he is beginning to conceive a unity of himself by regarding certain activity as especially important or indicative. Not so quick to jump to a conclusion on a matter of some concern to him, the subject awaits further evidence. In his subsequent experience, he will be provided ample matter with which to reconsider his tentative resolution and considerable evidence with which to test the tenability of a provisional identity. To what more easily cultivated use can experience be put by a human subject? It comes so naturally he need hardly work at it.

Is he *essentially* a thief? This is not necessarily or ordinarily *the* question; still, it is *a* question. Consequently, that question, whatever its specific actual form, is kept in mind by the subject as he leaves the situation of apprehension and proceeds to or is restored to his ordinary world. There, undazzled by displays of authority, away from the initial shock of discovery, experience may help clarify matters one way or the other—or it may leave him in a condition of long or permanent uncertainty. As occasional writers on signification need to be reminded, it depends on what happens to him and the meaning he puts on those events.

The materials provided by experience include the eventuality of exclusion—if things actually come to that—but are by no means limited to that rather crude piece of evidence. Quite obviously, though, if he suffers the misfortune of being grossly excluded from all circles save that of thieves and is reasonably excluded from all occasions promising the temptation of theft, his provisional identity as thief receives considerable affirmation. And even if such misfortune occurs only irregularly or occasionally it must be counted as partial evidence. But exclusion and its converse—being embraced by more advanced exponents of the deviant activity—are only the most glaring

---

[27] Things can be indicative of larger tendencies only within a basic unity, or system. Without a basic unity, how could the self or anything else be represented by something?

events. With the question of provisional identity in mind, the deviant subject will be reminded of it in a few other ways. He may be treated differently even though not grossly or reasonably excluded—or so it may appear, since he may not have been so observant before the question arose in his own mind. Thus, for instance, the thief may be included in honest company, movable property not securely bolted, but the presence of at least a single observer seemingly constant; the homosexual maintained as a companion but not embraced or even touched so often; or in reverse fashion, it may appear to persons signified mentally ill that, though included, certain terms, expressions or jokes have disappeared from the repertoire of their associates, or slip through with the greatest of unease.[28]

These and other pieces of evidence may be utilized in reconsidering the provisional identity, but they will not suffice. There is another kind of evidence more relevant to the subject. It speaks more directly to the issue being reconsidered, it is less vulnerable to being negatived or discounted. Circumstantial to the core, it achieves the prominence of positive identification in court—with even less reason. Despite numerous deficiencies, it may be regarded as conclusive evidence—an acid test. The test is simple: does he do the damned thing again? Compared to this one, the other tests of provisional identity provided by experience have little significance. Their significance takes form within the context of repetition or its absence. Without the testimony of recurrent activity, exclusion or maltreatment can be discounted as prejudice. With regard to the growth of identity, the subject himself is the key witness. To understand how a provisional identity can become established, we must consider the possibility of the subject making himself an object, turning star witness—against himself. No better example of his collaborative tendencies can be imagined, for in truth it is not so easy. Consequently, the full and certain establishing of the provisional deviant identity is not very common. But by comprehending the kind of stuff it takes, those who fall short and never have their being completely cast will be better appreciated as permanently provisional. Once the illumination provided the ordinary by the ideal is granted—easy to do given Weber's blessing—the devilish method of the acid test can be considered.

The question that must be answered is deceptively simple: How can my recurrence as thief come to be regarded as conclusive evidence that *essentially* I am a thief? Logically, the conclusion hardly follows the premise. Naturally, then, the subject will have to provide some ordinary reasoning, or *common sense*. Not as refined as logic, common sense possesses its own methods of arriving at a conclusion. The lack of elegance is more than made up for by a kind of rough efficiency. In logic, we can only rarely arrive at meaningful conclusions. Logic's ambition has been to inform the common

[28] See E. Goffman, *Stigma: Notes on the Management of Spoiled Identity* (Englewood Cliffs, N.J.: Prentice-Hall, Inc. [Spectrum] 1963).

sense that in drawing or making conclusions it has been rough and fool-hardy. Undaunted by the admirable criticisms of logic, the common sense has persisted in coming to conclusions, if not jumping to them, with whatever materials happen to be at hand. Using common sense, the subject may be aided in coming to a conclusion on the question of his identity. This feat should not be surprising. Using the same common sense, he can even do what the logician shrieks is impermissible and impossible: derive normative conclusions from factual assertions.

Viewed negatively or unsympathetically, common sense includes many instances of what logicians call "fallacies." As logicians discovered each time they visited the world to collect their specimens, fallacies are the stuff that make logically unwarranted conclusions possible. Because they were too correctional in spirit to appreciate the beauty of ordinary reason, logicians tore numerous fallacies from their worldly context. Transformed into their current status as abstracted specimens to be memorized, discussed and then liquidated in college classrooms, fallacies fell into a certain disrepute. From the logical standpoint, fallacies became the methods of the devil, inadmissable in the hall of reason. Elsewhere, however, they persist in serving their traditional function of enabling one to derive a conclusion from whatever materials happen to be at hand—which returns us to the subject who, whatever his educational deficiencies, is certainly up to using common sense. In the common sense, fallacies are workaday methods of arriving to a conclusion. That is their positive nature; it is in the subject's nature to use them along with the rest of his common sense.

Signified during apprehension, taking the gravity imparted by authoritative being, referring consciousness of it to himself instead of to society, the subject was provided matter from which the meaning of deviant identity could be conceived and built. The edifice grew by the equating, or confusing, of gravity with indication. To continue the building of meaning —or to knock it all down—the subject reconsiders his provisional identity in the light of subsequent experience. Matters provided by experience are utilized as evidence and, as suggested, recurrence—whether the activity is done again—may come to be regarded as the acid test, the most compelling piece of evidence.

The very possibility of the subject's using such evidence may seem remote, since in the halls of reason—perhaps even in courts of law—the matter of recurrence would not be tolerated or admitted in a hearing on identity. It might take a moment or two because the question's phrasing has become quite elliptical by this stage of the building of meaning, but soon enough it would be clear that recurrence is not only unilluminating as evidence on the issue of identity; but infinitely more serious, it does not even speak to the issue. Put another way, the method used by the subject at this level of building the meaning of his deviant identity is to beg the real question. Masquerading as an answer, getting away with it because of a slight economy earlier instituted in the building of meaning, recurrence whatever its consequence remains unalterably a bogus. Taken by it, the subject can continue to build meaning. First, however, two more immediate questions must be briefly considered: How does the method work? In what sense does the subject err in even allowing recurrence to count as evidence and what prompted so meaningful a disservice?

The second question has already been partly answered: The context of signification prompts so meaningful a disservice. If he is never apprehended, the subject is unlikely to collaborate in the process of adding gravity to the meaning of his infraction. He may dislike his deviation, even dislike himself for doing it, but unsignified he may continue to regard the deviation as occasional or alien, unreflective of his better self. He is even less likely to build the meaning of identity around the activity if the activity itself is not signified or banned. Apprehended for doing a banned thing, the subject is prompted. If and when he has proceeded to the current level of building the meaning of deviant identity, he is ready to be taken further.

However, few members of society are so silly as to be taken by a guileless begging of the question. A very small child perhaps, but no one else, engages in open begging of questions. For everyone else the method depends on the institution of a bogus—an appearance of an answer that capitalizes on the way in which the question is framed. Thus, a few very small children may disingenuously answer, "because I went across the street" when asked "why did you go across the street?" Most others begin by introducing the simplest bogus: "I wanted to" or "I like to." Each appears an answer by capitalizing on the way in which the question was framed. Most often, though not always, the question "why did you cross the street?" exists with an economy already instituted—an ellipsis. The interrogator meant to say "why did you want to cross the street?" or "why do you like to?" Intention is taken for granted. From the simplest bogus, "I like to," to the most elaborate, "culture," the same principle remains in the art of begging questions. But there is a difference. The more intricate the bogus, the more useful its part in performing the function of common sense: easing the process of arriving at a conclusion with whatever materials happen to be at hand. Thus, it is the more intricate bogus that deserves attention, both generally and in the specific question before us.

Recurrence can only be seen for what it is—an intricate bogus—by slightly *disassembling* the building of meaning thus far described. In assembling meaning, the subject instituted certain economies of language. Those economies must now be retrieved; otherwise, the difference between the way in which the subject now puts the question and the way he meant to remains obscure. And obscured, the meaningful question can be begged. An appearance of an answer that capitalizes on the way in which a question is put—

the principle of bogus—can become a reality in the world, and not just in the classroom.

Currently, the subject has put the question in the form, "am I essentially a thief?" In truth, he is even closer to framing it in a form suited for begging, though the current formulation does well enough. The most suitable form for being begged is "am I *really* a thief?" It is more likely anyway than the more esoteric term, "essentially." The difference is small, however, since the economies instituted in building the meaning have in consequence already succeeded in converting the meaning of "essentially" to "really," and in pointing the subject to that meaning of "really" that is different from "essentially." Thus, we can continue using the term "essentially," whatever word the subject uses. He doesn't mean "essentially" any longer anyway. The most he means is "really."

To build the meaning of a deviant identity, the subject has had to grapple with matters of fundamental and genuine philosophy. Though partly implicitly, he can actually do those things; otherwise, he could never be described as someone who is "taking on an identity." Even to consider the question of his identity, the subject *has to* conceive of the difference between doing and being. To continue building the meaning of deviant identity, he has to uncover the idea of indication and glimpse the conception of unity that renders it sensible. And to reconsider the tenability of so shaky or provisional a building, he has to use subsequent experience in the manner of evidence. The entire project is genuinely philosophical. But somewhere in the project, an economy of language was instituted that could be fateful, which allows recurrence to masquerade as an answer and brings the subject one step closer to a completed building of the meaning of his own deviant identity. Busy doing other things—our subject is no mere philosopher—he did not reckon with the cost of such an economy. And as a result, he can be swayed by the enormous gravity of repeating the activity. If he had carefully checked his accounts, he would be able to see that he was under no logical obligation to repeat and further magnify the gravity his deviation incurred during apprehension. But with his accounts unchecked, he can obscure from himself the human way in which mountains are made from molehills.

The meaningful issue of identity is whether this activity, or any of my activities can stand for me, or be regarded as proper indications of my being. I have done a theft, been signified a thief; *Am* I a thief? To answer affirmatively, we must be able to conceive a special relationship between being and doing—a unity capable of being indicated. That building of meaning has a notable quality. Elaborate structure notwithstanding, it may be summarized in a single thought—even in a single word. *Essentially*— that is the economy. Thus summarized, the question of identity warrantedly becomes, "essentially, am I a thief?" The question is now well-framed for

being begged. For once it is instituted, the previously built meaning summarized by the economy can be obscured and forgotten.

Without that economy and where it can take the subject, it should be
clear to all that the fact of recurrence cannot yield meaningful evidence in
an inquiry devoted to the relation between doing and being—the question of
identity. Framed properly, before the economy and the equivocation that en-
sues, the question of identity could not be begged by the fact—or facts—of
recurrence.[29] Framed in full meaning—or uneconomically—the facts of subsequent commission can be seen for what they are: inadmissible as evidence on identity because they beg the question. But framed with economy,
the question is perfectly suited for a fate in which recurrence may play its
part as bogus. Once obscured by the economy of language, the meaningful
question of identity can be begged. The evidence of recurrence admitted,
the subject may continue coming to a conclusion.

By economizing language, substituting "essentially" for the elaborate
building of meaning it represents, the subject does two things: creates in his
own mind the thought or word that is among the most easily and commonly
equivocated in the world and places himself in a predicament that may later
become dizzying.[30] This is no ordinary equivocation. The difference between

[29] Of course, the whole matter could be framed differently and be quite ad-
missable as evidence. If relative frequency were the test rather than recurrence—
the two are quite distinct—no logical grounds for exclusion could be mustered. There
might be literary or aesthetic grounds, hostile as they are to careful counting, but
no logical basis. The test of relative frequency is direct, simple and, not unimportant, quite beneficent in consequence: The best indicator of my being is what I do
most often. So crude an indicator should not be seriously recommended, unless of
course we could devise a way of knowing what people were *actually* doing when
going about their business *apparently* doing other things, which gets us right back
to the question of identity. Still, as a matter of social policy, or therapy, the test of
relative frequency has much to recommend it. Far fewer persons than is currently
the case could conclude the possibility of their own deviant identity.

[30] Thus, it is not the word, thief, nor the potency of an accuser who utters it
that is dizzying but, instead, the final situation to which the subject may bring himself upon hearing the word. This view differs substantially from Sartre's rendition
and from that of sociologists who knowingly or unwittingly follow his lead on this
matter. In Sartre's essay, the child of ten is caught hand in open drawer. A voice
declares, "you're a thief." Genet's identity materializes.

> "It is the moment of awakening. The sleepwalking child opens his eyes and
> realizes he is stealing. It is revealed to him that he *is* a thief and [he] pleads
> guilty crushed by a fallacy he is unable to refute; he stole, he is therefore a
> thief. Can anything be more evident? Genet, thunderstruck, considers his act,
> looks at it from every angle. No doubt about it, it is a theft. And theft is an
> offense, a crime. What he *wanted* was to steal; what he *did*, a theft; what he
> *was*, a thief. . . . What happened? Actually, almost nothing: an action was
> undertaken without reflection, conceived and carried out in the secret, silent
> inwardness in which he often takes refuge. . . . Genet learns what he is *ob-
> jectively*. It is this *transition* that is going to determine his entire life."

From Jean-Paul Sartre, *Saint Genet* (New York: Mentor Books, 1964 [originally
published in 1952]), pp. 26–27.

the two meanings is staggering, as between a mountain and a molehill. Unequivocated, "essentially" is a warranted and impressive economy, summarizing one of the most profound relations man is capable of conceiving: the special relation in which an entire unity of being is indicated, revealed—apprehended wholly—by one small part of it. But equivocated, "essentially" is a molehill, an earthy and disappointing return from the mountain of created human meaning. Equivocated, "essentially" means next to nothing. It means simply "simply."

Turned into a molehill—something the sophists did long ago—"essentially" is drained of all meaning. The term and the thought it represented could come to mean "simply": *what is right there on the surface of things.* The mere face of things—plainly there for all to see—could be proposed as essence, since it bore surface resemblance to the tiny flash by which an entire unity of being is displayed, indicated, revealed and made apprehensible. But the face of things was to be simply essence, indicative of nothing but itself—next to nothing. Thus "essentially" comes to have a double meaning, one standing for the human creation of meaning, the other for next to nothing, a denial of constructive or symbolic meaning. With regard to the question of identity, the first suggests that one's appearance in the world may provide a flash that indicates or reveals an apprehensible unity of being; the second that one simply appears in the world. The trouble with the subject engaged in considering his identity is that in making the equivocation—if he does—he will receive a sophist treatment of a Platonic question—to this day an unpardonable abuse.

By begging the question, the subject allowed the fact of recurrence to appear or pose as evidence. And by equivocating the meaning of "essentially" he is making the transition from a Platonic to a sophist way of conceiving. The combination of the two philosophies and the consequence provide meaning of sufficient gravity to recurrence to complete the building of a deviant identity. If, during his apprehension, or shortly after, he could have withstood the display of authority and maintained a sophist attitude on the question of his identity, the building would never have begun. Sophistry sees no question of identity. Bureaucratically apprehended, the subject would remain immune from his own philosophical apprehension. And, later, if despite the economy of language that instituted the very possibility of so fateful an equivocation the subject were able to recollect the meaning thus summarized and remain Platonic in attitude, his consistency would nearly cancel his decision to allow recurrence to pose as evidence. He could beg the question, allow recurrence as evidence and still assign it little meaning, deem it inconsequential. Recurrence can be given a gravity only in the special combination of a sophist acceptance of the meaning of appearance with a Platonic quest for an apprehension of the *relation* between appearance and being. That sequence experienced, repeating the activity takes on additional meaning.

Sophist throughout, the subject would see that the appearance of his theft was reality only in the simple sense that at that moment no other surface doings were observable. But coming late to sophistry, imposing it on himself by equivocation and building it on to the Platonic context in which he has been dwelling, the appearance of his theft becomes reality in the profound sense of indicating or revealing his true being or identity. It is as plain as day, right there on the surface of things! He is "really" or "simply" or "just"—a thief. This time, no one else need be there. He can apprehend himself. In the light of the question of identity he thought he was asking himself, and in the darkness he imposed by equivocation and the subsequent shift in philosophical attitude, the subject during recurrence will find someone who is *essentially* a thief; and that someone will bear an amazing likeness to himself.

One question remains and its consideration brings us to a conclusion in which the subject completes the building of the meaning of his deviant identity. What would motivate the subject to become star-witness against himself? Why should he turn to sophistry at so late a point in the building of meaning? Why after going through the considerable trouble of being rather intelligent and creating a mountain of meaning should so silly a philosophy hold any appeal? The basic answer, I think, coincides with a general reason for the appeal of sophistry. With good intentions, and in too great a hurry, perhaps, to arrive at a conclusion, the subject engages in self-service. He turns to sophistry in order to expedite a comforting conclusion regarding the question of identity.

To understand what may motivate the subject to turn star-witness against himself in the event of recurrence, we must return and illuminate an earlier period when he was getting something out of it. Such a period is not difficult to locate. If at all a collaborator, the subject has just gone through a suitable period: the one between apprehension and the time of next commission. Thus far, that interim has been avoided. Consequently, the reader may have wondered why the subject did not utilize sophistry continuously to conclude—right up to the moment of next commission—that essentially he was *not* a thief. The most likely answer to that question may have occurred to the reader: In self-deception, that is precisely what the subject was doing. That comforting and desired conclusion prompts or motivates the subject to turn to sophistry after so promising a start as a genuine philosopher. Far from a mature, committed or professional thief, the subject must first be maneuvered into *realizing* a deviant identity. Later in life, perhaps, the identity will be embraced. More important, the period following apprehension and exposure as a thief contains a peculiarly dis-easing feature; and it is this feature more than his immaturity that will prompt a hurried and thus premature conclusion.

A consideration of the subject during this period of self-deception returns us to the basic idea of signification: the deviant subject's continuous bind with the state. Despite his creation of the meaning of a deviant identity through his own activity, and though he is the author of most of its acquired meaning and star-witness in the final inquest, the subject has not been free of the authoritative context of Leviathan from the moment he did the banned thing. Before apprehension he was merely bedevilled; after it, he lives in the shadow of a spell that is cast on him. His freedom persists but is bound by terms implicit in the effects of signification. Thus, the first thing he cannot do is to contain the sense of deviation to the act itself—how could he, having the sense to behave so deviously? The second thing he cannot do—not immediately after apprehension and for a time—is to pursue good intention without glimpsing his appearance as petty collaborator: one who refrains from doing bad deeds because he has been told to.[31] Caught in such binds, though none so crude as outright determination or preordination, the subject continues to exist in relation to instituted authority. He considers himself in the light of that relation.

This second bind—the subject's incapacity to pursue good intention without glimpsing his own appearance as petty collaborator—defines for a time the hold of Leviathan. Though the relation between Leviathan and the subject is objective, its method is to capitalize temporarily on the subjective capacity to see oneself in the eyes of another. But that puts it too weakly. More potent than that, the spell capitalizes on the subject's essential *incapacity:* He is *unable not to* see or glimpse himself as he appears in the eyes of another. As Mead taught, that is the way the subject is put together and thus part of the human nature. It is quite a capacity, but sometimes it is more usefully conceived as an incapacity or flaw.

Unable not to see himself in the eyes of another, the subject will glimpse his appearance as pettiest of collaborators. Ordinary members of society as well as men of authority see him in a very peculiar way, or so he glimpses under the spell. They will gaze at him as he plays baseball, or walks to school, or stands idly and they will literally observe someone in the act of refraining from doing bad things because he has been forcefully told to. And whether the peculiar observers say "good" or utter a sarcastic derogation, like "shit" is not the point. Under the spell—for they too are in its bind, they have noticed the subject "behaving himself," or as it is sometimes put, "keeping his nose clean." That those who say "good" are "glad to see that he is" and those who say "shit" are notably unimpressed is really of little relevance. The relevant matter is that *in his own mind,* the subject

[31] See Carl Werthman, *Delinquency and Authority* (Master's thesis, University of California, Berkeley, 1964), Chapter 5, p. 186.

has glimpsed society as it caught him in the act of collaborating. He was playing baseball and they saw him doing something quite different, "behaving himself."

To catch a glimpse of this, the subject must exist in a spell; and society too must be spellbound to be capable of perceiving in so curious a manner. Thus, I mean the term *spell* literally, not metaphorically. The perception which converts a person playing baseball into one who refrains from doing bad things because he has been forcefully told to, or converts the youth helping his mother with household chores into someone behaving himself or "keeping his nose clean" is unusual and warrants full appreciation. Such a conversion is not *just* a definition of a situation, though surely it is also that. To conceive it as merely a definition of the situation runs the risk of losing the real magic that continues to exist in the world and, as a corollary, reduces magic to the theatrical.

The subject and the society he glimpses exist in a spell that produces a shift in perception and thus appearance. Persons under the spell are literally *seen differently*. Because it is a real spell and not theatrical, the bind of Leviathan and the magic it works can be undone by the subject. He can be *dis*-spelled. Thus, the subject may try to disspell himself, rid himself of an unformulated sense of dis-ease. But there is a problem: Not conscious of the meaning of his situation, he may work himself further into its hold. That is the trouble with all real spells. Consequently, whether the subject breaks the spell or not is a bit uncertain.

A number of methods of breaking the spell can be suggested. One can only be imagined, the others exist in the world. But some activity may work the subject further into the grip of Leviathan's magical hold. The effective methods require only brief discussion. The other activity of disspelling needs fuller discussion, for during that period we can locate the subject's motives for later turning witness against himself. There we are provided with clues as to the motives for collaboration.

The imaginary method is to directly and explicitly put the question to the society that mind had glimpsed: "What do you mean" it could be indignantly asked, "taking my self who is plainly playing baseball to be someone who is refraining from doing bad things because he was told to, someone who is 'behaving himself!' Do you not see the two are altogether different phenomena, wholly apprehended?" But the question can never be put in the world. Even if it were not a *non sequitur* to develop direct and explicit questions from an unformulated sense of unease, even if the risk of being taken for mad seemed worth running, still, the imaginary method would have little use in the world. Society, too, is spell-bound. If ever asked what it meant by thinking or saying such a thing it would tell the truth—but be misunderstood. "It was just a manner of speaking," society would say, "and besides, you could be both at the same time, couldn't you?" It would say that, and being as spell-bound as the subject, neither would realize that the statement merely masquerades as a half-hearted apology. Behind the facade—and mockingly since the true meaning lies right at the surface—the statement reveals the very method of magic that makes the spell work, a method too ancient to warrant serious consideration in the modern world. Both subject and society would hear the statement and suppress its blatant or profound meaning: *the magic of words,* the capacity of words first to juggle reality by boggling the mind and subsequently shape reality by directing the mind. Through words, man can be magically persuaded, deceived first into believing he can be two wholly apprehended phenomena at the same time and then into conceiving himself the one he was not. By a manner of speaking and the construction of words, the baseball player can be transformed into one who is primarily behaving himself.

Shaping reality—structuring its appearance—through the magic of words is an ancient method and modernity has succeeded only in devising numerous ways—all called reason—of suppressing its persistence in the world. Reason points us away from an understanding of word-magic and the potent spells it can help produce by rendering wholly imaginary—useless in the world—the direct and explicit approach to detection and discovery. Reason does that by enunciating the *non sequitur* and banning it, by defining madness and confining it; but most of all, by its habit of losing profundity through mistaking surface-meaning for that which is blatant.[32] Having described the imaginary method and its results, we may return to our subject. Because he is in the world, the subject is effectively sealed off *by reason* from this method of breaking the spell. He simply cannot use it. His entire heritage, if it has accomplished nothing else, has seen to it that the escape of imagination is sealed from him. The force of centuries acting on him, he must search elsewhere for a way of breaking the spell.

The subject has been left hanging many times in this book, while I, the writer, have followed numerous digressions. Each digression was allegedly justified by my implicit claim that the process of becoming deviant made little human sense without understanding the philosophical inner life of the subject as he bestows meaning on the events and materials that beset him. He has now been left hanging once again, as I digressed to consider an imaginary method. Once again, I apologize and claim the same grounds in begging the reader's pardon. But this time, there is another excuse perhaps more compelling: the subject was left hanging because, currently, that is where he is, and for a time that is where he will be. Left hanging for a time, he searches for another method of breaking a spell he has been unable even to formulate.

The spell can be broken easily even though no exact moment of being

32 The obvious source of this uncomplimentary view of reason is Michel Foucault, *Madness and Civilization* (New York: Pantheon Books, Inc., 1965).

freed from its bind can be visualized, and even though the sorcerer—Leviathan—keeps its hand hidden throughout. The spell is broken when the subject comes to terms with the *actual,* the *objective* relation between Leviathan and himself: when, in other words, he concretely realizes that he is a *subject of Leviathan.* The concrete realization of that subjugation to Leviathan requires the subject's further, and this time massive, collaboration. He must accept the exact terms of the spell and its surreality; he must not be repelled by his glimpse of himself as petty collaborator, and not rebel against it. Concretely, the subject must make believe he is playing ball when, *really,* he is behaving himself, or keeping his nose clean. If for a time he impresses everyone, especially Leviathan, that he is actually collaborating in the massive deception, he will find himself released from the terms of the spell. One fine day, while behaving himself, he will glimpse society as, magically, it reconsiders and observes him playing baseball. Incessantly receiving its cues on matters such as these from organized authority, and as spellbound during the term as the subject, society reinvests its trust in him. Temporarily alienated or taken from him—those, existentially, are the terms of the spell—his good intentions are returned to him. Why regard Leviathan as the sorcerer? Mainly, because try as it may, it does not hide its hand completely. The spell began with Leviathan's apprehension of the subject. That awesome display created an apprehension or *distrust* of the subject in society. And though there is no certain or definite date on which the sorcerer's spell is broken, it is suspiciously around the time when Leviathan, persuaded of the subject's transformation, no longer bothers to call on *this* subject when seeking an offender of roughly that description or capacity. The spell appears broken when the subject is no longer considered a likely suspect.[33] And, finally, of course, Leviathan reveals its hand in a most telltale manner. Who else would have such powers?

Thus, the spell can be broken, the subject's good intentions restored. But before that happy ending is attained—and there should be little doubt that it happens often enough to sustain the thriving business of correction—the subject is left hanging. During the period of massive collaboration which may last weeks at least, perhaps many months, the subject has no possible way of knowing where "behaving himself" is going to lead. He is left hanging not only on the question of *how* to break a spell only vaguely sensed; more important, he is left hanging on the question of his identity—the same one that led him to this wilderness. And so *within* the terms set down by the spell, *within* the predicament of not knowing where the massive collaboration of behaving himself leads, *within* the quest for a more certain knowledge of his true identity, the subject hits upon on an apparent resolution: He becomes a sophist. All his philosophical problems are thereby reduced if

---

[33] Being a regular suspect will be discussed in the final part of this chapter, "Collective Representation."

not resolved. As a sophist, he can settle all questions—and so he proceeds to.

He takes his massive collaboration and tears it out of context. Easily —one might say slickly—he takes the self-deception that allowed him to trust the magical transformation of himself playing ball into himself behaving and translates the self-deception into a most unlikely thing: a true identity as good. Inspired by sophistry and beguiled by its flattery, he does not see his true identity at this moment—self-deceiver; instead, he takes the unquestionable recurrence of "behaving himself" as an indication of his identity, and he invests trust in what was inspired by sophistry. Why shouldn't he? There it is, plain and simple as the nose on his face! He does behave himself; therefore, and essentially, that is what he is.

It would be touching, and testimony to the just order of things, if the subject with his fatal flaw revealed were destined—preordained—to fall and be undone. That happens quite often and how it happens should be clear. Often, however, it does not happen. To succumb to romance in the form of pathetic fatality is a mistake. To succumb to such a temptation denies the plain fact that most sophists—even those who have sinned and repented— do quite well in the world; moreover, it obscures a main source of the plain hypocrisy evident in respectable quarters of society; finally, it implies that Leviathan does badly in carrying out its historic purpose of straightening evil out. One should never claim any of those, especially the last.

Thus, the process remains open even as the conclusion regarding the issue of identity approaches. Nothing of note has shifted or changed with regard to the "forces" driving the subject to commit the violation. That is still a matter of circumstance—no more preordained than humane conceptions of affinity and affiliation will countenance. What *has* shifted—and quite remarkably—is the meaning or the gravity that will be placed on deviating again if the subject should happen to. In all likelihood, the circumstantial context of the subject has remained nearly constant during the entire period being considered; it is his philosophical situation that has undergone radical alteration. Thus, the main shift has been in the subject's definition of a situation he *may* find himself in. But whether he finds himself in the situation of recurrence or in that of persistent good behavior remains a matter of circumstance governed as weakly or strongly as before by affinity and affiliation. The meaning of affinity and the meaning of affiliation become bloated—in the eyes of the subject. Small wonder thus that sociologists, too, bloat the meaning of affinity and affiliation; that they, too, take it out of context, though in a different way.

There is one minor problem with so static a formulation. A change has occurred in the circumstances in which the subject exists: A good behaver, his good intentions are alienated. In the measure, slight as it may be, that he is aware of so dis-easing an alienation, the subject now possesses a motive for deviation. By doing it again he may regain the human sense of intention—however bad. Good intentions alienated, bad intentions are still *easily* his. Hence the slight shift in his circumstances occurs, but only, as suggested, in the measure that the subject himself is dimly aware of the disease implicit in the predicament of the good behaver. With that provisional qualification, we may return to the sophist pretending to play baseball, his circumstances more or less intact but, in what is for him a novel philosophical situation produced by his collaboration with the signifier—Leviathan. It is in that sense among others that Leviathan is the neglected producer of a deviant cast.

The subject is prepared to be key witness against himself. In the context of sophistry, more profoundly in the context of the events that led the subject to sophistry, the subject may draw the conclusion of a deviant identity from the fact of recurrence. Whether recurrence derives from the special circumstance of seeking to restore his sense of intention by bad behavior or the general circumstances posed by affinity and affiliation is largely immaterial. In either case, the context of sophistry leads—*mis*leads would be more accurate—the subject to an abject conclusion. He has done the damned thing again; therefore, he is essentially, or simply, a thief. The subject has collaborated with a process signalled by Leviathan which maneuvered him into the acceptance of bogus evidence against himself. The petty collaborator becomes a massive collaborator. Essentially a good behaver the moment before, he now bestows himself with an essential deviant identity because of bad behavior. He ordains himself a thief.

But—alas—there is no finality in the tribulations of our subject. Key witness against himself during recurrence and shortly after, still, he is a Sophist. Consequently, he will bounce back and forth between conclusions —now a good behaver, now just a thief. Every self-conception he holds will be equally "sincere," but in the Sophist, not the Parisienne sense of that term. In bad faith, he will claim remorse if apprehended anew, and mean it; fulfill a deviant identity when doing the thing, and mean it. A Sophist, he will mean everything he says—in bad faith. That is the sense in which he becomes dizzy. Later perhaps, after being committed, he may commit himself to a life of bad intentions, but that need never happen. Unless he does, or unless circumstances spare him the fact of recurrence, he will never be straightened out regarding himself. Committed to a life of bad intentions, he may become, as Sartre has brilliantly shown, a Saint Genet. Not a way of being to hanker after, still it is straightly evil. And if spared the fact of recurrence by circumstance, the subject may continue the sophist for a while at any rate. Released from the spell in which his good intentions are alienated—something Leviathan will permit in due time —the good behaver can once again try his hand at merely playing ball. Only then will he know if he can be straightly good.

Our main concern, however, is not with the sophist who succeeds in the world. He is the main subject in other works. It is the other subject—the one who discovers his deviant identity—whom we must follow. Assuming my argument to be warranted, we are now possessed of a subject who, as much as could be expected, has taken on a deviant identity. He *is* a thief— when he steals or prepares for it. Let us not worry too much what he makes of himself when he is not stealing—nobody else seems to. A question suggests itself: Of what use is such a person and to whom?

Collective Representation

Without building and conceiving the meaning of his own deviant identity, the subject would be unprepared for the constructive use to which he is to be put. Just as, earlier, building the meaning of being devious prepared him for meaningful apprehension by compounding his deviation, in the same manner conceiving himself as an essential deviant prepares him for meaningfully representing the deviant enterprise. Apprehended by himself in the full philosophical sense, no longer simply one who has been bureaucratically apprehended, the subject has become suited for collective representation. The thief will stand for theft. Though he may resent the part he comes to play, the social use to which he will be put, though he may regard it as unjust, simultaneously he will concur in the common sense that, after all, there is a certain justice in employing an admitted thief whenever an account of theft is sought. Having been cast in a part, he should be put to work. The essential thief is employed as a regular suspect; so too is the one who has not concluded the building of a deviant identity, but being unprepared for such socially valuable work, to him the job will have different meaning. Only the ordained thief—one who has witnessed his own deviant identity— can see the limited justice of so strange an employment, only *he* can build and conceive its full meaning. Those who have *not* collaborated with Leviathan or have *not* suffered the misfortune of turning witness against themselves may easily and properly discount the unquestionable attempts by Leviathan to employ them too as regular suspects. With unmitigated indignation or carefree toleration, they—but not the essential thief—may regard such attempts as casual and thus meaningless employment, as a temporary mistake, as laughable or as irritating injustice. Their response may be likened to mine when as a doctor (but of the wrong sort) I am asked to prescribe a cure for delinquency. It is simply a case of mistaken identity, or so it may be conceived.

The indignation of the essential thief is marred by his concrete realization of a deviant identity; his toleration is ruined by the care he must take to keep his realization to himself. Innocent of the theft for which he is employed as a suspect, he has philosophically witnessed himself in another and thus he will concur in the poetic justice of being cast a thief by Leviathan. His sense of poetic justice will exist side-by-side with a more fully displayed sense of injustice. Thus complicated, he becomes even more devious.

Joined more closely to Leviathan than ever, the essential thief begins his career as an employee of the state. A suspect, he now works for the state, literally, though without adequate recognition or compensation. He *also* works for the society regulated by a state. To understand the curious nature of the suspect's employment, we need a fuller picture of Leviathan's policing task, a better appreciation of the inherent difficulties of that task, and a reminder of the *social contract* by which society permits but restricts Leviathan's power of police. Once those are provided, the suspect's employment will be clarified. Equally important, the irony of signification will come full circle: It will become clear that Leviathan's insidious production, too, is not without flawed reason, or cause. Bound by its purpose and by its contract with society, Leviathan will freely take an ordained thief, employ him as suspect and, eventually, produce a convict—unless, of course, the thief reconsiders himself in the light of all that has happened and stops doing the damned thing. Admittedly, such a reconsideration grows more difficult as the thief gets closer to being committed—but, a subject, he is still not actually imprisoned.

Because signified and signifier are so tightly-bound, an understanding of the meaning of being suspect presumes a comprehension of the police institution of suspicion and *its* foundations. It is here in the institution of suspicion that we approach the truthful element of the irony of "labeling" and separate it from the exaggerated romance by which subjects become deviant "because" such a status is conferred upon them. Actually, the only status thus far conferred on the subject is the dubious one of being employed as a regular suspect. And in reality, the reason suggested thus far for such an employment—the subject's partial willingness to collaborate in the part —leaves out the main foundation for Leviathan's suspicion.

The main foundation for the institution of suspicion lies in its workability as a tentative solution to the constant pressures to which police are subjected—and not in the existence of inevitable suspects who command or otherwise intimidate an institutional response. Suspects are utilized or employed by a police force as part of the method by which an uneasy accommodation with other elements of state and society is reached. Thus viewed, the institution of suspicion, which focusses attention on a regular but small criminal corps, is mainly based on the police pursuit of other socially valuable goals; taken by itself, the pursuit of thieves could be managed in quite different ways—as any reader of detective stories can imagine.

"To catch a thief" is only an abstracted version of the fundamental police function. Like all abstracted versions, it reckons without the working context that shapes practice and directs a choice of method. The institution of suspicion represents the historic choice of a main method over conceivable and extant others. Though the tendency to rely on the method of suspicion is perhaps always implicit, that of making it the pronounced routine of ordinary police operation develops within a specific context. The method of suspicion comes into use when police, faced with a considerable volume of crime, are asked to provide an account of their effectiveness along with an account of their propriety, or legality. Because of its un-rivaled scale of crime, its avid concern with effectiveness, and the rapid but controversial development of judicial standards of police legality, the United States has surpassed other nations in its current reliance on the method of suspicion.

Executive and judicial accountability in the face of a publicly con-ceived "crime problem" make up the working context that directs police to a workable solution: the method of suspicion. Through the use of suitable suspects, through an allegedly understandable and certainly invisible reduc-tion of their legal safeguards, the safeguards guaranteed the rest of society are upheld, a moderately acceptable account of police efficiency is provided —and a few convicts produced. Let us briefly explore the executive and judicial accountability of police and then proceed to the method of employ-ing suspects as a collective representation of the full criminal volume.

The introduction of police into society on a regular basis is a recent phenomenon, appearing for the most part in the first half of the nineteenth century. A regular martial presence insinuates danger or annoyance for the citizenry since there can be no guarantee that in protecting property and person police will leave untouched the good reputation or business of the law-abiding. Thus, Alan Silver's summary of the historic meaning of police in society evokes a proper sense of threat. "The police penetration of civil society . . . lay not only in its narrow application to crime and violence. In a broader sense, it represented the penetration and continual presence of . . . political authority in daily life."[34] One way of perceiving the contrac-tual protection of the citizenry from the threat implicit in police penetration is summarized in developments like procedural regularity, due process, judi-cial accountability or the codified regulation of police agents. However important the protection afforded by the promise of civil rights, it is aug-mented by a more basic safeguard. The more important way in which a citizen's rights are protected is the expectation that under ordinary circum-stances he will remain above suspicion. Most of us remain above suspicion as long as, apparently, we deserve to be.[35] The protection of due process is

---

[34] Alan Silver, "The Demand for Order in Civil Society," in David Bor-dua (ed.), *The Police* (New York: John Wiley and Sons, Inc., 1967), pp. 12–13.

[35] For a general discussion of the presumption of an immunity from penetra-tion, see Arthur Stinchecombe, "Institutions of Privacy in the Determination of Police Administrative Practice," *American Journal of Sociology*, LXIX (September 1963), 150–160.

at best a procedural probability; immunity from suspicion is substantial and certain because it is an absence. The absence of penetration protects us from finding out whether due process is full reality. And being above suspicion normally protects the apparently law-abiding from the possible embarrassment of apprehension.[36] The most compelling evidence for the approximate immunity of the law-abiding that can be mustered is the likely fact that most readers of this volume—like the writer—have never been suspected of substantial wrong-doing. By suggesting that, I do not mean the occasional incident in which a specific set of circumstances lead the police to question our doings. I mean something considerably more general: being regularly subjected to methodical suspicion. What is the difference between incidental and methodical suspicion?

To fall under suspicion, most members of society would have to go out of their way. They are subjected to police attention only under special circumstances. Actual policemen, except those dealing in traffic offenses and those concerned with homicide, rarely proceed in the classic manner in which the scene of the crime yields clues or certain knowledge of the identity of a culprit who, likely as not, is someone previously above suspicion.[37]

Because of the unusual nature of traffic violations and homicide—the two offenses coincidentally displayed to the public—our understanding of police practice is one-sided and our appreciation of the basic contribution of the method of suspicion dimmed. Neither traffic offense nor homicide reveals the *ordinary* method of investigation used by police. Their mundane method is best displayed in cases of larceny and burglary. Accordingly, most discussions of police bias or abuse of discretionary power miss the main point. Beginning too late in the process of investigation, these analyses point to the least consequential forms of bias. Moreover, having selected the wrong section of police work for observation and scrutiny, some writers even conclude that claims regarding police bias are exaggerated. Small wonder: The main bias of police operation has little to do with how policemen act when persons fall under incidental suspicion. Instead, it follows from how and where police look when *no one* has fallen under incidental suspicion. The main bias flows from the method of suspicion—a form of regular police practice that utilizes essential thieves and those resembling them as suspects.

Once a distinction between incidental and methodic suspicion is made, the issue regarding the existence or frequency of police bias can be clarified.

---

[36] For an elegant demonstration that the protection of the innocent has a different moral basis—and thus cannot be derived from the utilitarian quest of protecting society from harm, see H. L. A. Hart, *Punishment and Responsibility* (London: Oxford University Press, 1968), pp. 71–83.

[37] See Carl Werthman and Irving Piliavin, "Gang Members and the Police," in David Bordua (ed.), *The Police* (New York: John Wiley and Sons, Inc., 1967), pp. 68–69.

Everybody is subjected to incidental suspicion—the suspicion that flows from an incident of apparent dereliction. For purposes of argument, it could even be granted that police encounter and treat incidental suspects more or less even-handedly though, plainly, such a concession would strain the American reader's credulity. Thus, in traffic violations, the exemplification of incidental suspicion and arrest, the chances of encountering a public official or wealthy businessman are as great, in principle, as stopping a Negro pusher of narcotics or someone resembling him.[38] One need hardly conjure a policeman, hat in hand, saying, "Sorry, Sir, I didn't realize it was you I stopped" or an irate call to the lieutenant resulting in a police apology. Such bias, even if it happens, is quite incidental—like the temporary and specific suspicion under which the honest citizen may fall. It is the superficial bias of flaunted discrimination and *not* the profound bias covered by institutional arrangement.

Traffic offenders are suspected, interrogated and sanctioned through the method of direct police witness. Incidentally implicated, offenders are caught red-handed—though obviously evidence must be developed and be persuasive if the charge is denied. Not automated, as in the case of the parking violation, traffic offenses exemplify the method of direct witness.[39] Within the somewhat whimsical limits set by the traffic policeman's schedule, route and alleged quota, the reader's chances of being apprehended and sanctioned when violating traffic laws are about as great as those of a familiar criminal—at least in principle. Similarly, though through a different method, being suspected for homicide partly follows the classic model of detection. Just as in traffic offenses, the method of discovery exerts a tendency even if—as in the case of homicide—the classic method of detection is augmented by the more prosaic method of suspicion. In homicide, as in driving his car eighty miles an hour, the honest citizen may incidentally fall under suspicion even though he is usually above it.

The classic method of detection remains most entrenched in the most heinous of crimes. Otherwise, it appears important only in those lesser offenses that happen to evince public outcry in the mass media. Using the most dubious justification imaginable—debatable regularities produced partly by the very methods they use—police search in different ways for offenders depending on the nature of the offense. Putting aside direct witness, which is important only in the traffic offenses, the methods range from

---

[38] Small wonder thus that policemen regularly provide the citizenry with authentic tales of giving a traffic ticket to a dignitary. In that way they may establish their even-handed dispensation of justice. Such an account is provided to Michael Banton in *The Policeman in the Community* (London: Tavistock, 1964), p. 179.

[39] See Jerome Skolnick, *Justice Without Trial* (New York: John Wiley & Sons, Inc., 1966), pp. 73–76. For a general discussion of the ways in which offenses come to the attention of the police, see Albert Reiss and David Bordua, "Environment and Organization: A Perspective on the Police," in Bordua, *op. cit.*, pp. 42–43.

the classic mode, still apparent and important in homicide, to the bureaucratic mode, the main method for the staple offenses of larceny, burglary and even sexual deviation.

While not a murderer, I can be suspected, briefly at least, of murder if, incidentally, I should happen to possess hypothetical motive or access to an actual corpse. Politely or rudely—that is not the issue at this level of police operation—I may be interrogated about my knowledge of the deceased, my awareness of his other acquaintances and my whereabouts and activities. Being known to the victim—that crudely is the operative criterion in the classic mode—I am not beyond suspicion. While I am under suspicion, my guilt may be revealed—not especially likely if I am actually innocent; it is more likely and more relevant than an immunity from police penetration assiduously earned by years of decent behavior has been temporarily breached. As a by-product of some consequence, the fortuitous discovery of minor irregularities in the assumed round of decent existence is made uncomfortably possible. At the very least, the good citizen's business is interrupted by so free-wheeling a method; and at most, it may be pried into— almost as if he were not trustworthy. Consequently, his toleration of the classic method is rather low, actually reserved to the most heinous and least likely offenses and, otherwise, fancifully projected to the many crimes that appear before him as spectacle in mystery novel, cinema, theatre and television broadcast. The immunity desired by the good citizen is not merely from brutality or abuse of his civil rights; more profound, it is from an unsolicited police presence in his daily life. To an amazing extent he is granted approximately that measure of immunity—as if by social contract with an agency that penetrates civil life. In return, perhaps, the good citizen maintains trust in the decent and considerate manner in which police treat the rest of the population. Sometimes, he even urges the police to get tougher with the lawless elements.

In homicide, governed partly as it is by the classic mode of detection, possessing motive and access to a corpse is sufficient to excite incidental suspicion. Being known to the deceased *is* the incident. In other crimes, especially the staple offenses of larceny and burglary, a different knowledge provides the basic principle underlying the operative method. Standing alongside the classic method in the case of homicide—in the event neither clue nor informant appears—the bureaucratic method ascends to unrivaled position in most other crimes. In larceny, being known to the victim warrants no breach of our ordinary immunity from suspicion; *being known to the police,* however, does. Partly for reasons of apparent social contract—there would be no end to the interruption of decent business, no respite from endangered friendships, little relief from sustained inquiry into an impeachable round-of-life if every burglary or larceny in my vicinity or social circle breached my immunity—and partly for reasons of producing a somewhat spurious appearance of efficiency, a different principle and method apply. For those reasons—and not because of the dubious fact that he has not or does not steal—the reader will in all likelihood be spared an interrogation regarding a recent theft committed within his reach.[40]

On the one side, police are pushed toward the method of suspicion by the unquestionably accurate anticipation that an application of the classic method of detection would elicit a howl of unprecedented volume from good citizens who know their rights and have the wherewithal to enforce them; on the other side, police are pressured toward the very same method by the extension of techniques of cost-accounting and efficiency to their domain—as reasonable a development, probably, as their extension to any one of a dozen other public services. It is for this second reason that the

[40] As for the predictable and familiar claim that the difference in methods reasonably derives from a patent difference between patterns of offense, it is surprising that so unsustained a contention receives such uncritical support from citizens and professionals who seem informed and express avid concern about the control of crime. Though it can be fairly assumed that a large proportion of homicides are committed by persons known to the victim, it cannot be assumed that a large proportion of crimes against property—larceny, especially—is committed by persons known to the police. Ninety per cent of reported homicides are cleared by arrest—and there is good reason to suppose that the overwhelming number of homicides are reported to the police. Careful study as well as police experience indicates that being known to the victim is in fact a dominant pattern of offense. Thus, there is a *reason* for the chosen classic method of apprehending offenders in the case of homicide. That the method of suspicion is a reasoned response to the pattern of committing crimes against property is highly debatable. The point is moot and must remain so. There is simply no adequate knowledge of the pattern of larceny or other crimes against property. At the very most, only 25 per cent of reported offenses against property are cleared, and there is excellent reason to suppose that a great many thefts go unreported. Since even by the self-serving records collected by police, roughly seventy-five per cent of such crimes remain unaccounted-for with regard to the identity of the thief and since captured thieves are provided every motive to admit at least the number of thefts they have actually committed, it clearly remains possible that a majority or large plurality of thefts are committed by persons completely unknown to the police. It is even possible that the dominant pattern of offense in homicide prevails in many forms of crime against property. Persons known to the victim—but not the police—figure importantly in the many discussions of pilfering by employees at factory, shop, office, warehouse and department store. Such offenses go unreported. But, conceivably, their pattern could be taken as a clue to the identity of thieves in the clear majority of reported thefts that remain permanently unsolved. With the direction and insight provided by such a clue, suspicion in the event of thefts and burglaries committed in homes or other intimate places might fruitfully extend beyond the house-maid or cleaning-woman, currently the only member or visitor in respectable households brought under the shadow of regular suspicion. For reasons best known to themselves, members of society have chosen not to follow this promising lead and implicitly if not explicitly have told policemen not to. For an excellent statistical treatment of the way in which homicide is committed, see Marvin Wolfgang, *Patterns of Homicide* (Philadelphia: University of Pennsylvania Press, 1958). For a valuable discussion of the widespread prevalence of theft in the ordinary population, see Mary Owen Cameron, *The Booster and the Snitch* (New York: The Free Press of Glencoe, Inc., 1964). Besides her own research on shoplifting, Dr. Cameron includes a short summary of the research on employee pilfering.

method of suspicion may be termed bureaucratic. Allegedly, it yields a high level of return per unit cost. But, alas, the "returns" are cleared or accounted for complaints—less tangible than the actual commodity stolen. Moreover, no comparison with other possible methods exists. Thus, elements of intangibility, uncertainty and ignorance mar the claim to inherent superiority. As in many bogus systems of cost-accounting one is never quite sure which costs are assessed and which suppressed.

There are many reasons police provide an account of their performance, some external and related to the widespread civic expectation that a going concern appear accountable, and some internal and implicit in the scientistic checking procedures often associated with avid professionalization. Alan Silver summarized the first development, rightly stressing the transfer of accounting procedures and high levels of expected performance from other public or municipal institutions. Silver said:

> The character of police as a public bureaucracy may also raise expectations about the level of public peace it is possible to attain. As an instrument of public policy they are easily seen in terms of a naive instrumentalism—as technicians applying efficient means that are in principle capable of fully realizing their ends. Have not public bureaucracies eliminated plague, solved the enduring problem of urban sanitation, and prevented gross impurities in purchased food? Why cannot the police similarly "clean up" crime and control violence?[41]

The familiar internal tendency of incipient professions to develop accounting procedures serves to facilitate supervision and provides a certain spurious basis for promotion through a hierarchy. Moreover, in civic bureaucracies accounting may be useful in public relations, serving to mollify criticism and justify budgetary requests. Jerome Skolnick stressed internal reasons though relating them to an external expectation of accountability. He explained:

> Whether police are unusually sensitive to demands for efficiency, or whether they are actually required to demonstrate efficiency by means of "hard" criteria, in the absence of clear goals or specific criteria of competence, police in fact collect enormous quantities of data. Primarily, these data serve as a point of reference, the equivalent of a "set of books," permitting outsiders to rate the department.[42]

Subjected to special requests by central investigative offices like the Federal Bureau of Investigation, Department of Justice and countless state and

[41] Silver, *op. cit.*, p. 21.
[42] Jerome Skolnick, *op. cit.*, p. 166.

municipal authorities, police have been especially vulnerable to the blandishments of professional statisticians who have a special interest as well as a competence in the amassing of quantified records. Thus, Skolnick concludes his discussion of police accounting by summarizing the value accorded it by John Griffin, author of a textbook on police statistics. Griffin likens the records of police activity to "production or sales reports in a business organization." He commends the assiduous collection of data on the grounds that the account "can be used by administrative heads of departments" in assessing efficiency, it can be used to "keep the public informed of police activity," and finally, of course, as if such things could be foretold in advance, the account "may do much to create a favorable climate of public opinion."[43]

The pressure toward executive accountability, efficiency, judicial accountability, or legality is merely a specified assertion of the broader constraints in the context of police work. Legality is the lawful enforcement of law and efficiency in this context is the orderly demonstration of an accomplished order. Thus, the working context within which police are to catch a thief is just a somewhat specified rendition of the basic dilemma faced by police: law *and* order. Skolnick poses law and order as the basic police dilemma, and uses it to inform and organize his subsequent analysis of the police operation.

> *Thus, when law is used as the instrument of social order, it necessarily poses a dilemma. The phrase "law and order" is misleading because it draws attention away from the substantial incompatibilities existing between the two ideas. Order under law suggests procedures different from achievement of "social control" through threat of coercion and summary judgment. Order under law is concerned not merely with the achievement of regularized social activity but with the means used to come by peaceable behavior. . . . In short, "law" and "order" are frequently found to be in opposition, because law implies rational restraint upon the rules and procedures utilized to achieve order. Order under law, therefore, subordinates the ideal of conformity to the ideal of legality.[44]*

Skolnick's explicit tendency in describing the way in which police resolve the dilemma of law and order is difficult to summarize, but I think it is fair to say that he usually emphasizes the sense in which the dilemma remains un-

---

[43] Skolnick, p. 166 and pp. 236–238. Also, John Griffin, *Statistics Essential for Police Efficiency* (Springfield, Ill.: 1958), p. 31. And for a slightly greater stress on the external demand for accountability from local organizations, newspapers, and crime commissions, see Albert Reiss and David Bordua, "Environment and Organization: A Perspective on the Police," in David Bordua (ed.), *The Police* (New York: John Wiley & Sons, Inc., 1967), p. 35.

[44] Skolnick, *op. cit.*, p. 9.

resolved and police compromise between the contrasting ideals. Without disputing the shaky resolution of compromise and vacillation, I want to suggest that, simultaneously, another more stable device is instituted, one that is implicit in the excellent descriptions provided in Skolnick's study.

The dilemma of law and order may be met by the ingenious device of being two-faced. In duplicity, both law and order may be pursued—though in different populations. It is in that sense that both horns of the dilemma point in the same direction: toward the method of suspicion. By adopting it, the police may satisfy everyone—or at least everyone who *counts*.

Let us begin with an ideal statement of the two-faced resolution of the dilemma of law and order and then proceed to a less exaggerated portrayal. No better rendition of the thesis of two faces can be imagined than the instructive incident reported by McNamara of an unusually excitable patrolman in New York City. After a brief introduction that suggested its relevance, McNamara described the incident:

> *Data concerning the handling of citizens by the police do not justify the assumption that police are completely unable to allow conceptually for individual variation among persons labeled as wrongdoers, but the data do indicate that legal labels, independent of the actions of the citizen, often tend to govern the police officers decision regarding the proper handling of a situation. One striking instance of the principle operating retroactively involved a patrolman directing traffic in the middle of an intersection who fired his revolver at and hit an automobile whose driver had not heeded the officer's hand signals. The driver immediately pulled over to the side of the street and stopped the car. The officer then realized the inappropriateness of his action and began to wonder what he might offer as an explanation to his supervisors and to the citizen. The patrolman reported that his anxiety was dissipated shortly upon finding that the driver of the car was a person convicted of a number of crimes. The reader should understand that departmental policy did not specify that any person convicted of crimes in New York City thereby became a target for police pistol practice.[45]*

Though an actual occurrence, the incident is best regarded as a joke, partly because it strikes me, at least, as rather funny and partly because, through convolution, it exaggerates a truth and points the way to a tempered version. But to make that modification, the convolution must first be straightened, the joke explained—and thus lost.

The two-faced resolution of police can only be constructed retroactively. Neither in the joke nor in other actual happenings are the two faces of police authority clearly announced, simply there to see or witness. Each essential face may be glimpsed at the surface but an understanding of

[45] John McNamara, "Uncertainties in Police Work," in David Bordua (ed.), *The Police*, p. 171.

it requires going a bit deeper; like all things essential, legality for good citizens and an imposed order for the known criminal is best sought beneath the surface, in the latent *police attitude*.

In the joke, the point appears clear only at the end. What precedes the conclusion is "set-up" or misdirection. Upon learning the conclusion, the meaning is constructed, retroactively. The conclusion of this joke is the dissipation of anxiety felt by the patrolman "upon finding that the driver of the car was a person convicted of a number of crimes"—the retroactive sense of freedom from the bind of *lawfully* enforced law. The latent attitude of police is brought to the surface and suggests a new construction of the meaning of other elements of the reported incident. Thus, the reader may fully appreciate that "departmental policy did not specify that any person convicted of crimes in New York City thereby became a target for police pistol practice" and still understand that beneath that guaranteed protection of convicted criminals lurked a permission to do many things short of target practice in the *unlawful* enforcement of law. Similarly, though the reader is first misled into inferring a blanket brutality endangering good citizens as well as criminals, the point of the joke suggests the proper reconstruction. Beneath the fierce surface of an armed control of city traffic ready to fire at all offenders is something considerably more comforting: the essential face of legality for good citizens as indicated in the patrolman's anxious anticipation that an explanation of his misconduct would be demanded. The meaning of the incident is the police attitude of double-face, and not the even-handed announced legality of departmental policy or the blind—and thus equally even-handed—illegality of the patrolman's forceful method of traffic-regulation. The latter two prepare us for knowing laughter when the essential point—the police attitude of double-face—is revealed. Once explained, the joke is lost—as well it should be. A police tendency that countenances two faces is no laughing matter, and least of all for those effaced by imposed order. Besides, the joke exaggerates as well as convolutes elements of police reality. To be truthful, the police attitude and the double face it engenders must be rendered in more modulated fashion. But the exaggerated rendition should be kept in mind; otherwise the qualifications would be without principle.

The first qualification requires only brief discussion since it merely underscores the existence and partial institution of the standards of judicial accountability. Though begrudgingly, police must respect judicial standards of legality, anticipate their application and ponder their operative meaning. But the effect of these standards are matters to be assessed, not automatically succumbed to. The standards of legality are most apt to be followed when in reality—and not in abstraction—police anticipate an actual judicial accounting. When a contest in court can be anticipated as a possible or probable culmination of the criminal process, police are reminded of the single face established in the principle of legality. More generally, *publicity* works toward the maximal introduction of a single standard of lawfully enforced law. Extra-judicial institutions like the press, civilian review, and minority organizational pressure may augment the anticipated reality of a courtroom contest as guarantees of proper police conduct. But their efficacy depends finally on alerting police to the development of new ways of bringing judicial accountability to bear. It is the threat of the courtroom and the possible concrete materialization of forces intended to defend the accused that effectively check an unhampered tendency toward a two-faced application of law and order. Few nations in the world—and surely not ours—can yet depend on a flourishing of a cherished principle of legality among police themselves. Police professionalism includes many things, but rarely an unbounded faith in the preeminence of legality.[46]

Largely, legality is an externally imposed condition of police operation that is internally honored whenever publicity or its cutting instrument—the courtroom contest—can be realistically anticipated. When, however—as in the overwhelming proportion of police contacts—no adversity need be conjured, the two-faced tendency may emerge and serve to resolve the police dilemma. The courts themselves, in fear of being swamped by contested proceedings, give ample consideration to a plea of guilty, and thus to a police operation which skirts judicial accountability. The operative justice is, thus, in Skolnick's phrase, "without trial." The spectre of "delay in the courts," of which much has been written, the understandable judicial fear of a system perilously overworked by a mass utilization of adversity or contested cases, has provided a leeway for a subterranean justice arranged by police in their routine dealings with ordinary criminals. It provides a discretion, a wide area of police operation where the check of anticipated judicial accountability can be neglected and fall into virtual desuetude.

The second qualification is more subtle, not pertaining to a conflicting reality which serves to check or restrict the tendency of a two-faced police; and it develops within the very terms of a two-faced attitude. The restriction on being two-faced which is introduced by the threat of a judicial accounting and the leeway provided by the fear of "delay in the courts" is complicated by the reality of appearance or "resemblance."

In their area of wide discretion—the contacts where little anticipation of courtroom contests exist—police may employ suspects in an efficient manner and thus give a good executive accounting of themselves. But before proceeding too far in that endeavor, police must quickly assess the nature and character of the person standing before them. Which of the two faces— modulated as each may be—is to be presented? Is what stands before him essentially a good citizen or a suspect? Often the answer is clear since persons are already known to the police; but, often, in the metropolis or great

---

[46] See Skolnick, *op. cit.,* Chapters 9–11.

society, appearance or resemblance will play a part—and emerge as a modification of the two-faced attitude within its very terms. Thus, those who resemble *bona fide* suspects will often see the modulated face of imposed order; those who resemble the good citizen that of legality. Sometimes relying on resemblances, police have little choice but to familiarize themselves with—and apply—the ideas of affinity and affiliation. Indeed, they probably devised and circulated many of these ideas before sociologists—though in crude form, of course. Aided by resemblances in their workaday world, police produce an inner official basis for the social whereabouts of deviant subjects. Guided by crude conceptions of affinity and affiliation in the very issue of whether careful scrutiny and inspection is warranted, police do their part in bloating the potency of both processes. In that regard, they are like other conventional members of society.

The confidence man personifies the exploitation by intelligent criminals of police and public reliance on resemblance. To secure victims and escape police notice, the confidence man uses artifice and disguise in order to perfect his resemblance with the good citizen in business.[47] Contrarily, the aspiring juvenile "tough" and more recently the long-haired, unkempt "hippy" exemplify portions of the population who for reasons of gross resemblance are especially noticed and scrutinized by police. They are regarded as suspicious. Thus, at both extremes of staged demeanor or costumed appearance, resemblance figures in the police assessment. But between the extremes of intentional presentation of appearance is a matter of greater importance in the current American setting. Hardly subject to manipulation, race provides police with a patent resemblance—and thus a bit of staple guidance as to the character of the one who stands before them.

The modification of a method that focuses suspicion on known criminals by a reliance on resemblance is best appreciated by considering the situation of black Americans. Their appearance is unintentional; the incapacity to tell one from the other is clearly a defect in the eyes of the beholder. Once we understand the method of suspicion as qualified by the role of resemblance, we may return to its application to proper criminals.

The method of suspicion employs police knowledge of known criminals to expedite their apprehension and the subsequent clearing of complaints. It deploys the police strength towards a corps of suspects and uses a variety of means of associating offenses with a person who is methodically suspected. No incident excites police attention. The suspicion derives from police knowledge regarding identity and resemblance. Thus, the actual implementation of the method of suspicion is *outgoing,* it seeks a regular suspect in the hope that any one or a whole series of uncleared offenses can

---

[47] Classic discussions may be found in Herman Melville, *The Confidence Man,* E. Foster (ed.) (New York: Hendrick House, 1954); Thomas Mann, *Confessions of Felix Krull* (New York: Alfred A. Knopf, Inc., 1955); and David Maurer, *The Big Con* (Indianapolis: The Bobbs-Merrill Co., Inc., 1948).

be settled. In the somewhat stilted language of law, the way to implement the method of suspicion is to *harass*. But it is not considered harassment by police because they have an accredited reason for methodical suspicion: The suspect is known to them or resembles those who are known to them.

The outgoing maneuvers of many American police forces are described in the *Report of the National Advisory Commission on Civil Disorders*. Intended to shock the reader into a realization of his racist premises, the findings achieve an even more direct importance: The properly condemned reliance on the resemblance of race is accompanied by a matter-of-fact acceptance of harassment *if limited to proper suspects*. Reliance on resemblance breaks the social contract despite the fact that it is common. But the method of suspicion is the key to the social contract. The members of the commission summarized their findings on police patrol practices:

> *Although police administrators may take steps to attempt to eliminate misconduct by individual police officers, many departments have adopted patrol practices which in the words of one commentator, have . . . replaced harassment by individual patrolman with harassment by entire departments. These practices, sometimes known as "aggressive preventive patrol" take a number of forms, but invariably they involve a large number of police-citizen contacts initiated by police rather than in response to a call for help or service. One such practice utilizes a roving task force which moves into high-crime districts without prior notice, and conducts intense, often indiscriminate, street stops and searches. A number of persons who might legitimately be described as suspicious are stopped. But so also are persons whom the beat patrolman would know are respected members of the community. Such task forces are often deliberately moved from place to place making it impossible for its members to know the people with whom they come in contact.*
>
> *In some cities aggressive patrol is not limited to special task forces. The beat patrolman himself is expected to participate and to file a minimum number of stop-and-frisk or field interrogation reports from each tour of duty. The pressure to produce, or a lack of familiarity with the neighborhood and its people, may lead to widespread use of these techniques without adequate differentiation between genuinely suspicious behavior and behavior which is suspicious to a particular officer only because it is unfamiliar.*[48]

In distinguishing between those legitimately regarded as suspicious and those improperly stopped and thus harassed, the Commission offers little guidance; though, plainly, furtive movements, if nothing else, give a minimal substance to the idea that persons can behave in a suspicious manner. More to the point, however, are the guides provided by a person's known reputation in the community and it is on that basis that the Commission recommends a

---

[48] *Report of the National Advisory Commission on Civil Disorders* (New York: Bantam Books, Inc., 1968), p. 304.

way of separating those who may be legitimately subjected to "aggressive preventive patrol" from those who are harassed by such procedures. Quaintly bemoaning the passing of the beat patrolman, the members of the commission observed:

> *Loss of contact between the police officer and the community he serves adversely affects law enforcement. If an officer has never met, does not know, and cannot understand the language and habits of the people in the area he patrols, he cannot do an effective police job. His ability to detect truly suspicious behavior is impaired. . . . He fails to know those persons with an "equity" in the community—homeowners, small business-men, professional men, persons who are anxious to support proper law enforcement—and thus sacrifices the contributions they can make to maintaining community order.*[49]

However laudable the Commission's disapproval of a racist policy of harassing sections of the black Ghetto may be, it fails to reckon with the police methods that lead to such a practice. Resemblance is a qualification that derives its misguided sense and meaning from the principled acceptance of the method of suspicion. By implicitly pretending that "suspicious behavior" is the key guide for operative policemen in deciding whether scrutiny is warranted, the more usable matter of "suspicious persons" as those without "equity in the community" is overlooked and avoided.

To be stopped, frisked or interrogated for suspicious *behavior* is not harassment and, in the terms suggested here, it falls short of being subjected to methodical suspicion. But what of the suspicious *person,* a category known to police but not to court or federal commission? Is the juvenile who utters these words subjected to harassment?

> *"Every time something happens in this neighborhood, them mother fuckin' cops come looking for me! I may not be doing nothing, but if somebody gets beat or something gets stole they always be coming right to my place to find out what's going on."*[50]

Whether he is or not is a matter for courts to decide, though the point is highly likely to remain moot. If a confession is gained, an undeniable legitimacy is retroactively cast on the entire procedure; if it is not, the matter is unlikely to proceed much further. Thus, the police practice is well composed to avoid judicial accountability. Legally harassed or not, the subject is regularly employed as a suspect; effaced by imposed order, he becomes the focused object of police penetration; and protected by legality, the good

[49] *Ibid.,* p. 305.
[50] Werthman and Piliavin, *op. cit.,* p. 70.

citizen and those resembling him are subjected only to the minimal penetration of incidental suspicion.

To disconnect the reliance on resemblance from the principle of methodical suspicion is, furthermore, to obscure the sense in which the former is simply a logical outgrowth of the latter. Once the idea of a suspicious person has been instituted in practice—as a workable extension of suspicious behavior—common sense and the pressure for results can provide the justification for an additional guess regarding the social whereabouts of offenders. Resemblance is nothing more—or less—than falling under suspicion of being a suspect. It is not guilt but *suspicion by association*. Developing within the very terms of the method of suspicion, resemblance qualifies the principle by extending its logic.

The injustice of modifying the method of suspicion by relying on resemblances is easy to grant and thus its defense rests on the assertion of hidden criminality. Not only do the corps of regular suspects provide an account of the prevalence of crime which shields respectable citizens from interference and mistrust; additionally, they yield a similarly comforting clue regarding the actual perpetrators of uncleared offenses. Relying on the modification of resemblance, police act as if they were confident of the identity of those unknown culprits. Whatever they may say when directly questioned, their ordinary practice commits them to the theory that the bulk of the unsolved 75 per cent of crimes against property are committed by yet other known criminals and an unknown horde who resemble them. The reliance on resemblance receives justification because it is at least partly illegitimate. But the method of suspicion itself is taken for granted, assumed as commonplace and without need of defense. Cicourel points to the routines of police work and suggests that many features are regarded as "natural" and beyond question. Among these operational routines is the specially focused attention on persons who are known to the police. "Operationally, therefore, certain males are always watched at football games or dances, or questioned in connection with certain offenses, or picked up immediately when particular patterns of crime or 'bothering' are referred to a department."[51]

Conclusion

Though the method of suspicion contributes to the process of becoming deviant by continuously sustaining the conclusion of a deviant identity and by making eventual conviction more likely through the focused produc-

[51] Aaron Cicourel, *The Social Organization of Juvenile Justice* (New York: John Wiley & Sons, Inc., 1968), p. 173. Also, see the discussion of deviation "amplification" in Leslie Wilkens, *Social Deviance* (Englewood Cliffs, N.J.: Prentice-Hall, Inc., 1964), p. 85.

tion of a string of offenses, it is equally important to stress its contribution to the collective representation. Never completely successful, and rarely without an initial but weak basis in the facts of circumstance, the method of suspicion provides substance for a Manichean vision of society: The forces of evil are concentrated, their whereabouts known in principle; the task of law enforcement can proceed. And it proceeds in approximately the same direction as when police were first instituted—toward the "dangerous classes." Within a vision of concentrated evil, goodness may be conceived as pervasive.[52] Given so striking a division, what recourse remains but to convict persons who "have been given every chance" but continue amassing a record? Taking for granted the focused and instituted scrutiny to which they are subjected, they are made to appear strikingly different from the great majority who, as far as can be ascertained, have never done anything wrong. Society is driven to a conclusion that appears inevitable. So endangered are the decent majority that the visual division becomes concrete: The convict is confined, segregated from the rest of society in penal colonies. And there, he will come face to face with the imposed order of Leviathan, unmodulated by the possibility of judicial accounting, unmitigated by any resemblance with one who enjoys civil rights. Imprisoned, he may once again reconsider the path he has taken, aided by an immense assortment of techniques ranging from enforced isolation to group therapy, from forced labor to chronic idleness, though hampered, it is granted, by full-scale immersion in a society of captive criminals. But his reconsideration occurs within a new context. Convicted and imprisoned, he is committed to a world in which his identity will henceforth be cast retrospectively. Even when he has served his sentence his conviction persists: He becomes an ex-convict. Aside from that, the deviant subject is more or less back where he started. Not a prisoner of circumstance, nor even of affiliation, still, he was a prisoner. The context of signification—his continued bind with the state— develops a final meaning. As much as could be hoped for in an imprecise world, his deviant identity has been concluded. Once again but more ardently, men of authority hope he will "behave himself" and will watch closely to see if he does. The surprising thing is that sometimes he seems to. In that event, the lingering of identity implicit in being an ex-convict is augmented: A deviant subject has been corrected, mended or rehabilitated.

Even at the conclusion of the signification process—imprisonment and parole—the process of becoming deviant remains open. Reconsideration continues; remission remains an observable actuality. Nonetheless, signification implies a closure or finality, at least in the minds of conventional members of society and empowered officials, though not in the lives of deviant persons. The finished product of signification is the collective representation

---

[52] For a stimulating consideration of this and related points, see Kai Erikson, *Wayward Puritans* (New York: John Wiley & Sons, Inc., 1966).

of concentrated evil, or deviation, and pervasive good, or conformity. Guided by its imagery and eternally beguiled by the illusion that man has discovered the secret of correction, agents of signification complete the symbolic representation of a deviant person by claiming to cure or fix him. In that manner every contingency is covered. Apprehended again, the subject continues to be a thief; or, with his way of life changed, he may be known as one who used to be a thief but has reformed. The benevolence of society and the wisdom of the state—the positive sides of the collective representation—are affirmed.

In its avid concern for public order and safety, implemented through police force and penal policy, Leviathan is vindicated. By pursuing evil and producing the *appearance* of good, the state reveals its abiding method— the perpetuation of its good name in the face of its own propensities for violence, conquest, and destruction. Guarded by a collective representation in which theft and violence reside in a dangerous class, morally elevated by its correctional quest, the state achieves the legitimacy of pacific intention and the appearance of legality—even if it goes to war and massively perpetrates activities it has allegedly banned from the world. But, that, the reader may say, is a different matter altogether. So says Leviathan—and that is the final point of the collective representation.

Index

Lightning Source UK Ltd.
Milton Keynes UK
UKOW06f1855220515

252145UK00005B/351/P